SEND
Special Educational Needs and Disability Code of Practice: 0 to 25 years

Statutory guidance for organisations which work with and support children and young people who have special educational needs or disabilities

January 2015

GRANGIS UK Publishing

Adapted and Published by GRANGIS (Grand Register Library).
Online: www.grangis.com.
E-mail: contact@grangis.com.

In this version:
ISBN: 979-8-88559-080-8

Note: Title, sub-title and version of this publication is as described. For the most recent information please visit www.gov.uk.

Contents

Foreword

From the Parliamentary Under-Secretary of State for Health and the Parliamentary Under-Secretary of State for Children and Families

Our vision for children with special educational needs and disabilities is the same as for all children and young people – that they achieve well in their early years, at school and in college, and lead happy and fulfilled lives.

This new Special Educational Needs and Disability Code of Practice will play a vital role in underpinning the major reform programme.

For children and young people this means that their experiences will be of a system which is less confrontational and more efficient. Their special educational needs and disabilities will be picked up at the earliest point with support routinely put in place quickly, and their parents will know what services they can reasonably expect to be provided. Children and young people and their parents or carers will be fully involved in decisions about their support and what they want to achieve. Importantly, the aspirations for children and young people will be raised through an increased focus on life outcomes, including employment and greater independence.

Local authorities and their local health partners have been working together to prepare for the new arrangements, to jointly plan and commission services for children and young people who have special educational needs or are disabled. Those with more complex needs will have an integrated assessment and where appropriate a single Education, Health and Care plan for their support.

The Code of Practice is the product of extensive consultation, and draws on the experience of pathfinder local authorities which have been piloting new approaches with local communities. We have listened to a wide range of individuals and groups and the result is a Code which will help everyone working with children and young people with special educational needs and disability to secure for them the outcomes from education, health and social care which will make the biggest difference to their lives.

DR DAN POULTER
Parliamentary Under-Secretary of State for Health

EDWARD TIMPSON
Parliamentary Under-Secretary of State for Children and Families

Introduction

About this guidance

i. This Code of Practice provides statutory guidance on duties, policies and procedures relating to Part 3 of the Children and Families Act 2014 and associated regulations and applies to England. It relates to children and young people with special educational needs (SEN) and disabled children and young people. A 'young person' in this context is a person over compulsory school age and under 25. Compulsory school age ends on the last Friday of June in the academic year in which they become 16. For ease of reference, young people are referred to in this Code of Practice as 'over 16'.

In this Code of Practice, where the text uses the word '**must**' it refers to a statutory requirement under primary legislation, regulations or case law.

The bodies listed in paragraph iv. **must** have regard to the Code of Practice. This means that whenever they are taking decisions they **must** give consideration to what the Code says. They cannot ignore it. They **must** fulfil their statutory duties towards children and young people with SEN or disabilities in the light of the guidance set out in it. They **must** be able to demonstrate in their arrangements for children and young people with SEN or disabilities that they are fulfilling their statutory duty to have regard to the Code. So, where the text uses the word 'should' it means that the guidance contained in this Code **must** be considered and that those who **must** have regard to it will be expected to explain any departure from it.

Expiry or review date

ii. This guidance will be kept under review and updated when necessary.

To which legislation does this guidance refer?

iii. This guidance refers to Part 3 of the Children and Families Act 2014 and associated regulations. The regulations associated with the Children and Families Act 2014 are:

- The Special Educational Needs and Disability Regulations 2014
- The Special Educational Needs (Personal Budgets) Regulations 2014
- The Special Educational Needs and Disability (Detained Persons) Regulations 2015
- The Children and Families Act 2014 (Transitional and Saving Provisions)(No 2) Order 2014

Who must have regard to this guidance?

iv. This Code of Practice is statutory guidance for the following organisations:

- local authorities (education, social care and relevant housing and employment and other services)
- the governing bodies of schools, including non-maintained special schools
- the governing bodies of further education colleges and sixth form colleges
- the proprietors of academies (including free schools, university technical colleges and studio schools)
- the management committees of pupil referral units
- independent schools and independent specialist providers approved under Section 41 of the Children and Families Act 2014
- all early years providers in the maintained, private, voluntary and independent sectors that are funded by the local authority
- the National Health Service Commissioning Board
- clinical commissioning groups (CCGs)
- NHS Trusts
- NHS Foundation Trusts
- Local Health Boards
- Youth Offending Teams and relevant youth custodial establishments
- The First-tier Tribunal (Special Educational Needs and Disability) (see v.)

The First-tier Tribunal (Special Educational Needs and Disability)

v. When considering an appeal from a parent or young person the First-tier Tribunal (Special Educational Needs and Disability) ('the Tribunal') **must** have regard to this Code of Practice. The Tribunal will expect local authorities, early education settings, schools and colleges to be able to explain any departure from the Code, where it is relevant to the case it is considering.

Changes from the SEN Code of Practice (2001)

vi. The main changes from the SEN Code of Practice (2001) reflect the changes introduced by the Children and Families Act 2014. These are:

- The Code of Practice (2014) covers the 0-25 age range and includes guidance relating to disabled children and young people as well as those with SEN
- There is a clearer focus on the participation of children and young people and parents in decision-making at individual and strategic levels
- There is a stronger focus on high aspirations and on improving outcomes for children and young people
- It includes guidance on the joint planning and commissioning of services to ensure close co-operation between education, health and social care
- It includes guidance on publishing a Local Offer of support for children and young people with SEN or disabilities
- There is new guidance for education and training settings on taking a graduated approach to identifying and supporting pupils and students with SEN (to replace School Action and School Action Plus)
- For children and young people with more complex needs a co-ordinated assessment process and the new 0-25 Education, Health and Care plan (EHC plan) replace statements and Learning Difficulty Assessments (LDAs)
- There is a greater focus on support that enables those with SEN to succeed in their education and make a successful transition to adulthood
- Information is provided on relevant duties under the Equality Act 2010
- Information is provided on relevant provisions of the Mental Capacity Act 2005
- There is new guidance on supporting children and young people with SEN who are in youth custody.

Implementation of the Code of Practice

Implementation

vii. From 1 September 2014 the majority of Part 3 of the Children and Families Act 2014, its associated regulations and this Code of Practice will be in force, subject to any transitional arrangements.

viii. From 1 September 2014 all the organisations listed in paragraph iv. **must** have regard to this Code of Practice.

ix. Subject to any transitional arrangements made, from that date the following guidance will cease to have effect:

- SEN Code of Practice (2001)
- Inclusive Schooling (2001)
- Section 139A Learning Difficulty Assessments Statutory Guidance (2013)

Transitional arrangements

x. From 1 September 2014 transitional arrangements will be in place to support the changeover from the current system to the new system in a phased and ordered way. These arrangements, which are set out in a statutory transitional order and accompanied by transitional guidance, will facilitate the transfer of those with statements to EHC plans. They ensure that during the transition period local authorities must continue to comply with elements of the Education Act 1996 in relation to children with statements, and the Learning and Skills Act 2000 in relation to young people who have had Learning Difficulty Assessments and remain in education or training (provided they still have learning difficulties).

xi. The legal test of when a child or young person requires an EHC plan remains the same as that for a statement under the Education Act 1996. Therefore, it is expected that all those who have a statement and who would have continued to have one under the current system, will be transferred to an EHC plan – no-one should lose their statement and not have it replaced with an EHC plan simply because the system is changing. Similarly, local authorities have undertaken LDAs for young people either because they had a statement at school or because, in the opinion of the local authority, they are likely to need additional support as part of their further education or training and would benefit from an LDA to identify their learning needs and the provision required to meet those needs. Therefore, the expectation is that young people who are currently receiving support as a result of an LDA and remain in further education or training during the transition period, who request and need an EHC plan, will be issued with one.

xii. Guidance on the provisions in the Children and Families Act 2014 relating to those in youth custody, which came into force in April 2015, is set out in Chapter 10.

Special educational needs (SEN)

xiii. A child or young person has SEN if they have a learning difficulty or disability which calls for special educational provision to be made for him or her.

xiv. A child of compulsory school age or a young person has a learning difficulty or disability if he or she:

- has a significantly greater difficulty in learning than the majority of others of the same age, or
- has a disability which prevents or hinders him or her from making use of facilities of a kind generally provided for others of the same age in mainstream schools or mainstream post-16 institutions

xv. For children aged two or more, special educational provision is educational or training provision that is additional to or different from that made generally for other children or young people of the same age by mainstream schools, maintained nursery schools, mainstream post-16 institutions or by relevant early years providers. For a child under two years of age, special educational provision means educational provision of any kind.

xvi. A child under compulsory school age has special educational needs if he or she is likely to fall within the definition in paragraph xiv. above when they reach compulsory school age or would do so if special educational provision was not made for them (Section 20 Children and Families Act 2014).

xvii. Post-16 institutions often use the term learning difficulties and disabilities (LDD). The term SEN is used in this Code across the 0-25 age range but includes LDD.

Disabled children and young people

xviii. Many children and young people who have SEN may have a disability under the Equality Act 2010 – that is '...a physical or mental impairment which has a long-term and substantial adverse effect on their ability to carry out normal day-to-day activities'. This definition provides a relatively low threshold and includes more children than many realise: 'long-term' is defined as 'a year or more' and 'substantial' is defined as 'more than minor or trivial'. This definition includes sensory impairments such as those affecting sight or hearing, and long-term health conditions such as asthma, diabetes, epilepsy, and cancer. Children and young people with such conditions do not necessarily have SEN, but there is a significant overlap between disabled children and young people and those with SEN. Where a disabled child or young person requires special educational provision they will also be covered by the SEN definition.

xix. The Equality Act 2010 sets out the legal obligations that schools, early years providers, post-16 institutions, local authorities and others have towards disabled children and young people:

- They **must not** directly or indirectly discriminate against, harass or victimise disabled children and young people

- They **must not** discriminate for a reason arising in consequence of a child or young person's disability

- They **must** make reasonable adjustments, including the provision of auxiliary aids and services, to ensure that disabled children and young people are not at a substantial disadvantage compared with their peers. This duty is anticipatory – it requires thought to be given in advance to what disabled children and young people might require and what adjustments might need to be made to prevent that disadvantage

- Public bodies, including further education institutions, local authorities, maintained schools, maintained nursery schools, academies and free schools are covered by the public sector equality duty and, when carrying out their functions, **must** have regard to the need to eliminate discrimination, promote equality of opportunity and foster good relations between disabled and non-disabled children and young people. Public bodies also have specific duties under the public sector equality duty and **must** publish information to demonstrate their compliance with this general duty and **must** prepare and publish objectives to achieve the core aims of the general duty. Objectives **must** be specific and measurable. The general duty also applies to bodies that are not public bodies but that carry out public functions. Such bodies include providers of relevant early years education, non-maintained special schools, independent specialist providers and others making provision that is funded from the public purse.

xx. The duties cover discrimination in the provision of services and the provision of education, including admissions and exclusions. All providers **must** make reasonable adjustments to procedures, criteria and practices and by the provision of auxiliary aids and services. Most providers **must** also make reasonable adjustments by making physical alterations. Schools and local authority education functions are not covered by this last duty, but they **must** publish accessibility plans (and local authorities, accessibility strategies) setting out how they plan to increase access for disabled pupils to the curriculum, the physical environment and to information.

xxi. School governing bodies and proprietors **must** also publish information about the arrangements for the admission of disabled children, the steps taken to prevent disabled children being treated less favourably than others, the facilities provided to assist access of disabled children, and their accessibility plans.

xxii. Where a child or young person is covered by SEN and disability legislation, reasonable adjustments and access arrangements should be considered as part of SEN planning and review. Where school governors are publishing information about their arrangements for disabled children and young people, this should be brought together with the information required under the Children and Families Act 2014.

xxiii. Here, and throughout this Code the term 'parent' includes all those with parental responsibility, including parents and those who care for the child.

Related legislation and guidance

xxiv. Where appropriate, references are made in this Code to other relevant legislation. The Code does not give guidance in relation to that legislation but signals where it can be found in the References section at the end of this Code.

xxv. Organisations may find it helpful to consider the following related guidance:

- **Working Together to Safeguard Children (2013):** Statutory guidance from the Department for Education which sets out what is expected of organisations and individuals to safeguard and promote the welfare of children

- **The Children Act 1989 Guidance and Regulations Volume 2 (Care Planning Placement and Case Review)** and **Volume 3 (Planning Transition to Adulthood for Care Leavers):** Guidance setting out the responsibilities of local authorities towards looked after children and care leavers

- **Equality Act 2010: Advice for schools:** Non-statutory advice from the Department for Education, produced to help schools understand how the Equality Act affects them and how to fulfil their duties under the Act

- **Reasonable adjustments for disabled pupils (2012):** Technical guidance from the Equality and Human Rights Commission

- **Supporting pupils at school with medical conditions (2014):** statutory guidance from the Department for Education

- **The Mental Capacity Act Code of Practice: Protecting the vulnerable (2005)**

1 Principles

What this chapter covers

Section19 of the Children and Families Act 2014 sets out the principles underpinning the legislation and the guidance in this Code of Practice. This chapter sets out those principles and how they are reflected in the chapters that follow.

Relevant legislation

Section 19 of the Children and Families Act 2014

Principles underpinning this Code of Practice

1.1 Section 19 of the Children and Families Act 2014 makes clear that local authorities, in carrying out their functions under the Act in relation to disabled children and young people and those with special educational needs (SEN), **must** have regard to:

- the views, wishes and feelings of the child or young person, and the child's parents
- the importance of the child or young person, and the child's parents, participating as fully as possible in decisions, and being provided with the information and support necessary to enable participation in those decisions
- the need to support the child or young person, and the child's parents, in order to facilitate the development of the child or young person and to help them achieve the best possible educational and other outcomes, preparing them effectively for adulthood

1.2 These principles are designed to support:

- the participation of children, their parents and young people in decision-making
- the early identification of children and young people's needs and early intervention to support them
- greater choice and control for young people and parents over support
- collaboration between education, health and social care services to provide support
- high quality provision to meet the needs of children and young people with SEN

- a focus on inclusive practice and removing barriers to learning
- successful preparation for adulthood, including independent living and employment

The principles in practice

Participating in decision making

1.3 Local authorities **must** ensure that children, their parents and young people are involved in discussions and decisions about their individual support and about local provision.

1.4 Early years providers, schools and colleges should also take steps to ensure that young people and parents are actively supported in contributing to needs assessments, developing and reviewing Education, Health and Care (EHC) plans.

Specifically, local authorities **must**

- ensure the child's parents or the young person are fully included in the EHC needs assessment process from the start, are fully aware of their opportunities to offer views and information, and are consulted about the content of the plan (Chapter 9)
- consult children with SEN or disabilities, and their parents and young people with SEN or disabilities when reviewing local SEN and social care provision (Chapter 4)
- consult them in developing and reviewing their Local Offer (Chapter 4)
- make arrangements for providing children with SEN or disabilities, and their parents, and young people with SEN or disabilities with advice and information about matters relating to SEN and disability (Chapter 2)

1.5 Clinical Commissioning Groups (CCGs), NHS Trusts or NHS Foundation Trusts who are of the opinion that a child under compulsory school age has or probably has SEN or a disability **must** give the child's parents the opportunity to discuss their opinion with them before informing the local authority (see paragraph 1.16).

1.6 Children have a right to receive and impart information, to express an opinion and to have that opinion taken into account in any matters affecting them from the early years. Their views should be given due weight according to their age, maturity and capability (Articles 12 and 13 of the United Nations Convention on the Rights of the Child).

1.7 Parents' views are important during the process of carrying out an EHC needs assessment and drawing up or reviewing an EHC plan in relation to a child. Local authorities, early years providers and schools should enable parents to share their knowledge about their child and give them confidence that their views and contributions are valued and will be acted upon. At times, parents, teachers and others may have differing expectations of how a child's needs are best met. Sometimes these discussions can be challenging but it is in the child's best interests for a positive dialogue between parents, teachers and others to be maintained, to work through points of difference and establish what action is to be taken.

1.8 The Children and Families Act 2014 gives significant new rights directly to young people once they reach the end of compulsory school age (the end of the academic year in which they turn 16). When a young person reaches the end of compulsory school age, local authorities and other agencies should normally engage directly with the young person rather than their parent, ensuring that as part of the planning process they identify the relevant people who should be involved and how to involve them. Chapter 8 sets out how some decision-making rights transfer from parents to young people at this stage and how families will continue to play a critical role in supporting a young person with SEN. Most young people will continue to want, or need, their parents and other family members to remain involved in discussions and decisions about their future. Some young people, and possibly some parents, will not have the mental capacity to make certain decisions or express their views. Provision is made in the Children and Families Act (Section 80) to deal with this and Annex 1 to this Code provides further details.

Supporting children, young people and parents to participate in decisions about their support

1.9 Local authorities **must** ensure that children, young people and parents are provided with the information, advice and support necessary to enable them to participate in discussions and decisions about their support. This should include information on their rights and entitlements in accessible formats and time to prepare for discussions and meetings. From Year 9 onwards, particularly for those with Education, Health and Care plans, local authorities, schools, colleges and other agencies will be involved in the planning for their transition to adult life, the future and how to prepare for it, including their health, where they will live, their relationships, control of their finances, how they will participate in the community and achieve greater independence. Further details are given in Chapter 8. Local authorities should help children and their families prepare for the change in status under SEN law that occurs once the child reaches the end of compulsory school age.

1.10 Local authorities should consider whether some young people may require support in expressing their views, including whether they may need support from an advocate (who could be a family member or a professional). Local authorities **must not** use the views of parents as a proxy for young people's views. Young people will have their own perspective and local authorities should have arrangements in place to engage with them directly.

Involving children, young people and parents in planning, commissioning and reviewing services

1.11 Local authorities **must** consult children with SEN or disabilities, their parents, and young people with SEN or disabilities in reviewing educational and training provision and social care provision and in preparing and reviewing the Local Offer. It is important that they participate effectively in decisions about support available to them in their local area. Chapters 3 and 4 provide guidance on these duties.

1.12 Effective participation should lead to a better fit between families' needs and the services provided, higher satisfaction with services, reduced costs (as long-term benefits emerge) and better value for money. Local authorities should work with children, young people and parents to establish the aims of their participation, mark progress and build trust. They should make use of existing organisations and forums which represent the views of parents – and those which represent the views of children and young people directly – and where these do not exist, local authorities should consider establishing them. Effective participation happens when:

- it is recognised, valued, planned and resourced (for example, through appropriate remuneration and training)
- it is evident at all stages in the planning, delivery and monitoring of services
- there are clearly described roles for children, young people and parents
- there are strong feedback mechanisms to ensure that children, young people and parents understand the impact their participation is making

Parent Carer Forums

1.13 Parent Carer Forums are representative local groups of parents and carers of children and young people with disabilities who work alongside local authorities, education, health and other service providers to ensure the services they plan, commission, deliver and monitor meet the needs of children and families. Parent Carer Forums have been established in most local areas and local authorities are actively encouraged to work with them. More information about Parent Carer Forums is available from the websites of Contact a Family and the National Network of

Parent Carer Forums. Links to them can be found in the References section under Chapter 1.

Identifying children and young people's needs

1.14 Local authorities **must** carry out their functions with a view to identifying all the children and young people in their area who have or may have SEN or have or may have a disability (Section 22 of the Children and Families Act 2014).

1.15 Local authorities may gather information on children and young people with SEN or disabilities in a number of ways. Anyone can bring a child or young person who they believe has or probably has SEN or a disability to the attention of a local authority (Section 24 of the Children and Families Act 2014) and parents, early years providers, schools and colleges have an important role in doing so.

1.16 CCGs, NHS Trusts and NHS Foundation Trusts **must** inform the appropriate local authority if they identify a child under compulsory school age as having, or probably having, SEN or a disability (Section 23 of the Children and Families Act 2014).

1.17 A child's parents, young people, schools and colleges have specific rights to request a needs assessment for an EHC plan and children and their parents and young people should feel able to tell their school or college if they believe they have or may have SEN. The legal test of when a child or young person requires an EHC plan remains the same as that for a statement under the Education Act 1996. Therefore, it is expected that all those who have a statement and who would have continued to have one under the current system, will be transferred to an EHC plan – no-one should lose their statement and not have it replaced with an EHC plan simply because the system is changing. Similarly, local authorities have undertaken LDAs for young people either because they had a statement at school or because, in the opinion of the local authority, they are likely to need additional support as part of their further education or training and would benefit from an LDA to identify their learning needs and the provision required to meet those needs. Therefore, the expectation is that young people who are currently receiving support as a result of an LDA and remain in further education or training during the transition period, who request and need an EHC plan, will be issued with one.

1.18 Chapters 5, 6 and 7 provide guidance for early years providers, schools and colleges on identifying children and young people's SEN and making provision to meet those needs as early as possible.

1.19 Local authorities, CCGs and other partners **must** work together in local Health and Wellbeing Boards to assess the health needs of local people, including those with SEN or who are disabled. This assessment, the Joint Strategic Needs Assessment, informs a local Health and Wellbeing Strategy which sets priorities for those who commission services. Local authorities **must** keep their educational and training provision and social care provision for children and young people with SEN or disabilities under review (Section 27 of the Children and Families Act 2014). In carrying out this duty, the local authority will gather information from early years providers, schools and post-16 institutions. In most cases, those institutions **must**, in turn, co-operate with the local authority. The local authority **must** publish and keep under review its Local Offer of provision in consultation with children, their parents and young people. Guidance on these matters is given in Chapters 3 and 4.

Greater choice and control for parents and young people over their support

1.20 A local authority's Local Offer should reflect the services that are available as a result of strategic assessments of local needs and reviews of local education and care provision (Section 27 of the Children and Families Act 2014) and of health provision (Joint Strategic Needs Assessments and Joint Commissioning arrangements (Section 26 of the Children and Families Act 2014). Linking these assessments and reviews to the Local Offer will help to identify gaps in local provision. Local authorities **must** involve children and young people with SEN or disabilities and the parents of children with SEN or disabilities in the development and review of the Local Offer. This will help to ensure it is responsive to local families. Guidance on the Local Offer is provided in Chapter 4.

1.21 Parents of children who have an EHC plan and young people who have such a plan have a right to ask for a particular educational institution to be named in the plan and for a Personal Budget for their support. Guidance is given in Chapter 9.

Collaboration between education, health and social care services to provide support

1.22 If children and young people with SEN or disabilities are to achieve their ambitions and the best possible educational and other outcomes, including getting a job and living as independently as possible, local education, health and social care services should work together to ensure they get the right support.

1.23 When carrying out their statutory duties under the Children and Families Act 2014, local authorities **must** do so with a view to making sure that services work together where this promotes children and young people's wellbeing or improves the quality of special educational provision (Section 25 of the Children and Families Act 2014). Local authorities **must** work with one another to assess local needs. Local authorities and health bodies **must** have arrangements in place to plan and commission education, health and social care services jointly for children and young people with SEN or disabilities (Section 26). Chapter 3 gives guidance on those duties.

High quality provision to meet the needs of children and young people with SEN

1.24 High quality teaching that is differentiated and personalised will meet the individual needs of the majority of children and young people. Some children and young people need educational provision that is additional to or different from this. This is special educational provision under Section 21 of the Children and Families Act 2014. Schools and colleges **must** use their best endeavours to ensure that such provision is made for those who need it. Special educational provision is underpinned by high quality teaching and is compromised by anything less.

1.25 Early years providers, schools and colleges should know precisely where children and young people with SEN are in their learning and development. They should:

- ensure decisions are informed by the insights of parents and those of children and young people themselves
- have high ambitions and set stretching targets for them
- track their progress towards these goals
- keep under review the additional or different provision that is made for them
- promote positive outcomes in the wider areas of personal and social development, and
- ensure that the approaches used are based on the best possible evidence and are having the required impact on progress

Chapters 5, 6 and 7 give guidance on identifying and supporting children and young people with SEN or disabilities.

A focus on inclusive practice and removing barriers to learning

1.26 As part of its commitments under articles 7 and 24 of the United Nations Convention of the Rights of Persons with Disabilities, the UK Government is committed to inclusive education of disabled children and young people and the progressive removal of barriers to learning and participation in mainstream education. The Children and Families Act 2014 secures the general presumption in law of mainstream education in relation to decisions about where children and young people with SEN should be educated and the Equality Act 2010 provides protection from discrimination for disabled people.

1.27 Where a child or young person has SEN but does not have an EHC plan they **must** be educated in a mainstream setting except in specific circumstances (see below).

The School Admissions Code of Practice requires children and young people with SEN to be treated fairly. Admissions authorities:

- **must** consider applications from parents of children who have SEN but do not have an EHC plan on the basis of the school's published admissions criteria as part of normal admissions procedures

- **must not** refuse to admit a child who has SEN but does not have an EHC plan because they do not feel able to cater for those needs

- **must not** refuse to admit a child on the grounds that they do not have an EHC plan

1.28 The Equality Act 2010 prohibits schools from discriminating against disabled children and young people in respect of admissions for a reason related to their disability. Further education (FE) colleges manage their own admissions policies and are also prohibited from discriminating against disabled young people in respect of admissions. Students will need to meet the entry requirements for courses as set out by the college, but should not be refused access to opportunities based on whether or not they have SEN.

1.29 Children and young people without an EHC plan can be placed in special schools and special post-16 institutions only in the following exceptional circumstances:

- where they are admitted to a special school or special post-16 institution to be assessed for an EHC plan with their agreement (in the case of a young person) or the agreement of their parent (in the case of a child), the local authority, the head teacher or principal of the special school or special post-16 institution and anyone providing advice for the assessment

- where they are admitted to a special school or special post-16 institution following a change in their circumstances with their agreement (in the case of a young person) or the agreement of their parent (in the case of a child), the local authority and the head teacher or principal of the special school or special post-16 institution. Where an emergency placement of this kind is made the local authority should immediately initiate an EHC needs assessment or re-assessment

- where they are in hospital and admitted to a special school which is established in a hospital, or

- where they are admitted to a special academy (including a special free school) whose academy arrangements allow it to admit children or young people with SEN who do not have an EHC plan

1.30 The last of these provisions enables the Secretary of State to approve academy arrangements for individual special academies or special free schools that are innovative and increase access to specialist provision for children and young people without EHC plans. Those academies the Secretary of State authorises will make clear through their Funding Agreement that a child or young person with SEN but no EHC plan should be placed there only at the request of their parents or at their own request and with the support of professional advice such as a report from an educational psychologist. A special academy or special free school with these arrangements will be able to admit only those children who have a type of SEN for which they are designated. They will have adopted fair practices and arrangements that are in accordance with the Schools Admission Code for the admission of children without an EHC plan.

1.31 The leaders of early years settings, schools and colleges should establish and maintain a culture of high expectations that expects those working with children and young people with SEN or disabilities to include them in all the opportunities available to other children and young people so they can achieve well.

1.32 There is a significant overlap between children and young people with SEN and those with disabilities and many such children and young people are covered by both SEN and equality legislation.

1.33 The Equality Act 2010 and Part 3 of the Children and Families Act 2014 interact in a number of important ways. They share a common focus on removing barriers to learning. In the Children and Families Act 2014 duties for planning, commissioning and reviewing provision, the Local Offer and the duties requiring different agencies to work together apply to all children and young people with SEN or disabilities. In carrying out the duties in the Children and Families Act 2014, local authorities and others with responsibilities under that Act, are covered by the Equality Act.

1.34 In practical situations in everyday settings, the best early years settings, schools and colleges do what is necessary to enable children and young people to develop, learn, participate and achieve the best possible outcomes irrespective of whether that is through reasonable adjustments for a disabled child or young person or special educational provision for a child or young person with SEN.

1.35 Much of the guidance in this Code of Practice focuses on the individual duties owed to children and young people with SEN. When early years settings, schools and colleges, local authorities and others plan and review special educational provision and make decisions about children and young people with SEN (chapters 5 to 7) and 9) they should consider, at the same time, the reasonable adjustments and access arrangements required for the same child or young person under the Equality Act.

1.36 The presumption of mainstream education is supported by provisions safeguarding the interests of all children and young people and ensuring that the preferences of the child's parents or the young person for where they should be educated are met wherever possible.

1.37 Special schools (in the maintained, academy, non-maintained and independent sectors), special post-16 institutions and specialist colleges all have an important role in providing for children and young people with SEN and in working collaboratively with mainstream and special settings to develop and share expertise and approaches.

1.38 Children and young people with SEN have different needs and can be educated effectively in a range of mainstream or special settings. Alongside the general presumption of mainstream education, parents of children with an EHC plan and young people with such a plan have the right to seek a place at a special school, special post-16 institution or specialist college. Further details of the arrangements for Education, Health and Care Plans are set out in Chapter 9.

Supporting successful preparation for adulthood

1.39 With high aspirations, and the right support, the vast majority of children and young people can go on to achieve successful long-term outcomes in adult life. Local authorities, education providers and their partners should work together to help children and young people to realise their ambitions in relation to:

- higher education and/or employment – including exploring different employment options, such as support for becoming self-employed and help from supported employment agencies
- independent living – enabling people to have choice and control over their lives and the support they receive, their accommodation and living arrangements, including supported living
- participating in society – including having friends and supportive relationships, and participating in, and contributing to, the local community
- being as healthy as possible in adult life

1.40 All professionals working with families should look to enable children and young people to make choices for themselves from an early age and support them in making friends and staying safe and healthy. As children grow older, and from Year 9 in school at the latest, preparing for adult life should be an explicit element of conversations with children and their families as the young person moves into and through post-16 education. For children and young people in or beyond Year 9 with

EHC plans, local authorities have a legal duty to include provision to assist in preparing for adulthood in the EHC plan review.

1.41 Chapter 8 provides further guidance on how to support children and young people in preparing for adult life. Provision required for preparation for adulthood should inform joint commissioning of services, the Local Offer, EHC needs assessments and plans, and education and training provision for all children and young people with SEN.

2 Impartial information, advice and support

What this chapter covers

This chapter is about the information, advice and support which local authorities **must** provide for children, young people and parents, covering special educational needs (SEN), disability, health and social care.

Relevant legislation

Primary

Sections 19(c), 26(3), 32 and 49 of the Children and Families Act 2014

Regulations

The Special Educational Needs and Disability Regulations 2014

The Special Educational Needs (Personal Budgets) Regulations 2014

Introduction

2.1 Local authorities **must** arrange for children with SEN or disabilities for whom they are responsible, and their parents, and young people with SEN or disabilities for whom they are responsible, to be provided with information and advice about matters relating to their SEN or disabilities, including matters relating to health and social care. This **must** include information, advice and support on the take-up and management of Personal Budgets. In addition, in carrying out their duties under Part 3 of the Children and Families Act 2014, local authorities **must** have regard to the importance of providing children and their parents and young people with the information and support necessary to participate in decisions.

2.2 Local authorities **must** take steps to make these services known to children, their parents and young people in their area; head teachers, proprietors and principals of schools and post-16 institutions in their area, and others where appropriate.

2.3 They **must** ensure that their Local Offer includes details of how information, advice and support related to SEN and disabilities can be accessed and how it is resourced (Chapter 4, The Local Offer).

2.4 Information, advice and support should be provided through a dedicated and easily identifiable service. Local authorities have established Information, Advice and Support Services (formerly known as Parent Partnership services) to provide information, advice and support to parents in relation to SEN. In addition, many local authorities provide or commission information, advice and support services for young people. Local authorities should build on these existing services to provide the information, advice and support detailed in this chapter.

2.5 Information, Advice and Support Services should be impartial, confidential and accessible and should have the capacity to handle face-to-face, telephone and electronic enquiries.

2.6 Local authorities should involve children, young people and parents (including local Parent Carer Forums and Youth Forums) in the design or commissioning of services providing information, advice and support in order to ensure that those services meet local needs. Local authorities should do this in a way which ensures that children, young people and parents feel they have participated fully in the process and have a sense of co-ownership. Chapters 3 and 4 give further detail on how local authorities should engage these groups in planning, commissioning and reviewing services, and in developing the Local Offer.

2.7 The joint arrangements that local authorities and Clinical Commissioning Groups (CCGs) **must** have for commissioning education, health and care provision for children and young people with SEN or disabilities **must** include arrangements for considering and agreeing what information and advice about education, health and care provision is to be provided, by whom and how it is to be provided. These joint arrangements should consider the availability of other information services in their area (services such as youth services, Local Healthwatch, the Patient Advice and Liaison Service (PALS) and the Family Information Service) and how these services will work together.

2.8 When designing Information, Advice and Support Services, local authorities should take into account the following principles:

- The information, advice and support should be impartial and provided at arm's length from the local authority and CCGs
- The information, advice and support offered should be free, accurate, confidential and in formats which are accessible and responsive to the needs of users
- Local authorities should review and publish information annually about the effectiveness of the information, advice and support provided, including customer satisfaction (see also Chapter 4, The Local Offer)
- Staff providing information, advice and support should work in partnership with children, young people, parents, local authorities, CCGs and other relevant partners

- The provision of information, advice and support should help to promote independence and self-advocacy for children, young people and parents

- Staff providing information, advice and support should work with their local Parent Carer Forum and other representative user groups (such as Youth Forums) to ensure that the views and experiences of children, young people and parents inform policy and practice

Who are information, advice and support for?

2.9 Local authorities should recognise the different needs of children, young people and parents.

Children

2.10 The Children and Families Act 2014 requires local authorities to provide children with information, advice and support relating to their SEN or disability. Many children will access information, advice and support via their parents. However, some children, especially older children and those in custody, may want to access information, advice and support separately from their parents, and local authorities **must** ensure this is possible.

Parents

2.11 Staff working in Information, Advice and Support Services should be trained to support, and work in partnership with, parents.

2.12 As a child reaches the end of compulsory school age (the end of the academic year in which they turn 16), some rights to participate in decision-making about Education Health and Care (EHC) plans transfer from the parent to the young person, subject to their capacity to do so, as set out in the Mental Capacity Act 2005 (See Chapter 8 for more information). Parents of young people can still access information, advice and support on behalf of, or with, the young person. Staff should be clear about the transfer of some rights and responsibilities to young people, and work sensitively with parents to help them understand their role.

2.13 There may be cases where the young person and the parents do not agree on an issue. Legally, it is the young person's decision which prevails, subject to their capacity. Where there are disagreements, staff providing information, advice and support should work impartially and separately with both the parents and the young person.

Young people

2.14 Young people are entitled to the same quality and level of information, advice and support as parents. Local authorities should recognise the specific needs of this group, while ensuring co-ordination and consistency in what is offered to children, young people and parents.

2.15 Young people **must** have confidence that they are receiving confidential and impartial information, advice and support. Staff working directly with young people should be trained to support them and work in partnership with them, enabling them to participate fully in decisions about the outcomes they wish to achieve. Young people may be finding their voice for the first time, and may need support in exercising choice and control over the support they receive (including support and advice to take up and manage Personal Budgets). Advocacy should be provided where necessary. Local authorities **must** provide independent advocacy for young people undergoing transition assessments, provided certain conditions are met (see section 67 of the Care Act 2014).

2.16 The service should direct young people to specialist support to help them prepare for employment, independent living (including housing) and participation in society and should provide access to careers advice where needed. Duties on schools and colleges to give impartial careers advice are covered in Chapter 8, Preparing for adulthood from the earliest years.

What needs to be provided?

2.17 The scope of this information, advice and support should cover initial concerns or identification of potential SEN or disabilities, through to ongoing support and provision, which may include an EHC plan. The local authority **must** ensure children, young people and parents are provided with information and advice on matters relating to SEN and disability. This should include:

- local policy and practice
- the Local Offer
- personalisation and Personal Budgets
- law on SEN and disability, health and social care, through suitably independently trained staff
- advice for children, young people and parents on gathering, understanding and interpreting information and applying it to their own situation
- information on the local authority's processes for resolving disagreements, its complaints procedures and means of redress

2.18 Local Healthwatch offers advice to patients and their families in relation to health services, and CCGs and local authorities should ensure that this information is clearly available to families, including through the Local Offer.

2.19 To meet local needs, local authorities should provide the following forms of support through their Information, Advice and Support Service(s):

- Signposting children, young people and parents to alternative and additional sources of advice, information and support that may be available locally or nationally
- Individual casework and representation for those who need it, which should include:
    - support in attending meetings, contributing to assessments and reviews and participating in decisions about outcomes for the child or young person
    - directing children, young people, parents and those who support and work with them to additional support services where needed, including services provided by the voluntary sector. These services should include support relating to preparing for adulthood, including housing support, careers advice and employment support
- Help when things go wrong, which should include:
    - supporting children, young people and parents in arranging or attending early disagreement resolution meetings
    - supporting children, young people and parents in managing mediation, appeals to the First-tier Tribunal (Special Educational Needs and Disability), exclusions and complaints on matters related to SEN and disability
    - making children, young people and parents aware of the local authority's services for resolving disagreements and for mediation, and on the routes of appeal and complaint on matters related to SEN and disability (see Chapter 11, Resolving disagreements)
- Provision of advice through individual casework and through work with parent carer support groups, local SEN youth forums or disability groups, or training events

Additional support

2.20 Families may receive help from an independent supporter, provided by private voluntary and community sector organisations, who is independent of the local authority. Independent supporters will be recruited locally and receive accredited training, including legal training, to help any family going through an EHC needs assessment and the process of developing an EHC plan. Local authorities should work with organisations that are providing independent supporters to ensure there are arrangements agreed locally to offer help from an independent supporter to as many families as possible who require it.

2.21 Local authorities should adopt a key working approach, which provides children, young people and parents with a single point of contact to help ensure the holistic provision and co-ordination of services and support. Key working may be provided by statutory services in health, social care and education, or by the voluntary, community, private or independent sectors. Key working can be offered to any family where children and young people have SEN or disabilities, for example if they receive SEN support in schools or nurseries or in preparing for adulthood. Approaches will vary locally, but the main functions of key working support should include some or all of the following:

- emotional and practical support as part of a trusting relationship
- enabling and empowering for decision-making and the use of Personal Budgets
- co-ordinating practitioners and services around the child or young person and their family
- being a single point of regular and consistent contact
- facilitating multi-agency meetings
- supporting and facilitating a single planning and joint assessment process
- identifying strengths and needs of family members
- providing information and signposting
- advocating on behalf of the child, young person and/or their family
- facilitating the seamless integration of clinical and social care services with specialist and universal services

2.22 Guidance and examples of best practice on key working approaches are available from the Early Support website (see the References section under Chapter 2) and the Pathfinder information packs (see the References section under General). Further non-statutory guidance on how to deliver impartial information, advice and support for children, young people and parents can be found on the Information,

Advice and Support Services Network website – see the References section under Chapter 2 for a link.

Support for parents in HM Armed Forces

2.23 Parents serving in HM Armed Forces can also access the Children's Education Advisory Service (CEAS) – an information, advice and support service established specifically for Service parents. It covers any issue relating to their children's education, including SEN. More information about CEAS may be found on the CEAS website – a link is given in the References section under Chapter 2.

Support for children and young people in custody

2.24 When securing a detained person's EHC needs assessment the local authority **must** consider whether the child, the child's parent or the young person requires any information, advice and support in order to enable them to take part effectively in the assessment. If it considers that such information, advice or support is necessary the local authority **must** provide it. Further guidance in respect of children and young people who are in custody is in Chapter 10.

3 Working together across education, health and care for joint outcomes

What this chapter covers

This chapter explains the duties local authorities and their partner commissioning bodies have for developing joint arrangements for commissioning services to improve outcomes for 0 to 25-year-old children and young people who have special educational needs (SEN) or disabilities, including those with Education Health and Care (EHC) plans.

It explains:

- the scope of joint commissioning arrangements
- how local partners should commission services to meet local needs and support better outcomes
- how partnership working should inform and support the joint commissioning arrangements
- the role that children, young people, parents and representative groups such as Parent Carer Forums and Youth Forums have in informing commissioning arrangements
- responsibility for decision-making in joint commissioning arrangements
- how partners should develop a joint understanding of the outcomes that their local population of children and young people with SEN and disabilities aspires to, and use it to produce a joint plan, which they then deliver jointly, and review jointly
- how joint commissioning draws together accountability arrangements for key partners
- the role of colleges as commissioners

Relevant legislation

Primary

Sections 23, 25, 28 and 31 of the Children and Families Act 2014

The Care Act 2014

Section 2 of the Chronically Sick and Disabled Persons Act 1970

Schedule 2, Sections 17 and section 47 of the Children Act 1989

Section 2 of the Children Act 2004

National Health Service Act 2006 (Part 3, section 75 and 14Z2)

Local Government and Public Involvement in Health Act 2007

Equality Act 2010 (including disability equality duty under s149)

Health and Social Care Act 2012

The legal framework

3.1 Section 25 of the Children and Families Act 2014 places a duty on local authorities that should ensure integration between educational provision and training provision, health and social care provision, where this would promote wellbeing and improve the quality of provision for disabled young people and those with SEN.

3.2 The Care Act 2014 requires local authorities to ensure co-operation between children's and adults' services to promote the integration of care and support with health services, so that young adults are not left without care and support as they make the transition from children's to adult social care. Local authorities **must** ensure the availability of preventative services for adults, a diverse range of high quality local care and support services and information and advice on how adults can access this universal support.

3.3 Local authorities and clinical commissioning groups (CCGs) **must** make joint commissioning arrangements for education, health and care provision for children and young people with SEN or disabilities (Section 26 of the Act). The term 'partners' refers to the local authority and its partner commissioning bodies across education, health and social care provision for children and young people with SEN or disabilities, including clinicians' commissioning arrangements, and NHS England for specialist health provision.

3.4 Joint commissioning should be informed by a clear assessment of local needs. Health and Wellbeing Boards are required to develop Joint Strategic Needs Assessments and Joint Health and Wellbeing Strategies, to support prevention, identification, assessment and early intervention and a joined-up approach. Under section 75 of the National Health Service Act 2006, local authorities and CCGs can pool resources and delegate certain NHS and local authority health-related functions to the other partner(s) if it would lead to an improvement in the way those functions are exercised.

3.5 To take forward the joint commissioning arrangements for those with SEN or disabilities described in this chapter, partners could build on any existing structures established under the Children Act 2004 duties to integrate services.

3.6 The NHS Mandate, which CCGs **must** follow, contains a specific objective on supporting children and young people with SEN or disabilities, including through the offer of Personal Budgets.

3.7 Joint commissioning arrangements should enable partners to make best use of all the resources available in an area to improve outcomes for children and young people in the most efficient, effective, equitable and sustainable way (*Good commissioning: principles and practice, Commissioning Support Programme, (Rev) September 2010*). Partners **must** agree how they will work together. They should aim to provide personalised, integrated support that delivers positive outcomes for children and young people, bringing together support across education, health and social care from early childhood through to adult life, and improves planning for transition points such as between early years, school and college, between children's and adult social care services, or between paediatric and adult health services.

3.8 Under the Public Sector Equality Duty (Equality Act 2010), public bodies (including CCGs, local authorities, maintained schools, maintained nursery schools, academies and free schools) **must** have regard to the need to eliminate discrimination, promote equality of opportunity and foster good relations between disabled and non-disabled children and young people when carrying out their functions. They **must** publish information to demonstrate their compliance with this general duty and **must** prepare and publish objectives to achieve the core aims of the general duty. Objectives **must** be specific and measurable.

Scope of joint commissioning arrangements

3.9 Joint commissioning arrangements **must** cover the services for 0-25 year old children and young people with SEN or disabilities, both with and without EHC plans. Services will include specialist support and therapies, such as clinical treatments and delivery of medications, speech and language therapy, assistive technology, personal care (or access to it), Child and Adolescent Mental Health Services (CAMHS) support, occupational therapy, habilitation training, physiotherapy, a range of nursing support, specialist equipment, wheelchairs and continence supplies and also emergency provision. They could include highly specialist services needed by only a small number of children, for instance children with severe learning disabilities or who require services which are commissioned centrally by NHS England (for example some augmentative and alternative communication systems, or health provision for children and young people in the secure estate or secure colleges).

3.10 Local authorities, NHS England and their partner CCGs **must** make arrangements for agreeing the education, health and social care provision reasonably required by local children and young people with SEN or disabilities. In doing so they should take into account provision being commissioned by other agencies, such as schools, further education colleges and other education settings. Partners should commission provision for children and young people who need to access services swiftly, for example because they need emergency mental health support or have sustained a serious head injury.

3.11 Joint commissioning **must** also include arrangements for:

- securing EHC needs assessments
- securing the education, health and care provision specified in EHC plans, and
- agreeing Personal Budgets

3.12 Local joint commissioning arrangements **must** consider:

- what advice and information is to be provided about education, health and care provision for those who have SEN or are disabled and by whom it is to be provided
- how complaints about education, health and social care provision can be made and are dealt with, and
- procedures for ensuring that disagreements between local authorities and CCGs (and NHS England for specialist services) are resolved as quickly as possible

The outputs of this work **must** be presented publicly in the Local Offer (see Chapter 4, The Local Offer, paragraphs 4.30 and 4.31).

The joint commissioning cycle

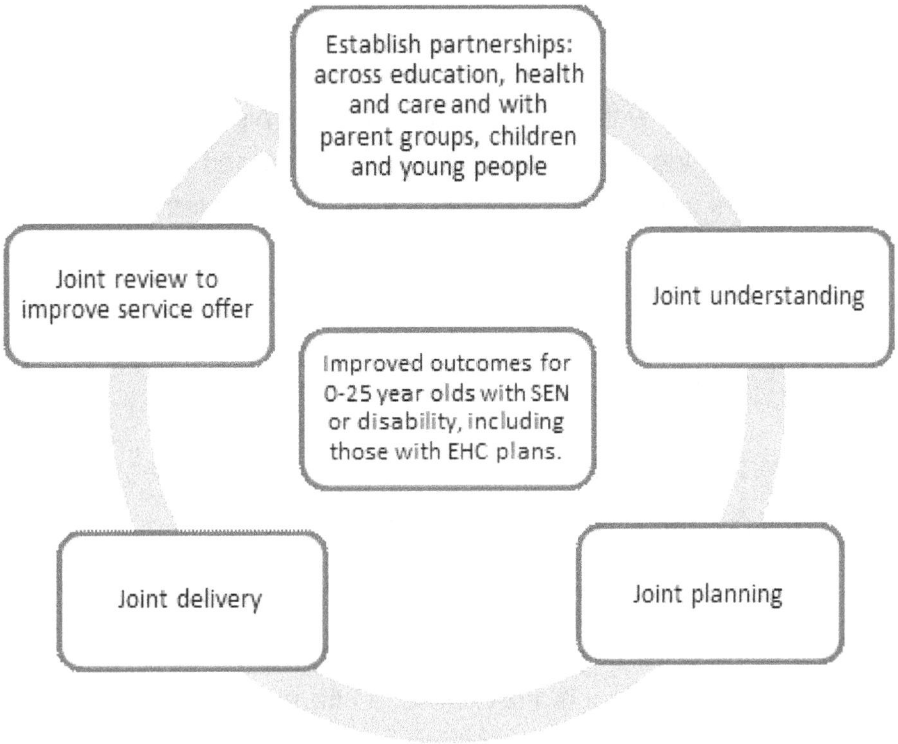

Establishing effective partnerships across education, health and care

3.13 Local authorities **must** work to integrate educational provision and training provision with health and social care provision where they think that this would promote the wellbeing of children and young people with SEN or disabilities, or improve the quality of special educational provision. Local partners **must** co-operate with the local authority in this. The NHS Mandate, NHS Act 2006 and Health and Social Care Act 2012 make clear that NHS England, CCGs and Health and Wellbeing Boards **must** promote the integration of services.

3.14 The Care Act 2014 also requires local authorities to work to promote the integration of adult care and support with health services.

3.15 *Working Together to Safeguard Children (2013)* includes requirements for local agencies to work together to assess the social care needs of individual children and young people who may benefit from early help, and for local authorities and their partners to have a clear line of accountability for the commissioning and/or provision of services designed to safeguard and promote the welfare of children and young people.

3.16 The local authority **must** review its educational, training and social care provision, consulting a range of partners including children and young people with SEN or disabilities, and their parents and carers. This consultation will inform the development and review of the Local Offer (Section 27 of the Children and Families Act 2014).

3.17 The local authority **must** engage other partners it thinks appropriate to support children and young people with SEN and disabilities. This might include voluntary organisations, CAMHS, local therapists, Jobcentre Plus and their employment support advisers, training/apprenticeship/supported employment providers, housing associations, careers advisers, leisure and play services. Local authorities and CCGs should consider the role that private, voluntary and community sector providers can play in delivering services. More information is given on roles and responsibilities of key agencies from paragraph 3.70 onwards.

Partnership with children, young people and parents

3.18 At a strategic level, partners **must** engage children and young people with SEN and disabilities and children's parents in commissioning decisions, to give useful insights into how to improve services and outcomes. Local authorities, CCGs and NHS England **must** develop effective ways of harnessing the views of their local communities so that commissioning decisions on services for those with SEN and disabilities are shaped by users' experiences, ambitions and expectations. To do this, local authorities and CCGs should engage with local Healthwatch organisations, patient representative groups, Parent Carer Forums, groups representing young people with SEN and disabilities and other local voluntary organisations and community groups.

3.19 Under Section 14Z2 of the NHS Act 2006 each CCG **must** exercise its functions to secure that individuals to whom the services are being, or may be, provided, are involved in in planning commissioning arrangements, in the development and consideration of proposals for change, and in decisions affecting the operation of commissioning arrangements where implementation would have an impact on the manner in which services are delivered or the range of services available. Links to a range of useful resources to help them do this are provided in the References section under Chapter 3.

Joint understanding: Joint Strategic Needs Assessments

3.20 There is a clear relationship between population needs, what is procured for children and young people with SEN and disabilities, and individual EHC plans.

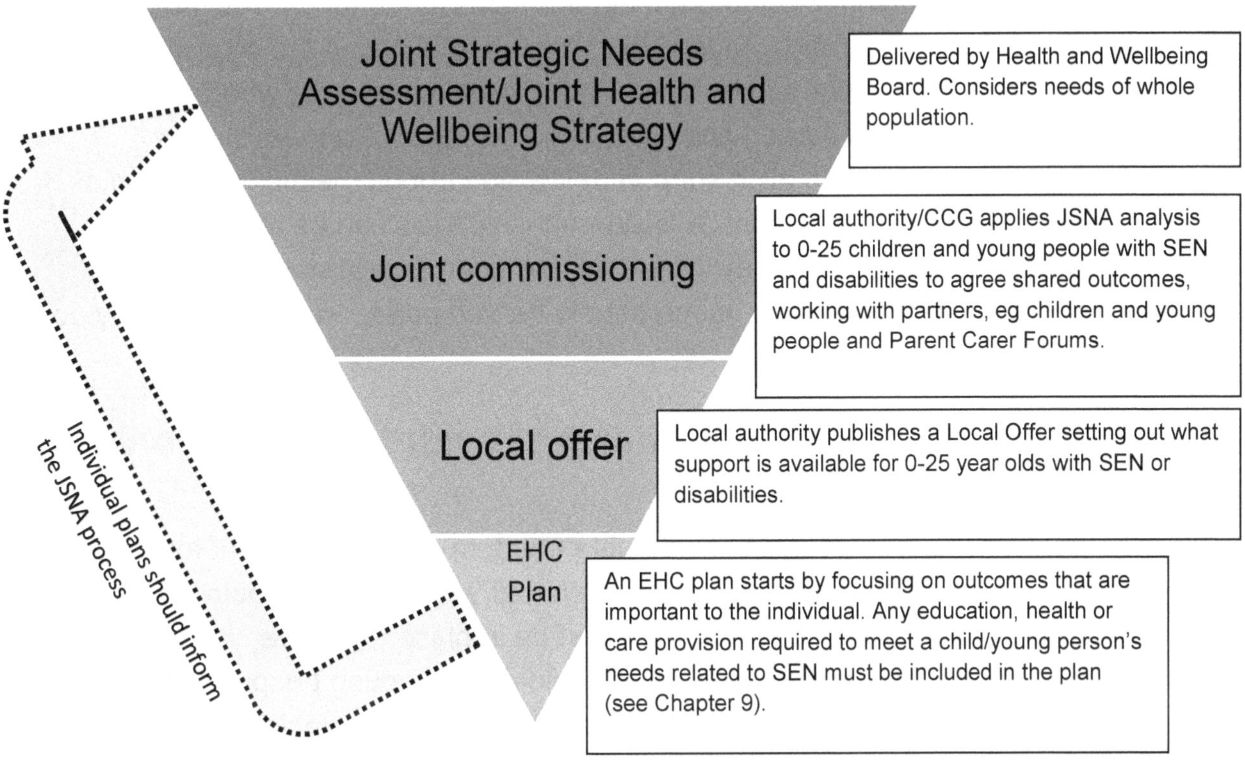

3.21 Each upper tier local authority (county council or unitary authority) has a Health and Wellbeing Board. The Health and Wellbeing Board is a strategic forum which provides leadership across the health, public health and social care systems. The board's job is to improve the health and wellbeing of the local population and reduce health inequalities. Health and Wellbeing Boards have a duty to promote greater integration and partnership working, including through joint commissioning, integrated provision and pooled budgets. The membership of the board **must** include the Director of Children's Services, Director of Public Health, Director of Adult Social Services and a minimum of one elected member from the local authority, a CCG representative and a local Healthwatch representative. Membership from communities and wider partners is decided locally.

3.22 The Joint Strategic Needs Assessment (JSNA) is the means by which the Board understands and agrees the needs of all local people. It is the basis for the joint health and wellbeing strategy which sets the priorities for joint action. Further information about the JSNA is available on the GOV.UK website – a link is given in the References section under Chapter 3.

3.23 The JSNA considers the needs of the local community as a whole, including specific analysis of the needs of vulnerable groups including disabled children and young people and those with SEN, those needing palliative care and looked after children. Local partners across education, health and social care should work together to establish what targeted commissioning is needed to address the needs identified.

3.24 The JSNA will inform the joint commissioning decisions made for children and young people with SEN and disabilities, which will in turn be reflected in the services set out in the Local Offer. At an individual level, services should co-operate where necessary in arranging the agreed provision in an EHC plan. Partners should consider how they will work to align support delivered through mechanisms such as the early help assessment and how SEN support in schools can be aligned both strategically and operationally. They should, where appropriate, share the costs of support for individual children and young people with complex needs, so that they do not fall on one agency.

Responsibility for decision-making in joint commissioning arrangements

3.25 Local authorities and CCGs have considerable freedom in how they work together to deliver integrated support that improves children and young peoples' outcomes. However, local governance arrangements **must** be in place to ensure clear accountability for commissioning services for children and young people with SEN and disabilities from birth to the age of 25. There **must** be clear decision-making structures so that partners can agree the changes that joint commissioning will bring in the design of services. This will help ensure that joint commissioning is focused on achieving agreed outcomes. Partners **must** also be clear about who is responsible for delivering what, who the decision-makers are in education, health and social care, and how partners will hold each other to account in the event of a disagreement. The partners **must** be able to make a decision on how they will meet the needs of children and young people with SEN or disabilities in every case.

3.26 Elected members, governing bodies of CCGs and chief executives across education, health and social care should provide leadership for integrated working. Arrangements for children and young people with SEN or disabilities should be specifically accountable to Lead Members for Children's Services and Directors for Children's Services in line with their statutory duties. It should be clear who can make decisions both operationally (for example, deciding what provision should be put in an EHC plan) and strategically (for example, what provision will be commissioned locally for disabled children and young people and those with SEN) in exercising statutory duties.

Using information to understand and predict need for services

3.27 To inform commissioning decisions, partners should draw on the wide range of local data sets as well as qualitative information about the likely education, health and social care needs of children and young people with SEN or disabilities.

3.28 Data-sets include but are not restricted to:

- population and demographic data
- prevalence data for different kinds of SEN and disability among children and young people at national level – for example through the Child and Maternal Health Intelligence Network (CHiMat)
- numbers of local children and young people with EHC plans and their main needs
- use of out-of-area placements for those with low-incidence needs
- analysis of key performance indicators that are shared across health, education and social care as part of the new joint commissioning arrangements
- the outcomes of developmental assessments (including the two-year-old check)
- information from the Early Years Foundation Stage (EYFS) profile
- where children or young people with SEN or disabilities are educated
- an analysis of local challenges and sources of health inequalities – for example, the level of local economic deprivation, historic data about previous support offered through statements and EHC plans, and the education and health needs of young offenders
- employment rates for young people leaving education
- local data on disabled children from the register of disabled children in their area (including those with impaired hearing and vision) which local authorities are required to keep under Schedule 2 of the Children Act 1989. Local authorities should ensure that registers of disabled children and young people, and particularly details of those with a vision or hearing impairment, are kept accurate and up to date, as such low-incidence needs are particularly difficult to plan for from national data sets

3.29 Local authorities **must** review their provision, taking into consideration the experiences of children, young people and families (including through representative groups such as Parent Carer Forums), voluntary and community sector providers and local Healthwatch. Information from such reviews will contribute to future arrangements and the effectiveness of local joint working.

3.30 Joint commissioning arrangements should be based on evidence about which services, support and interventions are effective. Local areas should maintain up-to-date information on research and guidance about good practice, for example through referring to NICE guidance and Campbell collaboration/Cochrane collaboration.

Joint planning

Deciding on shared outcomes

3.31 Local partners should identify the outcomes that matter to children and young people with SEN or disabilities to inform the planning and delivery of services and the monitoring of how well services have secured those outcomes. Outcomes refer to the benefit or difference made to an individual as a result of an intervention at three levels:

- **Individual outcomes** such as might be set out in an EHC plan: for example, Martha can communicate independently with her friends at playtime
- **Service level outcomes:** for example, paternal mental health has improved in 10 families
- **Strategic outcomes:** for example, there has been a 10% increase in young people supported into employment and independent living

3.32 To achieve such outcomes, provision has to be put in place. In the examples above, a speech and language and social skills programme, a short breaks programme and a newly commissioned transitions strategy, respectively.

3.33 Partners should use their joint understanding to determine the shared outcomes they seek to achieve, for example improvement in educational attainment, levels of mental health and wellbeing and reductions in health inequalities. They should draw on national priorities (for example, those set through the NHS Outcomes Framework), local priorities (for example, the JSNA and Joint Health and Wellbeing Strategy). This should be a transparent process – the local community should be aware both of what the shared outcomes are and the plan to achieve them. This requirement could be discharged through the requirement to consult publicly on the Local Offer.

3.34 The Children and Young People's Outcome Forum report *Improving Children and Young People's Health Outcomes: a system wide response* is a useful resource that partners should draw upon. It is available from the GOV.UK website (see References section under Chapter 3 for a link).

Making best use of resources

3.35 Joint commissioning arrangements should help partners identify scope for working more efficiently together. Partners should assess the extent to which activities contribute to their local priorities and outcomes and decide which services should be commissioned or decommissioned, in consultation with children and young people with SEN or disabilities, their parents, or representative groups such as Parent Carer Forums.

3.36 Under Section 10 of the Children Act 2004 and Section 75 of the National Health Service Act 2006 local authorities and CCGs have a statutory duty to consider the extent to which children and young people's needs could be met more effectively through integrating services and aligning or pooling budgets in order to offer greater value for money, improve outcomes and/or better integrate services for children and young people with SEN or disabilities. Under the Care Act 2014, local authorities **must** ensure the provision of preventative services, the diversity and quality of care and support services for adults, and the provision of information and advice on care and support locally.

3.37 To make the best use of resources, partners should consider how an integrated approach can best support:

- prevention – for example using the outcomes of developmental assessments as outlined in the EYFS to target early help for children experiencing developmental delay can reduce the need for specialist services later on
- early identification of needs
- the resilience of families and local services to enable children and young people with more complex needs to participate actively in their local community
- better access to services
- the development of good language, communication and mental health through universal services so that effective use is made of specialist speech and language therapy services and CAMHS

- better transitions between life stages and settings, including from early years to primary education, primary to secondary and secondary to further education (FE), and
- children and young people in preparing for adult life

Personal Budgets

3.38 Young people and parents of children who have EHC plans have the right to request a Personal Budget, which may contain elements of education, social care and health funding. Partners **must** set out in their joint commissioning arrangements their arrangements for agreeing Personal Budgets. They should develop and agree a formal approach to making fair and equitable allocations of funding and should set out a local policy for Personal Budgets that includes:

- a description of the services across education, health and social care that currently lend themselves to the use of Personal Budgets
- the mechanisms of control for funding available to parents and young people including:
    - direct payments – where individuals receive the cash to contract, purchase and manage services themselves
    - an arrangement – whereby the local authority, school or college holds the funds and commissions the support specified in the EHC plan (these are sometimes called notional budgets)
    - third party arrangements – where funds (direct payments) are paid to and managed by an individual or organisation on behalf of the child's parent or the young person
    - a combination of the above
- clear and simple statements of eligibility criteria and the decision-making processes that underpin them

3.39 To do this, partners should:

- identify and agree the funding streams and services for inclusion and develop the necessary infrastructure to support their inclusion
- identify the links to be made locally between the SEN offer and Personal Health Budgets for children and adults

- identify and establish the information, advice and support necessary at an area and individual level to help families consider options for, and to take up and manage, Personal Budgets

- develop a pathway for Personal Budgets within the process of EHC needs assessment and EHC plan development and the workforce and cultural changes necessary for a person-centred approach

- identify how the new joint commissioning strategies will support greater choice and control year on year, as the market is developed and funding streams are freed from existing contractual arrangements

- as an integral part of this, partners should ensure children, young people and families are involved in the decision-making processes at both an individual and a strategic level

Joint delivery

3.40 At a strategic level, when commissioning training for professionals partners should consider whether combined service delivery, training or a common set of key skills would help professionals and providers adapt to meeting the needs of children and young people with SEN or disabilities in a more personalised way. This could include commissioning 'key working' roles to support children and young people with SEN and disabilities and their parents, particularly at key points such as diagnosis, EHC plan development and transition.

3.41 Partners should also consider whether and how specialist staff can train the wider workforce so they can better identify need and offer support earlier – for example, educational psychologists or speech and language therapists training professionals such as teachers or GPs to identify and support children and young people with mental health problems or speech and language difficulties, respectively. This may involve NHS Local Education and Training Boards. Some areas have involved parent carers in delivery of workforce development programmes.

Joint review to improve service offered

3.42 Joint commissioning is an ongoing improvement cycle. Over time, partners may shift the focus of their activity as the needs of the local population change and delivery of services improves.

3.43 Partners should agree how they will work together to monitor how outcomes in education, health and care are being improved as a result of the provision they make. Partners should monitor the changing needs of the local population of children and young people with SEN and disabilities closely and, crucially, establish whether or not the provision arranged for them is improving outcomes. EHC plans for individual children and young people **must** be similarly reviewed to see if they are enabling the child or young person to achieve their desired outcomes, so that where appropriate the commissioned provision can be changed. Feedback from children, young people and families is useful in identifying gaps in provision. Any changes in provision commissioned locally should be reflected in the Local Offer.

3.44 Local authorities **must** review the special educational provision and social care provision in their areas for children and young people who have SEN or disabilities and the provision made for local children and young people who are educated out of the area, working with the partners to their joint commissioning arrangements. The local authority **must** consult with children and young people with SEN or disabilities and their parents and as part of this should consult with family representatives such as Parent Carer Forums. Joint commissioning arrangements **must** consider the needs of children and young people with SEN and disabilities. Partners should also work with commissioners of adult services to ensure that there are smooth transitions between children's and adult services. This will involve working with a range of professionals in the public, private, voluntary and community sectors and will help those with SEN or disabilities prepare for adulthood, including living independently and employment.

Education, Health and Care: roles and responsibilities

Designated Medical/Clinical Officer

3.45 Partners should ensure there is a Designated Medical Officer (DMO) to support the CCG in meeting its statutory responsibilities for children and young people with SEN and disabilities, primarily by providing a point of contact for local partners, when notifying parents and local authorities about children and young people they believe have, or may have, SEN or a disability, and when seeking advice on SEN or disabilities. This does not alter the CCG's responsibility for commissioning health provision.

3.46 The DMO provides the point of contact for local authorities, schools and colleges seeking health advice on children and young people who may have SEN or disabilities, and provides a contact (or contacts) for CCGs or health providers so that appropriate notification can be given to the local authority of children under compulsory school age who they think may have SEN or disabilities. The DMO can support schools with their duties under the 'Supporting Pupils with Medical Conditions' guidance. The DMO would not routinely be involved in assessments or planning for individuals, except in the course of their usual clinical practice, but would be responsible for ensuring that assessment, planning and health support is carried out. Some CCGs may delegate key decisions to the DMO (for example, agreeing the health services in an EHC plan).

3.47 The DMO should have an appropriate level of clinical expertise to enable them to exercise these functions effectively, and should be designated as the DMO in their job description. There may be one DMO for several CCGs and local authorities, where there are joint arrangements or shared commissioning responsibilities, and given the age range of EHC plans from birth to 25, the DMO may need to liaise with colleagues outside paediatrics.

3.48 This is a non-statutory role which would usually be carried out by a paediatrician, but there is local flexibility for the role to be undertaken by a suitably competent qualified and experienced nurse or other health professional (in which case the role would be the Designated Clinical Officer). The person in this role should have appropriate expertise and links with other professionals to enable them to exercise it in relation to children and young adults with EHC plans from the age of 0 to 25 in a wide range of educational institutions.

Children's social care

3.49 Where a child or young person has been assessed as having social care needs in relation to their SEN or disabilities social care teams:

- **must** secure social care provision under the Chronically Sick and Disabled Persons Act (CSDPA) 1970 which has been assessed as being necessary to support a child or young person's SEN and which is specified in their EHC plan
- should provide early years providers, schools and colleges with a contact for social care advice on children and young people with SEN and disabilities
- **must** undertake reviews of children and young people with EHC plans where there are social care needs
- should make sure that for looked after children and care leavers the arrangements for assessing and meeting their needs across education, health and social care are co-ordinated effectively within the process of care and pathway planning, in order to avoid duplication and delay, to include in particular liaising with the Virtual School Head (VSH) for looked after children

3.50 Where children or young people with SEN or disabilities also have a child in need or child protection plan, the social worker within the SEN team should ensure the statutory timescales for social care assessments are met and any assessments are aligned with EHC needs assessments wherever possible. *Working Together to Safeguard Children* (2013) gives full details. A link is available in the References section under Chapter 3.

Adult social care

3.51 Young people with SEN or disabilities turning 18 may become eligible for adult social care services, regardless of whether they have an EHC plan or whether they have been receiving services from children's social care.

3.52 The Care Act 2014 and the associated regulations and guidance set out the requirements on local authorities when young people are approaching, or turn, 18 and are likely to require an assessment for adult care and support. These are intended to support effective transition from children's to adult social care services. For those already receiving support from children's services, the Care Act makes it clear that local authorities **must** continue to provide children's services until adult provision has started or a decision is made that the young person's needs do not meet the eligibility criteria for adult care and support following an assessment. Children's services **must not** be discontinued simply because a young person has reached their 18th birthday. More information on this is given in Chapter 8, Preparing for Adulthood.

3.53 Local authorities and their partners **must** co-operate in the provision of adult care and support in promoting the individual's wellbeing and local authorities **must**:

- promote the integration of adult care and support and health services
- arrange the provision of preventative resources that can be accessed by those who require support but who do not have eligible needs (under the Care Act 2014).
- ensure a diverse and high quality range of services to meet assessed care and support needs

3.54 Local authorities **must** provide information and advice on the range of services available. They should include in their Local Offer relevant information and advice on local provision and how to receive an assessment for transition to adult care and support.

3.55 The transition from children's to adult services needs to be well managed and should take place at a time that is appropriate for the individual. This is particularly important where young people's assessed needs do not meet eligibility criteria for adult services.

3.56 Local authorities and their partners should work together to ensure effective and well supported transition arrangements are in place; that assessment and review processes for both Care plans and EHC plans are aligned; that there is effective integration with health services, and that there is a good range of universal provision for inclusion in the Local Offer. Young people and their families should not be expected to repeatedly provide duplicate information to different services, or to attend numerous reviews, or receive support that is not co-ordinated and joined up. There should be clear and joined-up decision-making processes and lines of accountability for considering when the transition to adult services should take place and ensuring that children's services continue to be in place for as long as required.

3.57 Local authorities should consider ways of supporting carers. Parent carers have often had to give up paid work after their child leaves full time education. Loss of paid employment can have a significant impact on the carer's wellbeing and self-esteem as well as a significant impact on the family's financial circumstances. Taking a whole family approach to care and support planning that sets out a 'five-day offer' for a young person and support for a carer to manage an increased caring role (which ideally allows them to stay in paid work if they wish to do so) can help families manage the transition and save money by avoiding costly out-of-area placements. More information on this is provided in the Care Act Statutory Guidance. Chapter 8 of this Code provides guidance on packages of provision across five days for young people with EHC plans.

3.58 Support for carers includes any support assessed as being reasonably required by the learning difficulties and disabilities which result in the child or young person having SEN. It can include any services assessed under an early help assessment and/or under Section 17 or Section 47 of the Children Act 1989 or eligible needs identified by assessments under adult care provisions. It can also include services for parents and carers which will support the child's outcomes, such as mental health support.

Health services for children and young people with SEN and disabilities and their families

3.59 Health services for children and young people with SEN or disabilities provide early identification, assessment and diagnosis, intervention and review for children and young people with long-term conditions and disabilities, for example chronic fatigue syndrome, anxiety disorders or life-threatening conditions such as inoperable heart disease. Services are delivered by health professionals including paediatricians, psychiatrists, nurses and allied health professionals such as occupational therapists, speech and language therapists, habilitation trainers, physiotherapists and psychologists. In addition, public health services for children ensure a whole population approach to health and wellbeing including preventative services such as immunisation for the whole population and targeted immunisation for the most vulnerable.

3.60 Health services support early identification of young children who may have SEN, through neonatal screening programmes, the Healthy Child Programme, and specialist health and developmental assessment where concerns have been raised. Community paediatricians in conjunction with other health professionals, particularly therapists, are often the first people to notify young children with SEN to local authorities. They provide diagnostic services and health reports for EHC needs assessments. CCGs, NHS Trusts, and NHS Foundation Trusts **must** inform the appropriate local authority if they identify a child under compulsory school age as having, or probably having, a disability or SEN (Section 23 of the Children and Families Act 2014).

3.61 The multi-disciplinary child health team, including paediatricians, therapists, clinical psychologists, dieticians and specialist nurses such as health visitors, school nurses and community children's nursing teams, provide intervention and review for children and young people with SEN and disabilities and should contribute to supporting key transition points, including to adulthood. They aim to provide optimum health care for the children, addressing the impact of their conditions, managing consequences for the families and preventing further complications.

3.62 Health professionals advise education services on managing health conditions such as epilepsy and diabetes, and health technologies such as tube feeding, tracheostomy care and ventilation in schools. They are able to provide an ongoing overview of health and wellbeing. They seek advice from paediatric specialists when necessary and facilitate training for education staff.

3.63 Therapists have important and specific roles in supporting children and young people with SEN or disabilities, working directly with children and young people, advising and training education staff and setting programmes for implementation at home and in school.

Local authorities' role in delivering health services

3.64 Local authorities and CCGs should consider how best to integrate the commissioning of services for children and young people who have SEN with the CCG's broad responsibility for commissioning health services for other groups, including preventative services, and the local authority's responsibility for health protection and health improvement for the local population. The local authority in particular has responsibility for securing a range of public health services which may be relevant for children and young people, and should consider how this can be aligned with the arrangements for commissioning services for children and young people who are disabled or who have SEN – for example, the Healthy Child Programme for pre-school and school-age children, including school nursing. A factsheet has been produced on the public health responsibilities of local authorities and is available from the GOV.UK website (see References section under Chapter 3 for a link).

The health commissioning duty

3.65 As health service commissioners, CCGs have a duty under Section 3 of the NHS Act 2006 to arrange health care provision for the people for whom they are responsible to meet their reasonable health needs. (NHS England may also have commissioning responsibility for some children and young people – for example in some secure children's homes – and therefore a similar duty to meet their reasonable needs.) This is the fundamental basis of commissioning in the NHS. Where there is provision which has been agreed in the health element of an EHC plan, health commissioners **must** put arrangements in place to secure that provision. This issue is explored in more detail in Chapter 9.

Schools and post-16 settings as commissioners

3.66 Schools, including early years providers, and post-16 settings can also be commissioners in their own right. Schools have a notional SEN budget and many schools will commission services (such as speech and language therapy, pastoral care and counselling services) to support pupils. Schools **must** work with the local authority in developing the Local Offer, which could include school-commissioned services. The school **must** set out its SEN policy and information on its approach to supporting children and young people with SEN. The school's governing body **must** ensure that arrangements are in place in schools to support pupils at school with medical conditions and should ensure that school leaders consult health and social care professionals, pupils and parents to make sure that the needs of children with medical conditions are effectively supported.

3.67 Joint commissioning arrangements should reflect this local commissioning and should ensure services being commissioned by schools are suitably supported to deliver positive outcomes for children and young people.

Regional commissioning: meeting the needs of children and young people with highly specialised and/or low-incidence needs

3.68 Partners should consider strategic planning and commissioning of services or placements for children and young people with high levels of need across groups of authorities, or at a regional level. The benefits include:

- greater choice for parents and young people, enabling them to access a wider range of services or educational settings

- greater continuity of support for children and young people in areas where there is a great deal of movement across local authorities (for example, in London)

NHS England already commissions specialist health services at a regional and national level, so local partners will need to engage and integrate these arrangements to support local joint commissioning activity.

3.69 When a health body is considering a placement that includes an education commitment, such as a placement in residential care, they should consult the local authority prior to the decision being made (see Chapter 10, paragraph 10.49). The Winterbourne View Concordat emphasised the need for high quality local provision – local authorities and CCGs should work together to consider how they will reduce out-of-area placements. Regional commissioning may help them to do this. Statutory guidance on long-term residential care is available on the GOV.UK website (see References section under Chapter 3 for a link).

Local accountability

3.70 The roles and responsibilities of bodies involved in joint commissioning arrangements are summarised below:

Agency	**Key responsibilities for SEN or Disability**	**Accountability**
Local authority	Leading integration arrangements for Children and Young People with SEN or disabilities	Lead Member for Children's Services and Director for Children's Services (DCS)
Children's and adult social care	Children's and adult social care services **must** co-operate with those leading the integration arrangements for children and young people with SEN or disabilities to ensure the delivery of care and support is effectively integrated in the new SEN system.	Lead Member for Children and Adult Social Care, and Director for Children's Services (DCS), Director for Adult Social Services (DASS).
Health and Wellbeing Board	The Health and Wellbeing Board **must** ensure a joint strategic needs assessment (JSNA) of the current and future needs of the whole local population is developed. The JSNA will form the basis of NHS and local authorities' own commissioning plans, across health, social care, public health	Membership of the Health and Wellbeing Board **must** include at least one local elected councillor, as well as a representative of the local Healthwatch organisation. It **must** also include the local DCS, DASS, and a senior CCG

Agency	Key responsibilities for SEN or Disability	Accountability
	and children's services. This is likely to include specific needs of children and young people with SEN or disabilities.	representative and the Director of Public Health. In practice, most Health and Wellbeing Boards include more local councillors, and many are chaired by cabinet members.
Clinical Commissioning Group	To co-operate with the local authority in jointly commissioning services, ensuring there is sufficient capacity contracted to deliver necessary services, drawing the attention of the local authority to groups and individual children and young people with SEN or disabilities, supporting diagnosis and assessment, and delivering interventions and review.	CCGs will be held to account by NHS England. CCGs are also subject to local accountability, for example, to the Health and Wellbeing Board for how well they contribute to delivering the local Health and Wellbeing Strategy. Each CCG has a governing body and an Accountable Officer who are responsible for ensuring that the CCG fulfils its duties to exercise its functions effectively, efficiently and economically and to improve the quality of services and the health of the local population whilst maintaining value for money.
NHS England	NHS England commissions specialist services which need to be reflected in local joint commissioning arrangements (for example augmentative and alternative communication systems, or provision for detained children and young people in relevant youth accommodation).	Secretary of State for Health
Healthwatch	Local Healthwatch organisations are a key mechanism for enabling people to share their views and concerns – to ensure that commissioners have a clear	Local Healthwatch organisations represent the voice of people who use health and social care on

Agency	Key responsibilities for SEN or Disability	Accountability
	picture of local communities' needs and that this is represented in the planning and delivery of local services. This can include supporting children and young people with SEN or disabilities.	the Health and Wellbeing Board. They are independent, but funded by local authorities.
Maintained nurseries and schools (including academies)	Mainstream schools have duties to use best endeavours to make the provision required to meet the SEN of children and young people. All schools **must** publish details of what SEN provision is available through the information report and co-operate with the local authority in drawing up and reviewing the Local Offer. Schools also have duties to make reasonable adjustments for disabled children and young people, to support medical conditions and to inform parents and young people if SEN provision is made for them. More information about the role of early years settings, schools and post-16 institutions is given in Chapters 5 to 7.	Accountability is through Ofsted and the annual report that schools have to provide to parents on their children's progress.
Colleges	Mainstream colleges have duties to use best endeavours to make the provision required to meet the SEN of children and young people. Mainstream and special colleges **must** also co-operate with the local authority in drawing up and reviewing the Local Offer. All colleges have duties to make reasonable adjustments for disabled children and young people. More information about duties on the further education sector is in Chapter 7.	Accountable through Ofsted and performance tables such as destination and progress measures.

3.71 These arrangements do not affect the disagreement resolution and complaints procedures described in Chapter 11. Local authorities **must** include in their Local Offer information on how complaints can be made about services.

4 The Local Offer

What this chapter covers

This chapter explains the statutory duties on local authorities to develop and publish a Local Offer setting out the support they expect to be available for local children and young people with special educational needs (SEN) or disabilities. It covers:

- preparing and reviewing the Local Offer, including involving children, young people and parents and those providing services
- publishing the Local Offer
- publishing comments on the Local Offer and the action to be taken in response
- what **must** be included in the Local Offer
- information, advice and support

Relevant legislation

Primary

Sections 27, 28, 30, 32, 41, 49, and 51-57 of the Children and Families Act 2014

Equality Act 2010

Regulations

The Special Educational Needs and Disability Regulations 2014 (Part 4)

What is the Local Offer?

4.1 Local authorities **must** publish a Local Offer, setting out in one place information about provision they expect to be available across education, health and social care for children and young people in their area who have SEN or are disabled, including those who do not have Education, Health and Care (EHC) plans. In setting out what they 'expect to be available', local authorities should include provision which they believe will actually be available.

4.2 The Local Offer has two key purposes:

- To provide clear, comprehensive, accessible and up-to-date information about the available provision and how to access it, and

- To make provision more responsive to local needs and aspirations by directly involving disabled children and those with SEN and their parents, and disabled young people and those with SEN, and service providers in its development and review

4.3 The Local Offer should not simply be a directory of existing services. Its success depends as much upon full engagement with children, young people and their parents as on the information it contains. The process of developing the Local Offer will help local authorities and their health partners to improve provision.

4.4 The Local Offer **must** include provision in the local authority's area. It **must** also include provision outside the local area that the local authority expects is likely to be used by children and young people with SEN for whom they are responsible and disabled children and young people. This could, for example, be provision in a further education college in a neighbouring area or support services for children and young people with particular types of SEN that are provided jointly by local authorities. It should include relevant regional and national specialist provision, such as provision for children and young people with low-incidence and more complex SEN.

4.5 Local authorities and those who are required to co-operate with them need to comply with the Equality Act 2010, including when preparing, developing and reviewing the Local Offer.

4.6 The Special Educational Needs and Disability Regulations 2014 provide a common framework for the Local Offer. They specify the requirements that all local authorities **must** meet in developing, publishing and reviewing their Local Offer, and cover:

- the information to be included
- how the Local Offer is to be published
- who is to be consulted about the Local Offer
- how children with SEN or disabilities and their parents and young people with SEN or disabilities will be involved in the preparation and review of the Local Offer, and
- the publication of comments on the Local Offer and the local authority's response, including any action it intends to take in relation to those comments

4.7 The Local Offer should be:

- **collaborative:** local authorities **must** involve parents, children and young people in developing and reviewing the Local Offer. They **must** also co-operate with those providing services

- **accessible:** the published Local Offer should be easy to understand, factual and jargon free. It should be structured in a way that relates to young people's and parents' needs (for example by broad age group or type of special educational provision). It should be well signposted and well publicised

- **comprehensive**: parents and young people should know what support is expected to be available across education, health and social care from age 0 to 25 and how to access it. The Local Offer **must** include eligibility criteria for services where relevant and make it clear where to go for information, advice and support, as well as how to make complaints about provision or appeal against decisions

- **up to date**: when parents and young people access the Local Offer it is important that the information is up to date

- **transparent:** the Local Offer should be clear about how decisions are made and who is accountable and responsible for them

Preparing and reviewing the Local Offer

Involving children and young people and parents

4.8 Local authorities **must** involve children with SEN or disabilities and their parents and young people with SEN or disabilities in:

- planning the content of the Local Offer

- deciding how to publish the Local Offer

- reviewing the Local Offer, including by enabling them to make comments about it

4.9 Local authorities should do this in a way which ensures that children, young people and parents feel they have participated fully in the process and have a sense of co-ownership. This is often referred to as 'co-production'. Local authorities should take steps to ensure that their arrangements for involving children, young people and parents include a broadly representative group of the children with SEN or disabilities and their parents and young people with SEN or disabilities in their area.

Parent Carer Forums, young people's forums and other local groups are useful ways to engage families.

4.10 Local authorities should publicise in their Local Offer the ways in which they will involve children, young people and parents in developing and reviewing it. Local authorities should ensure that they provide support that enables children, young people and parents to contribute to decision-making at this strategic level and the Local Offer should include details of this support, which should include Parent Carer Forums and local voluntary organisations.

Young people

4.11 Local authorities **must** engage young people directly in developing and reviewing the Local Offer and should consider setting up a forum, or a range of forums, to do so. Local authorities should make every effort to engage a cross-section of young people with a range of SEN and disabilities, in a variety of settings and circumstances and at different ages within the 16–25 age range. Local authorities should make every effort to establish the issues on which young people most want to be engaged. They should also consider using a variety of methods to engage young people. These could include surveys and social media or young people's forums, and making existing consultation groups, such as a local youth council, accessible to young people with SEN or disabilities. Young people should also have opportunities to be engaged independently of their parents.

4.12 When organising participation events for young people, local authorities should endeavour to ensure full accessibility by considering:

- **timing:** holding events when young people are most likely to be free and not when they are likely to be in education (unless arrangements have been made with their education providers)
- **transport:** explaining to young people how to travel to an event, with clear instructions, maps and, particularly in rural areas, details of a taxi service which is accessible to those with disabilities
- **physical accessibility:** for example, access for a number of wheelchair users
- **accessibility of content:** providing materials in different formats and tailored to meet different cognitive abilities and reading skills and supporting different communication needs, avoiding jargon and acronyms wherever possible and where this is not possible, explaining terms used

- **age appropriateness:** keeping membership of young people's forums under review as the participants get older, and bearing in mind the very different stages that young people will be at from the age of 16 to 25

Whatever the means of consultation and engagement local authorities should let participants know the outcome of discussions so that they will know what will happen as a result of their contribution.

Parents

4.13 Effective parent participation can lead to a better fit between families' needs and the services provided, higher satisfaction with services, reduced costs (as long-term benefits emerge), better value for money and better relationships between those providing services and those using them. Local authorities and parents should work together to establish the aims of parent participation, to mark progress and build trust. To enable effective parental participation, local authorities should consider in particular the timing of events and meetings – for example, organising them during the school day while children are at school and ensuring that parents have enough notice to allow them to organise childcare.

Involving schools, colleges, health services and others

4.14 Local authorities and their partner bodies and agencies **must** co-operate with each other in the development and review of the Local Offer. This is essential so that the Local Offer provides a comprehensive, transparent and accessible picture of the range of services available.

4.15 The most relevant local partners who are required to co-operate with the local authority in relation to the Local Offer include:

- the governing bodies of schools that the local authority maintains
- the proprietors of academies and free schools in the local authority's area
- the proprietors of non-maintained special schools that are in the local authority's area or provide education or training for children and young people in the local authority's area
- the governing bodies of further education colleges and sixth form colleges that are in the local authority's area or are attended or likely to be attended by young people from their area
- the management committees of pupil referral units that are in the local authority's area or are attended or likely to be attended by young people from their area

- the proprietors of independent specialist colleges and independent schools specially organised to make provision for children and young people with SEN which have been included on the list of institutions approved by the Secretary of State for the purpose of enabling parents and young people to request that they are named on an EHC plan and are in the local authority's area or are attended or likely to be attended by children and young people in their area

- any other person (other than a school or college) that makes special educational provision for children or young people for whom the local authority is responsible, including providers of relevant early education

- NHS England and any relevant health bodies including:

    - clinical commissioning groups (CCGs) whose areas coincide with or fall within the local authority's area or which have a duty under section 3 of the National Health Service Act 2006 to arrange for the provision of services for any children or young people for whom the local authority is responsible

    - an NHS Trust or NHS Foundation Trust which provides services in the local authority's area or for children and young people for whom the authority is responsible, or

    - a Local Health Board with functions in relation to children and young people for whom the local authority is responsible

4.16 The local authority should engage with the providers of relevant early years education, particularly those in receipt of early education funding.

4.17 The local authority must also ensure that all its officers co-operate with each other in respect of the Local Offer. This must include those whose roles relate to social services or who will contribute to helping young people make a successful transition to adulthood – for example those working in housing and economic regeneration.

Keeping the Local Offer under review

4.18 The requirement on local authorities to publish comments on their Local Offer and their response to those comments is relevant to their duty to keep under review the educational and training provision and social care provision for children and young people with SEN or disabilities and their role in contributing, with their partner CCGs, to Joint Strategic Needs Assessments and the development of local Health and Wellbeing Strategies (see chapter 3).

4.19 Local authorities **must** keep their educational and training provision and social care provision under review and this includes the sufficiency of that provision. When considering any reorganisation of SEN provision decision makers **must** make clear how they are satisfied that the proposed alternative arrangements are likely to lead to improvements in the standard, quality and/or range of educational provision for children with SEN (School organisation (maintained schools), Annex B: Guidance for Decision-makers, DfE 2014 – see the References section under Chapter 4 for a link).

4.20 Local authorities should link reviews of education, health and social care provision to the development and review of their Local Offer and the action they intend to take in response to comments. This will help to identify gaps in provision and ensure that the Local Offer is responsive to the needs of local children and young people and their families. At a strategic level local authorities should share what they have learned from the comments they receive with local Health and Wellbeing Boards where appropriate, to help inform the development of Health and Wellbeing Strategies and the future provision of services for children and young people with or without EHC plans.

Publishing comments about the Local Offer

4.21 Local authorities **must** publish comments about their Local Offer received from or on behalf of children with SEN or disabilities and their parents and young people with SEN or disabilities.

4.22 Comments **must** be published if they relate to:

- the content of the Local Offer, which includes the quality of existing provision and any gaps in the provision
- the accessibility of information in the Local Offer
- how the Local Offer has been developed or reviewed

4.23 It is up to local authorities to decide on the format for publishing comments but they should consult children and young people with SEN or disabilities and parents and representative organisations such as Parent Carer Forums and local organisations providing information, advice and support to parents, children and young people about this, including the local authority's Information, Advice and Support Service. They should make clear how they have sought comments about the Local Offer.

4.24 Local authorities **must** publish a summary of comments at least annually, although this is expected to be an ongoing process. They **must** ensure that comments are published in a form that does not enable any individual to be identified.

4.25 Local authorities are not expected to publish responses to every comment individually but could, for example, adopt a 'you said, we did' approach. They are not required to publish abusive or vexatious comments or complaints about the service provided to an individual since there are established routes to bring such complaints. The Local Offer should make clear what these routes are and how to access them.

Taking action in response to comments about the Local Offer

4.26 Local authorities **must** publish their response to comments received within the Local Offer and this **must** include details of the action they intend to take. They should consult children and young people with SEN or disabilities and the parents of children with SEN or disabilities in relation to the action they intend to take.

4.27 Where appropriate, local authorities should also feed back comments to commissioners of services and the services themselves, including those in neighbouring local authorities. Comments should be used to inform commissioning decisions and decisions about the specific nature and type of provision that local families want.

4.28 Local authorities should ensure they have access to good quality data to inform their decisions when reviewing provision and taking action to develop their Local Offer.

What must be included in the Local Offer?

4.29 Local authorities **must** include information about all the areas specified in the Special Educational Needs and Disability Regulations 2014. They may wish to include wider information, taking account of their discussions with children with SEN or disabilities and their parents and young people with SEN or disabilities.

4.30 The Local Offer **must** include information about:

- special educational, health and social care provision for children and young people with SEN or disabilities – this should include online and blended learning
- details of how parents and young people can request an assessment for an EHC plan
- arrangements for identifying and assessing children and young people's SEN – this should include arrangements for EHC needs assessments
- other educational provision, for example sports or arts provision, paired reading schemes
- post-16 education and training provision
- apprenticeships, traineeships and supported internships

- information about provision to assist in preparing children and young people for adulthood (see paragraphs 4.52 to 4.56)
- arrangements for travel to and from schools, post-16 institutions and early years providers
- support to help children and young people move between phases of education (for example from early years to school, from primary to secondary)
- sources of information, advice and support in the local authority's area relating to SEN and disabilities including information and advice provided under Section 32 of the Children and Families Act 2014, forums for parents and carers and support groups
- childcare, including suitable provision for disabled children and those with SEN
- leisure activities
- support available to young people in higher education, particularly the Disabled Students Allowance (DSA) and the process and timescales for making an application for DSA
- arrangements for resolving disagreements and for mediation, and details about making complaints
- parents' and young people's rights to appeal a decision of the local authority to the First-tier Tribunal (SEN and disability) in respect of SEN and provision
- the local authority's accessibility strategy (under paragraph 1 Schedule 10 to the Equality Act 2010)
- institutions approved under Section 41 of the Children and Families Act 2014

4.31 The Local Offer should cover:

- support available to all children and young people with SEN or disabilities from universal services such as schools and GPs
- targeted services for children and young people with SEN or disabilities who require additional short-term support over and above that provided routinely as part of universal services
- specialist services for children and young people with SEN or disabilities who require specialised, longer term support

Educational, health and care provision

Educational and training provision

4.32 The local authority **must** set out in its Local Offer an authority-wide description of the special educational and training provision it expects to be available in its area and outside its area for children and young people in its area who have SEN or disabilities from providers of relevant early years education, maintained schools, non-maintained special schools, pupil referral units, independent institutions approved under section 41 of the Children and Families Act 2014, and the full range of post-16 providers. This includes information about the arrangements the local authority has for funding children and young people with SEN, including any agreements about how providers will use any budget that has been delegated to them.

It includes the arrangements providers have in place for:

- identifying the particular SEN of children and young people
- consulting with parents of disabled children with SEN and disabled young people with SEN or disabilities
- securing the services, provision and equipment required by children and young people with SEN or disabilities
- supporting disabled children and young people and those with SEN in moving between phases of education and preparing for adulthood and independent living

and information about:

- approaches to teaching, adaptations to the curriculum and the learning environment for children and young people with SEN or disabilities and additional learning support for those with SEN
- enabling available facilities to be accessed by disabled children and young people and those with SEN (this should include ancillary aids and assistive technology, including Augmentative and Alternative Communication (AAC))
- assessing and reviewing pupils' and students' progress towards outcomes, including how providers work with parents and young people in doing so
- securing expertise among teachers, lecturers or other professionals to support children and young people with SEN or disabilities – this should include professional development to secure expertise at different levels:

- **awareness** (to give a basic awareness of a particular type of SEN, appropriate for all staff who will come into contact with a child or young person with that type of SEN)
- **enhanced** (how to adapt teaching and learning to meet a particular type of SEN, for early years practitioners, class and subject teachers/lecturers and teaching assistants working directly with the child or young person on a regular basis), and
- **specialist** (in-depth training about a particular type of SEN, for staff who will be advising and supporting those with enhanced-level skills and knowledge)

- assessing and evaluating the effectiveness of the education and training provision the local authority makes for children and young people with SEN or disabilities
- activities that are available to disabled children and young people and those with SEN, including physical activities and extra-curricular activities, and
- supporting the emotional, mental and social development of disabled children and young people and those with SEN (this should include extra pastoral support arrangements for listening to the views of pupils and students with SEN and measures to prevent bullying)

4.33 The above will include arrangements for supporting children who are looked after by the local authority and have SEN.

Schools

4.34 Schools have additional duties under the Special Educational Needs and Disability Regulations 2014. Schools **must** publish more detailed information about their arrangements for identifying, assessing and making provision for pupils with SEN (see Chapter 6, Schools).

4.35 The information **must** also include information about the arrangements for the admission of disabled pupils, the steps taken to prevent disabled pupils from being treated less favourably than other pupils, the facilities provided to assist access for disabled pupils and the schools' accessibility plans. The school-specific information should relate to the schools' arrangements for providing a graduated response to children's SEN. It should elaborate on the information provided at a local authority wide level in the Local Offer.

4.36 The Local Offer **must** make clear where this information can be found and **must** make clear how young people and parents can find relevant information published by post-16 institutions about their SEN provision (see Chapter 7).

Early years

4.37 When securing funded early education for two-, three- and four-year-olds local authorities **must** promote equality of opportunity for disabled children. This should include securing relevant expertise among early years providers and working with parents to ensure that appropriate provision is in place to enable each child to flourish. Local authorities **must** also secure sufficient childcare for working parents and **must** work with providers to plan and manage local provision to meet the needs of families and children in their area.

4.38 Local authorities **must** publish in their Local Offer information about childcare options available to parents including the range of expertise to support children with SEN or disabilities and should publish information about:

- free early education places and eligibility criteria
- relevant services from other agencies such as Portage, Health Visitors and Early Support
- arrangements for identifying and assessing children's needs in the early years
- support available to parents to aid their child's development at home, and
- arrangements for reviewing children's progress, including progress checks and health and development reviews between the ages of 2 and 3

Other educational provision

4.39 Information about educational provision **must** include where to find the list of non-maintained special schools and independent schools catering wholly or mainly for children with SEN, and Independent Specialist Colleges in England, including details of which institutions have been approved by the Secretary of State, to give parents and young people a statutory right to request that they are named on an EHC plan. It should also include:

- the special educational provision (including Area SEN co-ordinators (SENCOs), and SEN support or learning support services, sensory support services or specialist teachers, and therapies such as speech and language therapy where they educate or train a child or young person) made available to mainstream schools, early years providers, special units, alternative provision and other settings (including home-based services), whether provided by the local authority or others

- local arrangements for collaboration between institutions to support those with SEN (for example, cluster or partnership working between post-16 institutions or shared services between schools)
- the local authority's arrangements for providing top-up funding for children and young people with high needs in mainstream and specialist settings
- support for children and young people who have been released from custody – this should include support offered by Youth Offending Teams in relation to education

Health

4.40 Building on the Joint Strategic Needs Assessment the Local Offer **must** include information about provision made by health professionals for children and young people with SEN or disabilities. This **must** include:

- services assisting relevant early years providers, schools and post-16 institutions to support children and young people with medical conditions, and
- arrangements for making those services which are available to all children and young people in the area accessible to those with SEN or disabilities

It should also include:

- speech and language therapy and other therapies such as physiotherapy and occupational therapy and services relating to mental health (these **must** be treated as special educational provision where they educate or train a child or young person (see Chapter 9 paragraphs 9.73 to 9.76)
- wheelchair services and community equipment, children's community nursing, continence services
- palliative and respite care and other provision for children with complex health needs
- other services, such as emergency care provision and habilitation support
- provision for children and young people's continuing care arrangements (including information on how these are aligned with the local process for developing EHC plans, which is described in Chapter 3), and

- support for young people when moving between healthcare services for children to healthcare services for adults

4.41 Local authorities and their partner CCGs **must** work together to ensure that this information is available through the Local Offer.

Social care and other provision

4.42 The Local Offer **must** include information about social care services and other provision supporting children and young people with SEN or disabilities. This should include:

- childcare
- leisure activities
- support for young people when moving between social care services for children to social care services for adults, including information on how and when the transfer is made
- support for young people in living independently and finding appropriate accommodation and employment

4.43 Under the Care Act 2014 local authorities **must** provide an information and advice service on the adult care and support system. This should include information on types of care and support, local provision and how to access it, accessing financial advice in relation to it and how to raise concerns**.** Local authorities **must** indicate in their Local Offer where this information can be found.

4.44 Local authorities **must** provide a range of short breaks for disabled children, young people and their families, and prepare a short breaks duty statement giving details of the local range of services and how they can be accessed, including any eligibility criteria (The Breaks for Carers of Disabled Children Regulations 2011). Local authorities **must** publish a short breaks statement on their website and review it on a regular basis, taking account of the needs of local parents and carers. The statement will therefore form a core part of the Local Offer.

4.45 Parent carers of disabled children often have significant needs for support, to enable them to support their children effectively. It is important that children's and adult services work together to ensure needs are met. The Local Offer **must** set out the support groups and others who can support parent carers of disabled children and how to contact them. Part 3 of the Children Act 1989 gives individuals with parental responsibility for a disabled child the right to an assessment of their needs by a local authority. Local authorities **must** assess on the appearance of need, as well as on request, and **must** explicitly have regard to the wellbeing of parent carers in undertaking an assessment of their needs. Following a parent carer's needs assessment, the local authority **must** decide whether the parent carer needs support to enable them to support their disabled child and, if so, decide whether to provide services under section 17 of the Children Act 1989. Relevant services may include short breaks provision and support in the home.

Training and apprenticeships

4.46 The Local Offer **must** identify training opportunities, supported employment services, apprenticeships, traineeships, supported internships and support available from supported employment services available to young people in the area to provide a smooth transition from education and training into employment. This should include information about additional support available to young people – for example via the Department for Work and Pensions' Access to Work fund – such as teaching and learning support, job coaching in the workplace, and provision of specialist equipment. Local authorities should engage with providers of apprenticeships and traineeships and educational institutions offering supported internships to ensure that the information they publish is of good quality and to identify providers who have particular expertise relevant to young people with SEN or disabilities.

4.47 Local authorities should include information on how young people can apply for these opportunities or make clear in their Local Offer where this information can be found. The information should include any entry requirements, including age limits and educational attainment.

Transport

4.48 Transport can be an important factor in the support for children and young people with SEN or disabilities. The Local Offer **must** include information about arrangements for transport provision, including for those up to age 25 with an EHC plan, and this should include local authorities' policy statements.

4.49 Local authorities **must** ensure that suitable travel arrangements are made where necessary to facilitate an eligible child's attendance at school. Section 508B of the Education Act 1996 requires local authorities to make such school travel arrangements as they consider necessary for children within their area. Such arrangements **must** be provided free of charge. Section 508C of the Act gives local authorities discretionary powers to make school travel arrangements for other children not covered by section 508B. Such transport does not have to be provided free of charge.

4.50 Local authorities **must** publish a transport policy statement each year setting out the travel arrangements they will make to support young people aged 16-19 and learners with learning difficulties and/or disabilities (LDD) aged up to 25, to access further education. This should include any arrangements for free or subsidised transport.

4.51 Local authorities **must** include in their Local Offer information about:

- any specific arrangements for specialised transport (for example, specially fitted buses)
- any support available from the local authority or others with transport costs

and should include information about:

- any support that is offered to children and young people to help them use transport, including public transport, and
- any training given to aid independent travel

Support available to children and young people to help them prepare for adulthood

4.52 Local authorities **must** set out in the Local Offer the support available to help children and young people with SEN or disabilities move into adulthood. Support should reflect evidence of what works in achieving good outcomes and **must** include information about preparing for and finding employment, finding somewhere to live, and participating in the community.

4.53 Preparing for and finding employment should include information about:

- pathways to employment such as apprenticeships, traineeships and supported internships and how to apply for them
- support available from supported employment services, such as job coaches, and how to obtain that support
- support available from employment agencies
- support available from Year 8 to help children and young people plan their careers, including signposting to where they can obtain information and advice about setting up their own enterprise, and
- financial support available, including from the Department for Work and Pensions, when people with learning difficulties or disabilities are looking for work or once they are employed, including 'in work' benefit calculations and specialist advice on Work Choice, Residential Training, The Work Programme and Access to Work

4.54 Finding somewhere to live should include information about:

- finding accommodation, including information about different housing options such as social housing, housing association accommodation, private renting, shared housing and shared ownership
- how to apply for accommodation, and where to get financial and other support (such as a personal assistant, assistive technology or modifications to a home) and more detailed advice on accommodation
- advice, for people eligible for social care or health support, about what support is available to help them personally, for example in managing their Personal Budget or recruiting a personal assistant, and
- opportunities and support to learn the skills needed to live in supported, semi-supported or independent accommodation

4.55 Participating in the community should include information about:

- leisure and social activities, including opportunities for influencing local decision-making
- how young people can access mainstream community facilities and local youth services (for example, access to staff with expertise in supporting young people with different needs)
- volunteering opportunities and the support available to access them
- care support available to help young people access social opportunities (for example, a personal assistant or assistive technology) and develop friendships, and how to apply for that support, and
- support in using the internet and social media to find information and develop and maintain friendships, including where they can go for guidance on using the internet safely and how to protect themselves against cyber-bullying and exploitation

4.56 The Care Act 2014 requires local authorities to establish and maintain a service for providing people in its area with information and advice about the adult care and support system.

Information about how to seek an EHC needs assessment

4.57 The Local Offer **must** include information about how to request a needs assessment for an EHC plan. A request is likely to happen where special educational provision currently being made for them by their early years setting, school or college from their own resources, is not enabling the child or young person to make adequate progress.

4.58 The information should include:

- how the local authority will consider a request for an assessment and inform parents and young people of their decision
- how parents, children and young people will be involved in the assessment process
- what support is available to help families during the needs assessment process and the development of an EHC plan
- the timescales involved in the assessment process
- the process for making an EHC plan

and **must** include:

- information about the option of having a Personal Budget, including a local policy for Personal Budgets, produced with parents and young people. This should provide:
    - a description of the services across education, health and social care that currently lend themselves to the use of Personal Budgets
    - the mechanisms of control for funding available to parents and young people including direct payments, arrangements and third party arrangements (see Chapter 9, Education, Health and Care needs assessments and plans)
    - clear and simple statements setting out eligibility criteria and the decision-making processes that underpin them
    - the support available to help families manage a Personal Budget
- arrangements for complaints, mediation, disagreement resolution and appeals

Information, advice and support

4.59 The Local Offer **must** provide information for children, parents and young people about where to get information and advice.

4.60 All local authorities **must** have arrangements for information and advice and should ensure that advice and guidance for children and young people is tailored appropriately for them (see Chapter 2).

4.61 Clear, comprehensive and accessible information should be published about the support available to children and young people with SEN and disabled children and young people and the opportunities to participate in strategic decision-making. Local authorities and CCGs **must** ensure that they publicise the availability of information and advice and opportunities to participate in strategic decision-making. Early years providers, schools, colleges, and other relevant services should tell parents and young people about the availability of local impartial information, advice and support. For young people this should include access to information, advice and support on preparing for adulthood, such as advice and support on securing paid employment and/or meaningful occupation, independent living and finding accommodation, health and social care and participating actively in their local communities.

Publishing the Local Offer

4.62 Local authorities **must** make their Local Offer widely accessible and on a website. They **must** publish their arrangements for enabling those without access to the internet to get the information. They **must** also enable access for different groups, including disabled people and those with different types of SEN.

5 Early years providers

What this chapter covers

This chapter explains the action early years providers should take to meet their duties in relation to identifying and supporting all children with special educational needs (SEN), whether or not they have an Education, Health and Care (EHC) plan.

Relevant legislation

Primary

The following sections of the Children and Families Act 2014:

- Co-operating generally: governing body functions: Section 29
- Children and young people with SEN but no EHC plan: Section 34
- Children with SEN in maintained nurseries: Section 35
- Using best endeavours to secure special educational provision: Section 66
- SEN co-ordinators: Section 64
- Informing parents and young people: Section 68
- SEN information report: Section 69
- Duty to support pupils with medical conditions: Section 100

The Equality Act 2010

Regulations

The Statutory Framework for the Early Years Foundation Stage

The Special Educational Needs and Disability Regulations 2014

Improving outcomes: high aspirations and expectations for children with SEN

5.1 All children are entitled to an education that enables them to:

- achieve the best possible educational and other outcomes, and
- become confident young children with a growing ability to communicate their own views and ready to make the transition into compulsory education

5.2 Providers of early years education, that is all early years providers in the maintained, private, voluntary and independent sectors that a local authority funds, are required to have regard to this Code including the principles set out in Chapter 1.

5.3 The Early Years Foundation Stage (EYFS) is the statutory framework for children aged 0 to 5 years. All early years providers **must** follow the safeguarding and welfare requirements of the EYFS and the learning and development requirements, unless an exemption from these has been granted.

5.4 Providers **must** have arrangements in place to support children with SEN or disabilities. These arrangements should include a clear approach to identifying and responding to SEN. The benefits of early identification are widely recognised – identifying need at the earliest point, and then making effective provision, improves long-term outcomes for children.

5.5 All those who work with young children should be alert to emerging difficulties and respond early. In particular, parents know their children best and it is important that all practitioners listen and understand when parents express concerns about their child's development. They should also listen to and address any concerns raised by children themselves.

5.6 Maintained nursery schools **must**:

- use their best endeavours to make sure that a child with SEN gets the support they need
- ensure that children with SEN engage in the activities of school alongside children who do not have SEN
- designate a teacher to be responsible for co-ordinating SEN provision (the SEN co-ordinator, or SENCO)
- inform parents when they are making special educational provision for a child

They **must** also prepare a report on:

- the implementation of their SEN policy
- their arrangements for the admission of disabled children
- the steps being taken to prevent disabled children from being treated less favourably than others
- the facilities provided to enable access to the school for disabled children, and
- their accessibility plan showing how they plan to improve access over time

5.7 Early years providers **must** provide information for parents on how they support children with SEN and disabilities, and should regularly review and evaluate the quality and breadth of the support they offer or can access for children with SEN or disabilities. Maintained nursery schools and all providers of relevant early education to children with SEN **must** co-operate with the local authority in reviewing the provision that is available locally (see Chapter 3), and in developing the Local Offer (see Chapter 4). Providers should work in partnership with other local education providers to explore how different types of need can be met most effectively.

5.8 Local authorities **must** ensure that all providers they fund in the maintained, private, voluntary and independent sectors are aware of the requirement on them to have regard to the SEN Code of Practice and to meet the needs of children with SEN and disabilities. When securing funded early education for two-, three- and four-year-olds local authorities should promote equality and inclusion for children with disabilities or SEN. This includes removing barriers that prevent children accessing early education and working with parents to give each child support to fulfil their potential.

5.9 Where assessment indicates that support from specialist services is required, it is important that children receive it as quickly as possible. Joint commissioning arrangements should seek to ensure that there are sufficient services to meet the likely need in an area (Chapter 3, Working together across Education, Health and Care for joint outcomes). The Local Offer should set out clearly what support is available from different services, including early years, and how it can be accessed.

Equality Act 2010

5.10 All early years providers have duties under the Equality Act 2010. In particular, they **must not** discriminate against, harass or victimise disabled children, and they **must** make reasonable adjustments, including the provision of auxiliary aids and services for disabled children, to prevent them being put at substantial disadvantage. This duty is anticipatory – it requires thought to be given in advance to what disabled children and young people might require and what adjustments might need to be made to prevent that disadvantage. All publicly funded early years providers **must** promote equality of opportunity for disabled children. There is further detail on the disability discrimination duties under the Equality Act in Chapter 1, Introduction. The guidance in this chapter should be read in the light of the guidance in Chapter 1 which focuses on inclusive practice and removing barriers to learning.

Medical conditions

5.11 All early years providers should take steps to ensure that children with medical conditions get the support required to meet those needs. This is set out in the EYFS framework.

SEN in the early years

5.12 All early years providers are required to have arrangements in place to identify and support children with SEN or disabilities and to promote equality of opportunity for children in their care. These requirements are set out in the EYFS framework. The EYFS framework also requires practitioners to review children's progress and share a summary with parents. In addition, the 'Early years outcomes' is an aid for practitioners, including child minders, nurseries and others such as inspectors, to help them to understand the outcomes they should be working towards. Links to the EYFS framework and the guide to early years outcomes are provided in the References section under Chapter 5.

5.13 Some children need support for SEN and disabilities at home or in informal settings before, or as well as, the support they receive from an early years provider. Provision for children who need such support should form part of the local joint commissioning arrangements and be included in the Local Offer.

From birth to two – early identification

5.14 Parents' early observations of their child are crucial. Children with more complex developmental and sensory needs may be identified at birth. Health assessments, such as the hearing screening test, which is used to check the hearing of all new-born babies, enable very early identification of a range of medical and physical difficulties. Health services, including paediatricians, the family's general practitioner, and health visitors, should work with the family, support them to understand their child's needs and help them to access early support.

5.15 Where a health body is of the opinion that a young child under compulsory school age has, or probably has, SEN, they **must** inform the child's parents and bring the child to the attention of the appropriate local authority. The health body **must** also give the parents the opportunity to discuss their opinion and let them know about any voluntary organisations that are likely to be able to provide advice or assistance. This includes the educational advice, guidance and any intervention to be put in place at an early point and before the child starts school.

5.16 This support can take a number of forms, including:

- specialist support from health visitors, educational psychologists, speech and language therapists or specialist teachers, such as a teacher of the deaf or vision impaired. These specialists may visit families at home to provide practical support, answering questions and clarifying needs
- training for parents in using early learning programmes to promote play, communication and language development
- home-based programmes, such as Portage, which offer a carefully structured system to help parents support their child's early learning and development

5.17 Early Support supports the better delivery and co-ordination of services for disabled children, and their families, including training for professional or trained independent volunteers providing a single point of contact or key working. (See References section under Chapter 2 for a link to the Early Support Programme.)

5.18 From September 2014, 2-year-olds for whom Disability Living Allowance is paid will be entitled to free early education.

5.19 Information about these services should be included in the Local Offer.

Early years provision

5.20 The majority of 3- and 4-year-olds, and many younger children, attend some form of early years provision. The EYFS framework sets the standards that all Ofsted-registered early years providers, and schools offering early years provision, **must** meet to ensure that children learn and develop well and are kept healthy and safe. This includes ongoing assessment of children's progress. Early years providers and educational settings should have arrangements in place that include a clear approach to assessing SEN. This should be part of the setting's overall approach to monitoring the progress and development of all children.

5.21 In assessing progress of children in the early years, practitioners can use the non-statutory Early Years Outcomes guidance as a tool to assess the extent to which a young child is developing at expected levels for their age. The guidance sets out what most children do at each stage of their learning and development. These include typical behaviours across the seven areas of learning:

- communication and language

- physical development
- personal, social and emotional development
- literacy
- mathematics
- understanding of the world
- expressive arts and design

5.22 The EYFS framework includes two specific points for providing written assessments for parents and other professionals – when the child is aged two and at the end of the reception year – which are detailed below.

Progress check at age two

5.23 When a child is aged between two and three, early years practitioners **must** review progress and provide parents with a short written summary of their child's development, focusing in particular on communication and language, physical development and personal, social and emotional development. This progress check **must** identify the child's strengths and any areas where the child's progress is slower than expected. If there are significant emerging concerns (or identified SEN or disability) practitioners should develop a targeted plan to support the child, involving other professionals such as, for example, the setting's SENCO or the Area SENCO, as appropriate. The summary **must** highlight areas where:

- good progress is being made
- some additional support might be needed
- there is a concern that a child may have a developmental delay (which may indicate SEN or disability)

5.24 It **must** describe the activities and strategies the provider intends to adopt to address any issues or concerns. If a child moves settings between the ages of two and three it is expected that the progress check will be undertaken in the setting where the child has spent most time.

5.25 Health visitors currently check children's physical development milestones between ages two and three as part of the universal Healthy Child Programme. From 2015, it is proposed to introduce an integrated review that will cover the development areas in the Healthy Child Programme two-year review and the EYFS two-year progress check. The integrated review will:

- identify the child's progress, strengths and needs at this age in order to promote positive outcomes in health and wellbeing, learning and development
- enable appropriate intervention and support for children and their families, where progress is less than expected, and
- generate information which can be used to plan services and contribute to the reduction of inequalities in children's outcomes

Assessment at the end of the EYFS – the EYFS profile

5.26 The EYFS profile provides parents, practitioners and teachers with a well-rounded picture of a child's knowledge, understanding and abilities. A profile is usually completed for children in the final term of the year in which they turn five. It is particularly helpful for children with SEN and should inform plans for future learning and identify any additional needs for support.

Identifying needs in the early years

5.27 In addition to the formal checks, early years practitioners working with children should monitor and review the progress and development of all children throughout the early years.

5.28 Where a child appears to be behind expected levels, or where a child's progress gives cause for concern, practitioners should consider all the information about the child's learning and development from within and beyond the setting, from formal checks, from practitioner observations and from any more detailed assessment of the child's needs. From within the setting practitioners should particularly consider information on a child's progress in communication and language, physical development and personal, social and emotional development. Where any specialist advice has been sought from beyond the setting, this should also inform decisions about whether or not a child has SEN. All the information should be brought together with the observations of parents and considered with them.

5.29 A delay in learning and development in the early years may or may not indicate that a child has SEN, that is, that they have a learning difficulty or disability that calls for special educational provision. Equally, difficult or withdrawn behaviour does not necessarily mean that a child has SEN. However, where there are concerns, there should be an assessment to determine whether there are any causal factors such as an underlying learning or communication difficulty. If it is thought housing, family or other domestic circumstances may be contributing to the presenting behaviour, a multi-agency approach, supported by the use of approaches such as the Early Help Assessment, should be adopted.

5.30 Identifying and assessing SEN for young children whose first language is not English requires particular care. Early years practitioners should look carefully at all aspects of a child's learning and development to establish whether any delay is related to learning English as an additional language or if it arises from SEN or disability. Difficulties related solely to learning English as an additional language are not SEN.

5.31 Where a child has a significantly greater difficulty in learning than their peers, or a disability that prevents or hinders a child from making use of the facilities in the setting and requires special educational provision, the setting should make that provision. In all cases, early identification and intervention can significantly reduce the need for more costly interventions at a later stage.

5.32 Special educational provision should be matched to the child's identified SEN. Children's SEN are generally thought of in the following four broad areas of need and support – see Chapter 6, paragraph 6.28 onwards, for a fuller explanation:

- communication and interaction
- cognition and learning
- social, emotional and mental health
- sensory and/or physical needs

5.33 These areas give an overview of the range of needs that providers should plan for. However, individual children often have needs that cut across all these areas and their needs may change over time. For instance speech, language and communication needs can also be a feature of a number of other areas of SEN, and children with an Autism Spectrum Disorder may have needs across all areas. The special educational provision made for a child should always be based on an understanding of their particular strengths and needs and should seek to address them all, using well-evidenced interventions targeted at areas of difficulty and, where necessary, specialist equipment or software. This will help to overcome barriers to learning and participation. Support should be family centred and should consider the individual family's needs and the best ways to support them.

5.34 Reviewing the effectiveness of interventions in enabling children to make progress can itself be part of the assessment of need, informing the next steps to be taken as part of a graduated approach to support, as described in 'SEN support in the early years' below. It may be necessary to test out interventions as part of this process, both to judge their effectiveness for the child and to provide further information about the precise nature of their needs.

5.35 There is a wide range of information available on early years and early intervention and on different areas of need and the most effective interventions. For more information and links to useful resources see Annex 2: Improving practice and staff training in education settings.

SEN support in the early years

5.36 It is particularly important in the early years that there is no delay in making any necessary special educational provision. Delay at this stage can give rise to learning difficulty and subsequently to loss of self-esteem, frustration in learning and to behaviour difficulties. Early action to address identified needs is critical to the future progress and improved outcomes that are essential in helping the child to prepare for adult life (Chapter 8, Preparing for adulthood from the earliest years).

5.37 Where a setting identifies a child as having SEN they **must** work in partnership with parents to establish the support the child needs.

5.38 Where a setting makes special educational provision for a child with SEN they should inform the parents and a maintained nursery school **must** inform the parents. All settings should adopt a graduated approach with four stages of action: assess, plan, do and review.

Assess

5.39 In identifying a child as needing SEN support, the early years practitioner, working with the setting SENCO and the child's parents, will have carried out an analysis of the child's needs. This initial assessment should be reviewed regularly to ensure that support is matched to need. Where there is little or no improvement in the child's progress, more specialist assessment may be called for from specialist teachers or from health, social services or other agencies beyond the setting. Where professionals are not already working with the setting, the SENCO should contact them, with the parents' agreement.

Plan

5.40 Where it is decided to provide SEN support, and having formally notified the parents, (see 5.38 above), the practitioner and the SENCO should agree, in consultation with the parent, the outcomes they are seeking, the interventions and support to be put in place, the expected impact on progress, development or behaviour, and a clear date for review. Plans should take into account the views of the child. The support and intervention provided should be selected to meet the outcomes identified for the child, based on reliable evidence of effectiveness, and provided by practitioners with relevant skills and knowledge. Any related staff development needs should be identified and addressed.

5.41 Parents should be involved in planning support and, where appropriate, in reinforcing the provision or contributing to progress at home.

Do

5.42 The early years practitioner, usually the child's key person, remains responsible for working with the child on a daily basis. With support from the SENCO, they should oversee the implementation of the interventions or programmes agreed as part of SEN support. The SENCO should support the practitioner in assessing the child's response to the action taken, in problem solving and advising on the effective implementation of support.

Review

5.43 The effectiveness of the support and its impact on the child's progress should be reviewed in line with the agreed date. The impact and quality of the support should be evaluated by the practitioner and the SENCO working with the child's parents and taking into account the child's views. They should agree any changes to the outcomes and support for the child in light of the child's progress and development. Parents should have clear information about the impact of the support provided and be involved in planning next steps.

5.44 This cycle of action should be revisited in increasing detail and with increasing frequency, to identify the best way of securing good progress. At each stage parents should be engaged with the setting, contributing their insights to assessment and planning. Intended outcomes should be shared with parents and reviewed with them, along with action taken by the setting, at agreed times.

5.45 The graduated approach should be led and co-ordinated by the setting SENCO working with and supporting individual practitioners in the setting and informed by EYFS materials, the Early Years Outcomes guidance and Early Support resources (information is available at the National Children's Bureau website – see the References section under Chapter 5 for the link).

5.46 Where a child has an EHC plan, the local authority **must** review that plan as a minimum every twelve months. As part of the review, the local authority can ask settings, and require maintained nursery schools, to convene and hold the annual review meeting on its behalf. Further information about EHC plan reviews and the role of early years settings is in Chapter 9, Education, Health and Care needs assessments and plans.

Transition

5.47 SEN support should include planning and preparing for transition, before a child moves into another setting or school. This can also include a review of the SEN support being provided or the EHC plan. To support the transition, information should be shared by the current setting with the receiving setting or school. The current setting should agree with parents the information to be shared as part of this planning process

Involving specialists

5.48 Where a child continues to make less than expected progress, despite evidence-based support and interventions that are matched to the child's area of need, practitioners should consider involving appropriate specialists, for example, health visitors, speech and language therapists, Portage workers, educational psychologists or specialist teachers, who may be able to identify effective strategies, equipment, programmes or other interventions to enable the child to make progress towards the desired learning and development outcomes. The decision to involve specialists should be taken with the child's parents.

Requesting an Education, Health and Care needs assessment

5.49 Where, despite the setting having taken relevant and purposeful action to identify, assess and meet the special educational needs of the child, the child has not made expected progress, the setting should consider requesting an Education, Health and Care needs assessment (see Chapter 9, Education, Health and Care needs assessments and plans).

Record keeping

5.50 Practitioners **must** maintain a record of children under their care as required under the EYFS framework. Such records about their children **must** be available to parents and they **must** include how the setting supports children with SEN and disabilities.

Keeping provision under review

5.51 Providers should review how well equipped they are to provide support across the four broad areas of SEN. Information on these areas is collected through the Early Years Census, and forms part of the statutory publication '*Children and Young People with SEN: an analysis*' which is issued by DfE each year.

The role of the SENCO in early years provision

5.52 A maintained nursery school **must** ensure that there is a qualified teacher designated as the SENCO in order to ensure the detailed implementation of support for children with SEN. This individual should also have the prescribed qualification for SEN Co-ordination or relevant experience.

5.53 The EYFS framework requires other early years providers to have arrangements in place for meeting children's SEN. Those in group provision are expected to identify a SENCO. Childminders are encouraged to identify a person to act as SENCO and childminders who are registered with a childminder agency or who are part of a network may wish to share that role between them.

5.54 The role of the SENCO involves:

- ensuring all practitioners in the setting understand their responsibilities to children with SEN and the setting's approach to identifying and meeting SEN
- advising and supporting colleagues
- ensuring parents are closely involved throughout and that their insights inform action taken by the setting, and
- liaising with professionals or agencies beyond the setting

The role of the Area SENCO

5.55 To fulfil their role in identifying and planning for the needs of children with SEN, local authorities should ensure that there is sufficient expertise and experience amongst local early years providers to support children with SEN. Local authorities often make use of Area SENCOs to provide advice and guidance to early years providers on the development of inclusive early learning environments. The Area SENCO helps make the links between education, health and social care to facilitate appropriate early provision for children with SEN and their transition to compulsory schooling.

5.56 Typically, the role of the Area SENCO includes:

- providing advice and practical support to early years providers about approaches to identification, assessment and intervention within the SEN Code of Practice
- providing day-to-day support for setting-based SENCOs in ensuring arrangements are in place to support children with SEN
- strengthening the links between the settings, parents, schools, social care and health services
- developing and disseminating good practice

- supporting the development and delivery of training both for individual settings and on a wider basis
- developing links with existing SENCO networks to support smooth transitions to school nursery and reception classes, and
- informing parents of and working with local impartial Information, Advice and Support Services, to promote effective work with parents of children in the early years

5.57 The Area SENCO plays an important part in planning for children with SEN to transfer between early years provision and schools.

5.58 Where there is an Area SENCO in place, they will want to work with early years providers who are registered with either Ofsted or a childminder agency. They should consider how they work with and provide advice to childminder agencies and their registered providers in supporting children with SEN.

Funding for SEN support in the early years

5.59 Local authorities **must** ensure that all providers delivering funded early education places meet the needs of children with SEN and disabled children. In order to do this local authorities should make sure funding arrangements for early education reflect the need to provide suitable support for these children.

5.60 Early years providers should consider how best to use their resources to support the progress of children with SEN.

6 Schools

What this chapter covers

This chapter applies mostly to mainstream schools. The Equality Act duties described under 'Equality and inclusion' and the duty to publish an SEN information report under 'Publishing information: SEN information report' apply to special schools, as do schools' duties in respect of EHC needs assessments and plans (Chapter 9 – Education, Health and Care needs assessments and plans). The chapter explains the action that mainstream schools should take to meet their duties in relation to identifying and supporting all children with special educational needs (SEN) whether or not they have an Education, Health and Care (EHC) plan.

Relevant legislation

Primary

The following sections of the Children and Families Act 2014:

- Co-operating generally: governing body functions: Section 29
- Children and young people with special educational needs but no EHC plan: Section 29
- Children with SEN in maintained nurseries and mainstream schools: Section 35
- Using best endeavours to secure special educational provision: Section 66
- SEN co-ordinators: Section 67
- Informing parents and young people: Section 68
- SEN information report: Section 69
- Duty to support pupils with medical conditions: Section 100

The Equality Act 2010

Regulations

The Special Educational Needs and Disability Regulations 2014

Improving outcomes: high aspirations and expectations for children and young people with SEN

6.1 All children and young people are entitled to an appropriate education, one that is appropriate to their needs, promotes high standards and the fulfilment of potential. This should enable them to:

- achieve their best
- become confident individuals living fulfilling lives, and
- make a successful transition into adulthood, whether into employment, further or higher education or training

6.2 Every school is required to identify and address the SEN of the pupils that they support. Mainstream schools, which in this chapter includes maintained schools and academies that are not special schools, maintained nursery schools, 16 to19 academies, alternative provision academies and Pupil Referral Units (PRUs), **must**:

- use their best endeavours to make sure that a child with SEN gets the support they need – this means doing everything they can to meet children and young people's SEN
- ensure that children and young people with SEN engage in the activities of the school alongside pupils who do not have SEN
- designate a teacher to be responsible for co-ordinating SEN provision – the SEN co-ordinator, or SENCO (this does not apply to 16 to 19 academies)
- inform parents when they are making special educational provision for a child
- prepare an SEN information report (see 'Publishing information: SEN information report', paragraph 6.78 onwards) and their arrangements for the admission of disabled children, the steps being taken to prevent disabled children from being treated less favourably than others, the facilities provided to enable access to the school for disabled children and their accessibility plan showing how they plan to improve access progressively over time

6.3 There should be a member of the governing body or a sub-committee with specific oversight of the school's arrangements for SEN and disability. School leaders should regularly review how expertise and resources used to address SEN can be used to build the quality of whole-school provision as part of their approach to school improvement.

6.4 The quality of teaching for pupils with SEN, and the progress made by pupils, should be a core part of the school's performance management arrangements and its approach to professional development for all teaching and support staff. School leaders and teaching staff, including the SENCO, should identify any patterns in the identification of SEN, both within the school and in comparison with national data, and use these to reflect on and reinforce the quality of teaching. Many aspects of this whole school approach have been piloted by Achievement for All – for further details and links to other sources of training and support materials, see Annex 2: Improving practice and staff training in education settings.

6.5 The identification of SEN should be built into the overall approach to monitoring the progress and development of all pupils.

6.6 A mainstream school's arrangements for assessing and identifying pupils as having SEN should be agreed and set out as part of the Local Offer. A school should publish its arrangements as part of the information it makes available on SEN (see the Special Educational Needs and Disability Regulations 2014).

6.7 In fulfilling these duties schools should have regard to the principles set out in Chapter 1. In particular, they should ensure that children, parents and young people are actively involved in decision-making throughout the approaches set out in this chapter.

Equality and inclusion

6.8 Schools support pupils with a wide range of SEN. They should regularly review and evaluate the breadth and impact of the support they offer or can access. Schools **must** co-operate with the local authority in reviewing the provision that is available locally (Chapter 3) and in developing the Local Offer (Chapter 4). Schools should also collaborate with other local education providers to explore how different needs can be met most effectively. They **must** have due regard to general duties to promote disability equality.

6.9 All schools have duties under the Equality Act 2010 towards individual disabled children and young people. They **must** make reasonable adjustments, including the provision of auxiliary aids and services for disabled children, to prevent them being put at a substantial disadvantage. These duties are anticipatory – they require thought to be given in advance to what disabled children and young people might require and what adjustments might need to be made to prevent that disadvantage. Schools also have wider duties to prevent discrimination, to promote equality of opportunity and to foster good relations.

6.10 Further duties are referred to in the Introduction. The guidance in this chapter should be read in the light of the principle in Chapter 1 which focuses on inclusive practice and removing barriers to learning.

Medical conditions

6.11 The Children and Families Act 2014 places a duty on maintained schools and academies to make arrangements to support pupils with medical conditions. Individual healthcare plans will normally specify the type and level of support required to meet the medical needs of such pupils. Where children and young people also have SEN, their provision should be planned and delivered in a co-ordinated way with the healthcare plan. Schools are required to have regard to statutory guidance '*Supporting pupils at school with medical conditions*' (see the References section under Introduction for a link).

Curriculum

6.12 All pupils should have access to a broad and balanced curriculum. The National Curriculum Inclusion Statement states that teachers should set high expectations for every pupil, whatever their prior attainment. Teachers should use appropriate assessment to set targets which are deliberately ambitious. Potential areas of difficulty should be identified and addressed at the outset. Lessons should be planned to address potential areas of difficulty and to remove barriers to pupil achievement. In many cases, such planning will mean that pupils with SEN and disabilities will be able to study the full national curriculum.

Careers guidance for children and young people

6.13 Maintained schools and PRUs must ensure that pupils from Year 8 until Year 13 are provided with independent careers guidance. Academies are subject to this duty through their funding agreements. Chapter 8 provides more information about careers guidance for children and young people.

Identifying SEN in schools

6.14 All schools should have a clear approach to identifying and responding to SEN. The benefits of early identification are widely recognised – identifying need at the earliest point and then making effective provision improves long-term outcomes for the child or young person.

6.15 A pupil has SEN where their learning difficulty or disability calls for special educational provision, namely provision different from or additional to that normally available to pupils of the same age. Making higher quality teaching normally available to the whole class is likely to mean that fewer pupils will require such support. Such improvements in whole-class provision tend to be more cost effective and sustainable.

6.16 Schools should assess each pupil's current skills and levels of attainment on entry, building on information from previous settings and key stages where appropriate. At the same time, schools should consider evidence that a pupil may have a disability under the Equality Act 2010 and, if so, what reasonable adjustments may need to be made for them.

6.17 Class and subject teachers, supported by the senior leadership team, should make regular assessments of progress for all pupils. These should seek to identify pupils making less than expected progress given their age and individual circumstances. This can be characterised by progress which:

- is significantly slower than that of their peers starting from the same baseline
- fails to match or better the child's previous rate of progress
- fails to close the attainment gap between the child and their peers
- widens the attainment gap

6.18 It can include progress in areas other than attainment – for instance where a pupil needs to make additional progress with wider development or social needs in order to make a successful transition to adult life.

6.19 The first response to such progress should be high quality teaching targeted at their areas of weakness. Where progress continues to be less than expected the class or subject teacher, working with the SENCO, should assess whether the child has SEN. While informally gathering evidence (including the views of the pupil and their parents) schools should not delay in putting in place extra teaching or other rigorous interventions designed to secure better progress, where required. The pupil's response to such support can help identify their particular needs.

6.20 For some children, SEN can be identified at an early age. However, for other children and young people difficulties become evident only as they develop. All those who work with children and young people should be alert to emerging difficulties and respond early. In particular, parents know their children best and it is important that all professionals listen and understand when parents express concerns about their child's development. They should also listen to and address any concerns raised by children and young people themselves.

6.21 Persistent disruptive or withdrawn behaviours do not necessarily mean that a child or young person has SEN. Where there are concerns, there should be an assessment to determine whether there are any causal factors such as undiagnosed learning difficulties, difficulties with communication or mental health issues. If it is thought housing, family or other domestic circumstances may be contributing to the presenting behaviour a multi-agency approach, supported by the use of approaches such as the Early Help Assessment, may be appropriate. In all cases, early identification and intervention can significantly reduce the use of more costly intervention at a later stage.

6.22 Professionals should also be alert to other events that can lead to learning difficulties or wider mental health difficulties, such as bullying or bereavement. Such events will not always lead to children having SEN but it can have an impact on wellbeing and sometimes this can be severe. Schools should ensure they make appropriate provision for a child's short-term needs in order to prevent problems escalating. Where there are long-lasting difficulties schools should consider whether the child might have SEN. Further guidance on dealing with bullying issues can be found on the GOV.UK website – a link is given in the References section under Chapter 6.

6.23 Slow progress and low attainment do not necessarily mean that a child has SEN and should not automatically lead to a pupil being recorded as having SEN. However, they may be an indicator of a range of learning difficulties or disabilities. Equally, it should not be assumed that attainment in line with chronological age means that there is no learning difficulty or disability. Some learning difficulties and disabilities occur across the range of cognitive ability and, left unaddressed may lead to frustration, which may manifest itself as disaffection, emotional or behavioural difficulties.

6.24 Identifying and assessing SEN for children or young people whose first language is not English requires particular care. Schools should look carefully at all aspects of a child or young person's performance in different areas of learning and development or subjects to establish whether lack of progress is due to limitations in their command of English or if it arises from SEN or a disability. Difficulties related solely to limitations in English as an additional language are not SEN.

6.25 When reviewing and managing special educational provision the broad areas of need and support outlined from 6.28 below may be helpful, and schools should review how well equipped they are to provide support across these areas. Information on these areas of need and support is also collected through the School Census and forms part of the statutory publication '*Children and Young People with SEN: an analysis*' which is issued by DfE each year.

6.26 There is a wide range of information available on appropriate interventions for pupils with different types of need, and associated training which schools can use to ensure they have the necessary knowledge and expertise to use them. See the References section under Chapter 6 for links to organisations that provide this information.

6.27 These four broad areas give an overview of the range of needs that should be planned for. The purpose of identification is to work out what action the school needs to take, not to fit a pupil into a category. In practice, individual children or young people often have needs that cut across all these areas and their needs may change over time. For instance speech, language and communication needs can also be a feature of a number of other areas of SEN, and children and young people with an Autistic Spectrum Disorder (ASD) may have needs across all areas, including particular sensory requirements. A detailed assessment of need should ensure that the full range of an individual's needs is identified, not simply the primary need. The support provided to an individual should always be based on a full understanding of their particular strengths and needs and seek to address them all using well-evidenced interventions targeted at their areas of difficulty and where necessary specialist equipment or software.

Broad areas of need

Communication and interaction

6.28 Children and young people with speech, language and communication needs (SLCN) have difficulty in communicating with others. This may be because they have difficulty saying what they want to, understanding what is being said to them or they do not understand or use social rules of communication. The profile for every child with SLCN is different and their needs may change over time. They may have difficulty with one, some or all of the different aspects of speech, language or social communication at different times of their lives.

6.29 Children and young people with ASD, including Asperger's Syndrome and Autism, are likely to have particular difficulties with social interaction. They may also experience difficulties with language, communication and imagination, which can impact on how they relate to others.

Cognition and learning

6.30 Support for learning difficulties may be required when children and young people learn at a slower pace than their peers, even with appropriate differentiation. Learning difficulties cover a wide range of needs, including moderate learning difficulties (MLD), severe learning difficulties (SLD), where children are likely to need support in all areas of the curriculum and associated difficulties with mobility and communication, through to profound and multiple learning difficulties (PMLD), where children are likely to have severe and complex learning difficulties as well as a physical disability or sensory impairment.

6.31 Specific learning difficulties (SpLD), affect one or more specific aspects of learning. This encompasses a range of conditions such as dyslexia, dyscalculia and dyspraxia.

Social, emotional and mental health difficulties

6.32 Children and young people may experience a wide range of social and emotional difficulties which manifest themselves in many ways. These may include becoming withdrawn or isolated, as well as displaying challenging, disruptive or disturbing behaviour. These behaviours may reflect underlying mental health difficulties such as anxiety or depression, self-harming, substance misuse, eating disorders or physical symptoms that are medically unexplained. Other children and young people may have disorders such as attention deficit disorder, attention deficit hyperactive disorder or attachment disorder.

6.33 Schools and colleges should have clear processes to support children and young people, including how they will manage the effect of any disruptive behaviour so it does not adversely affect other pupils. The Department for Education publishes guidance on managing pupils' mental health and behaviour difficulties in schools – see the References section under Chapter 6 for a link.

Sensory and/or physical needs

6.34 Some children and young people require special educational provision because they have a disability which prevents or hinders them from making use of the educational facilities generally provided. These difficulties can be age related and may fluctuate over time. Many children and young people with vision impairment (VI), hearing impairment (HI) or a multi-sensory impairment (MSI) will require specialist support and/or equipment to access their learning, or habilitation support. Children and young people with an MSI have a combination of vision and hearing difficulties. Information on how to provide services for deafblind children and young people is available through the Social Care for Deafblind Children and Adults guidance published by the Department of Health (see the References section under Chapter 6 for a link).

6.35 Some children and young people with a physical disability (PD) require additional ongoing support and equipment to access all the opportunities available to their peers.

Special educational provision in schools

6.36 Teachers are responsible and accountable for the progress and development of the pupils in their class, including where pupils access support from teaching assistants or specialist staff.

6.37 High quality teaching, differentiated for individual pupils, is the first step in responding to pupils who have or may have SEN. Additional intervention and support cannot compensate for a lack of good quality teaching. Schools should regularly and carefully review the quality of teaching for all pupils, including those at risk of underachievement. This includes reviewing and, where necessary, improving, teachers' understanding of strategies to identify and support vulnerable pupils and their knowledge of the SEN most frequently encountered.

6.38 In deciding whether to make special educational provision, the teacher and SENCO should consider all of the information gathered from within the school about the pupil's progress, alongside national data and expectations of progress. This should include high quality and accurate formative assessment, using effective tools and early assessment materials. For higher levels of need, schools should have arrangements in place to draw on more specialised assessments from external agencies and professionals.

6.39 This information gathering should include an early discussion with the pupil and their parents. These early discussions with parents should be structured in such a way that they develop a good understanding of the pupil's areas of strength and difficulty, the parents' concerns, the agreed outcomes sought for the child and the next steps. A short note of these early discussions should be added to the pupil's record on the school information system and given to the parents. Schools should also tell children, parents and young people about the local authority's Information, Advice and Support Service.

6.40 Consideration of whether special educational provision is required should start with the desired outcomes, including the expected progress and attainment and the views and wishes of the pupil and their parents. This should then help determine the support that is needed and whether it can be provided by adapting the school's core offer or whether something different or additional is required.

6.41 More detailed information on what constitutes good outcome setting is given in Chapter 9, Education, Health and Care needs assessments and plans (paragraphs 9.64 to 9.69). These principles should be applied to planning for all children and young people with SEN. From Year 9 onwards, the nature of the outcomes will reflect the need to ensure young people are preparing for adulthood.

6.42 The outcomes considered should include those needed to make successful transitions between phases of education and to prepare for adult life. Schools should engage with secondary schools or FE providers as necessary to help plan for these transitions (see Chapter 8, Preparing for adulthood from the earliest years). The agreed actions may also include those taken to make sure the school meets its duty to ensure that pupils with SEN engage in school activities together with those who do not have SEN.

6.43 However support is provided, a clear date for reviewing progress should be agreed and the parent, pupil and teaching staff should each be clear about how they will help the pupil reach the expected outcomes. The overriding purpose of this early action is to help the pupil achieve the identified outcomes and remove any barriers to learning. Where it is decided that a pupil does have SEN, the decision should be recorded in the school records and the pupil's parents **must** be formally informed that special educational provision is being made. Arrangements for appropriate support should be made through the school's approach to SEN support.

SEN support in schools

6.44 Where a pupil is identified as having SEN, schools should take action to remove barriers to learning and put effective special educational provision in place. This SEN support should take the form of a four-part cycle through which earlier decisions and actions are revisited, refined and revised with a growing understanding of the pupil's needs and of what supports the pupil in making good progress and securing good outcomes. This is known as the graduated approach. It draws on more detailed approaches, more frequent review and more specialist expertise in successive cycles in order to match interventions to the SEN of children and young people.

Assess

6.45 In identifying a child as needing SEN support the class or subject teacher, working with the SENCO, should carry out a clear analysis of the pupil's needs. This should draw on the teacher's assessment and experience of the pupil, their previous progress and attainment, as well as information from the school's core approach to pupil progress, attainment, and behaviour. It should also draw on other subject teachers' assessments where relevant, the individual's development in comparison to their peers and national data, the views and experience of parents, the pupil's own views and, if relevant, advice from external support services. Schools should take seriously any concerns raised by a parent. These should be recorded and compared to the setting's own assessment and information on how the pupil is developing.

6.46 This assessment should be reviewed regularly. This will help ensure that support and intervention are matched to need, barriers to learning are identified and overcome, and that a clear picture of the interventions put in place and their effect is developed. For some types of SEN, the way in which a pupil responds to an intervention can be the most reliable method of developing a more accurate picture of need.

6.47 In some cases, outside professionals from health or social services may already be involved with the child. These professionals should liaise with the school to help inform the assessments. Where professionals are not already working with school staff the SENCO should contact them if the parents agree.

Plan

6.48 Where it is decided to provide a pupil with SEN support, the parents **must** be formally notified, although parents should have already been involved in forming the assessment of needs as outlined above. The teacher and the SENCO should agree in consultation with the parent and the pupil the adjustments, interventions and support to be put in place, as well as the expected impact on progress, development or behaviour, along with a clear date for review.

6.49 All teachers and support staff who work with the pupil should be made aware of their needs, the outcomes sought, the support provided and any teaching strategies or approaches that are required. This should also be recorded on the school's information system.

6.50 The support and intervention provided should be selected to meet the outcomes identified for the pupil, based on reliable evidence of effectiveness, and should be provided by staff with sufficient skills and knowledge.

6.51 Parents should be fully aware of the planned support and interventions and, where appropriate, plans should seek parental involvement to reinforce or contribute to progress at home. The information set out in 6.39 should be readily available to and discussed with the pupil's parents.

Do

6.52 The class or subject teacher should remain responsible for working with the child on a daily basis. Where the interventions involve group or one-to-one teaching away from the main class or subject teacher, they should still retain responsibility for the pupil. They should work closely with any teaching assistants or specialist staff involved, to plan and assess the impact of support and interventions and how they can be linked to classroom teaching. The SENCO should support the class or subject teacher in the further assessment of the child's particular strengths and weaknesses, in problem solving and advising on the effective implementation of support.

Review

6.53 The effectiveness of the support and interventions and their impact on the pupil's progress should be reviewed in line with the agreed date.

6.54 The impact and quality of the support and interventions should be evaluated, along with the views of the pupil and their parents. This should feed back into the analysis of the pupil's needs. The class or subject teacher, working with the SENCO, should revise the support in light of the pupil's progress and development, deciding on any changes to the support and outcomes in consultation with the parent and pupil.

6.55 Parents should have clear information about the impact of the support and interventions provided, enabling them to be involved in planning next steps.

6.56 Where a pupil has an EHC plan, the local authority **must** review that plan as a minimum every twelve months. Schools **must** co-operate with the local authority in the review process and, as part of the review, the local authority can require schools to convene and hold annual review meetings on its behalf. Further information about EHC plan reviews is given in Chapter 9, Education, Health and Care needs assessments and plans.

Transition

6.57 SEN support should include planning and preparation for the transitions between phases of education and preparation for adult life (see Chapter 8, Preparing for adulthood from the earliest years). To support transition, the school should share information with the school, college or other setting the child or young person is moving to. Schools should agree with parents and pupils the information to be shared as part of this planning process. Where a pupil is remaining at the school for post-16 provision, this planning and preparation should include consideration of how to provide a high quality study programme, as set out in paragraph 8.32.

Involving specialists

6.58 Where a pupil continues to make less than expected progress, despite evidence-based support and interventions that are matched to the pupil's area of need, the school should consider involving specialists, including those secured by the school itself or from outside agencies.

6.59 Schools may involve specialists at any point to advise them on early identification of SEN and effective support and interventions. A school should always involve a specialist where a pupil continues to make little or no progress or where they continue to work at levels substantially below those expected of pupils of a similar age despite evidence-based SEN support delivered by appropriately trained staff. The pupil's parents should always be involved in any decision to involve specialists.

The involvement of specialists and what was discussed or agreed should be recorded and shared with the parents and teaching staff supporting the child in the same way as other SEN support.

6.60 Where assessment indicates that support from specialist services is required, it is important that children and young people receive it as quickly as possible. Joint commissioning arrangements should seek to ensure that there are sufficient services to meet the likely need in an area. The Local Offer should set out clearly what support is available from different services and how it may be accessed.

6.61 Schools should work closely with the local authority and other providers to agree the range of local services and clear arrangements for making appropriate requests. This might include schools commissioning specialist services directly. Such specialist services include, but are not limited to:

- educational psychologists
- Child and Adolescent Mental Health Services (CAMHS)
- specialist teachers or support services, including specialist teachers with a mandatory qualification for children with hearing and vision impairment , including multi-sensory impairment, and for those with a physical disability. (Those teaching classes of children with sensory impairment **must** hold an appropriate qualification approved by the Secretary of State. Teachers working in an advisory role to support such pupils should also hold the appropriate qualification.)
- therapists (including speech and language therapists, occupational therapists and physiotherapists)

6.62 The SENCO and class teacher, together with the specialists, and involving the pupil's parents, should consider a range of evidence-based and effective teaching approaches, appropriate equipment, strategies and interventions in order to support the child's progress. They should agree the outcomes to be achieved through the support, including a date by which progress will be reviewed.

Requesting an Education, Health and Care needs assessment

6.63 SEN support should be adapted or replaced depending on how effective it has been in achieving the agreed outcomes. Where, despite the school having taken relevant and purposeful action to identify, assess and meet the SEN of the child or young person, the child or young person has not made expected progress, the school or parents should consider requesting an Education, Health and Care needs assessment (see Chapter 9). To inform its decision the local authority will expect to see evidence of the action taken by the school as part of SEN support.

Involving parents and pupils in planning and reviewing progress

6.64 Schools **must** provide an annual report for parents on their child's progress. Most schools will want to go beyond this and provide regular reports for parents on how their child is progressing.

6.65 Where a pupil is receiving SEN support, schools should talk to parents regularly to set clear outcomes and review progress towards them, discuss the activities and support that will help achieve them, and identify the responsibilities of the parent, the pupil and the school. Schools should meet parents at least three times each year.

6.66 These discussions can build confidence in the actions being taken by the school, but they can also strengthen the impact of SEN support by increasing parental engagement in the approaches and teaching strategies that are being used. Finally, they can provide essential information on the impact of SEN support outside school and any changes in the pupil's needs.

6.67 These discussions should be led by a teacher with good knowledge and understanding of the pupil who is aware of their needs and attainment. This will usually be the class teacher or form tutor, supported by the SENCO. It should provide an opportunity for the parent to share their concerns and, together with the teacher, agree their aspirations for the pupil.

6.68 Conducting these discussions effectively involves a considerable amount of skill. As with other aspects of good teaching for pupils with SEN, schools should ensure that teaching staff are supported to manage these conversations as part of professional development.

6.69 These discussions will need to allow sufficient time to explore the parents' views and to plan effectively. Meetings should, wherever possible, be aligned with the normal cycle of discussions with parents of all pupils. They will, however, be longer than most parent-teacher meetings.

6.70 The views of the pupil should be included in these discussions. This could be through involving the pupil in all or part of the discussion itself, or gathering their views as part of the preparation.

6.71 A record of the outcomes, action and support agreed through the discussion should be kept and shared with all the appropriate school staff. This record should be given to the pupil's parents. The school's management information system should be updated as appropriate.

Use of data and record keeping

6.72 It is for schools to determine their own approach to record keeping in line with the requirements of the Data Protection Act 1998. The provision made for pupils with SEN should be recorded accurately and kept up to date. As part of any inspection, Ofsted will expect to see evidence of pupil progress, a focus on outcomes and a rigorous approach to the monitoring and evaluation of any SEN support provided. Ofsted publish more detail about their expectations in their inspection guidelines.

6.73 Schools should particularly record details of additional or different provision made under SEN support. This should form part of regular discussions with parents about the child's progress, expected outcomes from the support and planned next steps. They should ensure that they have accurate information to evidence the SEN support that has been provided over the pupil's time in the school, as well as its impact. A local authority that is considering or is carrying out an assessment of the pupil's needs will wish to review such information (see Chapter 9). For children and young people detained in custody, a Youth Offending Team will seek information from the school to support their initial assessments. The school should respond to such requests as soon as possible (see Chapter 10).

6.74 Schools use information systems to monitor the progress and development of all pupils. Details of SEN, outcomes, teaching strategies and the involvement of specialists should be recorded as part of this overall approach.

6.75 As outlined in 'Involving parents and pupils in planning and reviewing progress' from paragraph 6.63 above, the school should readily share this information with parents. It should be provided in a format that is accessible (for example, a note setting out the areas of discussion following a regular SEN support meeting or tracking data showing the pupil's progress together with highlighted sections of a provision map that enables parents to see the support that has been provided).

6.76 Provision maps are an efficient way of showing all the provision that the school makes which is additional to and different from that which is offered through the school's curriculum. The use of provision maps can help SENCOs to maintain an overview of the programmes and interventions used with different groups of pupils and provide a basis for monitoring the levels of intervention.

6.77 Provision management can be used strategically to develop special educational provision to match the assessed needs of pupils across the school, and to evaluate the impact of that provision on pupil progress. Used in this way provision management can also contribute to school improvement by identifying particular patterns of need and potential areas of development for teaching staff. It can help the school to develop the use of interventions that are effective and to remove those that are less so. It can support schools to improve their core offer for all pupils as the most effective approaches are adopted more widely across the school.

6.78 The Department for Education publishes a helpful range of further information and resources about provision mapping (see the References section under Chapter 6 for a link).

Publishing information: SEN information report

6.79 The governing bodies of maintained schools and maintained nursery schools and the proprietors of academy schools **must** publish information on their websites about the implementation of the governing body's or the proprietor's policy for pupils with SEN. The information published should be updated annually and any changes to the information occurring during the year should be updated as soon as possible. The information required is set out in the Special Educational Needs and Disability Regulations 2014 and **must** include information about:

- the kinds of SEN that are provided for
- policies for identifying children and young people with SEN and assessing their needs, including the name and contact details of the SENCO (mainstream schools)
- arrangements for consulting parents of children with SEN and involving them in their child's education
- arrangements for consulting young people with SEN and involving them in their education
- arrangements for assessing and reviewing children and young people's progress towards outcomes. This should include the opportunities available to work with parents and young people as part of this assessment and review
- arrangements for supporting children and young people in moving between phases of education and in preparing for adulthood. As young people prepare for adulthood outcomes should reflect their ambitions, which could include higher education, employment, independent living and participation in society
- the approach to teaching children and young people with SEN
- how adaptations are made to the curriculum and the learning environment of children and young people with SEN

- the expertise and training of staff to support children and young people with SEN, including how specialist expertise will be secured

- evaluating the effectiveness of the provision made for children and young people with SEN

- how children and young people with SEN are enabled to engage in activities available with children and young people in the school who do not have SEN

- support for improving emotional and social development. This should include extra pastoral support arrangements for listening to the views of children and young people with SEN and measures to prevent bullying

- how the school involves other bodies, including health and social care bodies, local authority support services and voluntary sector organisations, in meeting children and young people's SEN and supporting their families

- arrangements for handling complaints from parents of children with SEN about the provision made at the school

6.80 The above should include arrangements for supporting children and young people who are looked after by the local authority and have SEN.

6.81 Schools should ensure that the information is easily accessible by young people and parents and is set out in clear, straightforward language. It should include information on the school's SEN policy and named contacts within the school for situations where young people or parents have concerns. It should also give details of the school's contribution to the Local Offer and **must** include information on where the local authority's Local Offer is published.

6.82 In setting out details of the broad and balanced curriculum provided in each year, schools should include details of how the curriculum is adapted or made accessible for pupils with SEN.

6.83 Schools should also make data on the levels and types of need within the school available to the local authority. This data will be required to inform local strategic planning of SEN support, and to enable the local authority to identify pupils who have or may have SEN. Such data, collected through the School Census, is also required to produce the national SEN information report.

The role of the SENCO in schools

6.84 Governing bodies of maintained mainstream schools and the proprietors of mainstream academy schools (including free schools) **must** ensure that there is a qualified teacher designated as SENCO for the school.

6.85 The SENCO **must** be a qualified teacher working at the school. A newly appointed SENCO **must** be a qualified teacher and, where they have not previously been the SENCO at that or any other relevant school for a total period of more than twelve months, they **must** achieve a National Award in Special Educational Needs Co-ordination within three years of appointment.

6.86 A National Award **must** be a postgraduate course accredited by a recognised higher education provider. The National College for Teaching and Leadership has worked with providers to develop a set of learning outcomes (see the References section under Chapter 6 for a link). When appointing staff or arranging for them to study for a National Award schools should satisfy themselves that the chosen course will meet these outcomes and equip the SENCO to fulfil the duties outlined in this Code. Any selected course should be at least equivalent to 60 credits at postgraduate study.

6.87 The SENCO has an important role to play with the headteacher and governing body, in determining the strategic development of SEN policy and provision in the school. They will be most effective in that role if they are part of the school leadership team.

6.88 The SENCO has day-to-day responsibility for the operation of SEN policy and co-ordination of specific provision made to support individual pupils with SEN, including those who have EHC plans.

6.89 The SENCO provides professional guidance to colleagues and will work closely with staff, parents and other agencies. The SENCO should be aware of the provision in the Local Offer and be able to work with professionals providing a support role to families to ensure that pupils with SEN receive appropriate support and high quality teaching.

6.90 The key responsibilities of the SENCO may include:

- overseeing the day-to-day operation of the school's SEN policy
- co-ordinating provision for children with SEN
- liaising with the relevant Designated Teacher where a looked after pupil has SEN
- advising on the graduated approach to providing SEN support

- advising on the deployment of the school's delegated budget and other resources to meet pupils' needs effectively
- liaising with parents of pupils with SEN
- liaising with early years providers, other schools, educational psychologists, health and social care professionals, and independent or voluntary bodies
- being a key point of contact with external agencies, especially the local authority and its support services
- liaising with potential next providers of education to ensure a pupil and their parents are informed about options and a smooth transition is planned
- working with the headteacher and school governors to ensure that the school meets its responsibilities under the Equality Act (2010) with regard to reasonable adjustments and access arrangements
- ensuring that the school keeps the records of all pupils with SEN up to date

6.91 The school should ensure that the SENCO has sufficient time and resources to carry out these functions. This should include providing the SENCO with sufficient administrative support and time away from teaching to enable them to fulfil their responsibilities in a similar way to other important strategic roles within a school.

6.92 It may be appropriate for a number of smaller primary schools to share a SENCO employed to work across the individual schools, where they meet the other requirements set out in this chapter of the Code. Schools can consider this arrangement where it secures sufficient time away from teaching and sufficient administrative support to enable the SENCO to fulfil the role effectively for the total registered pupil population across all of the schools involved.

6.93 Where such a shared approach is taken the SENCO should not normally have a significant class teaching commitment. Such a shared SENCO role should not be carried out by a headteacher at one of the schools.

6.94 Schools should review the effectiveness of such a shared SENCO role regularly and should not persist with it where there is evidence of a negative impact on the quality of SEN provision, or the progress of pupils with SEN.

Funding for SEN support

6.95 All mainstream schools are provided with resources to support those with additional needs, including pupils with SEN and disabilities. Most of these resources are determined by a local funding formula, discussed with the local schools forum, which is also applied to local academies. School and academy sixth forms receive an allocation based on a national funding formula.

6.96 Schools have an amount identified within their overall budget, called the notional SEN budget. This is not a ring-fenced amount, and it is for the school to provide high quality appropriate support from the whole of its budget.

6.97 It is for schools, as part of their normal budget planning, to determine their approach to using their resources to support the progress of pupils with SEN. The SENCO, headteacher and governing body or proprietor should establish a clear picture of the resources that are available to the school. They should consider their strategic approach to meeting SEN in the context of the total resources available, including any resources targeted at particular groups, such as the pupil premium.

6.98 This will enable schools to provide a clear description of the types of special educational provision they normally provide and will help parents and others to understand what they can normally expect the school to provide for pupils with SEN.

6.99 Schools are not expected to meet the full costs of more expensive special educational provision from their core funding. They are expected to provide additional support which costs up to a nationally prescribed threshold per pupil per year. The responsible local authority, usually the authority where the child or young person lives, should provide additional top-up funding where the cost of the special educational provision required to meet the needs of an individual pupil exceeds the nationally prescribed threshold.

7 Further education

What this chapter covers

This chapter explains and provides guidance on the statutory duties on further education colleges, sixth form colleges, 16-19 academies and some independent specialist colleges approved under Section 41 of the Children and Families Act 2014 to identify, assess and provide support for young people with special educational needs (SEN).

Relevant legislation

Primary

The following sections of the Children and Families Act 2014:

- Co-operating generally: local authority functions: Section 28
- Co-operating generally: governing body function: Section 29
- Children and young people with SEN but no plan: Section 34
- Independent specialist schools and special post-16 institutions – approval: Section 41
- Schools and other institutions named in EHC plan: duty to admit: Section 43
- Using best endeavours to secure special educational provision: Section 66
- Code of Practice: Section 77

The Equality Act 2010

Regulations

The Special Educational Needs and Disability Regulations 2014

Introduction

7.1 The post-16 education and training landscape is very diverse. It encompasses school sixth forms (both mainstream and special schools), sixth form colleges, general further education (FE) colleges, 16-19 academies, special post-16 institutions, and vocational learning and training providers in the private or voluntary sector. The range of available study programmes is broad and includes AS/A-levels, vocational qualifications at all levels, apprenticeships, traineeships, supported internships and bespoke packages of learning. School provision is covered in Chapter 6.

7.2 Mainstream providers include school sixth forms, general FE colleges, sixth form colleges, specialist art and design and land-based colleges and 16-19 academies. Colleges are usually very much larger than schools, and offer an extensive breadth of courses to young people and adults of all ages. Special school sixth forms, independent specialist colleges and many general FE colleges specialise in provision for students with SEN. Post-16 provision is also offered by not-for-profit and voluntary sector, independent and private training and employment services. Unless stated otherwise, the use of 'college' throughout this chapter encompasses general FE colleges, specialist art and design and land-based colleges, sixth form colleges, 16-19 academies and special post-16 institutions approved under section 41 of the Children and Families Act 2014.

Statutory duties on post-16 institutions

7.3 FE colleges, sixth form colleges, 16-19 academies and independent specialist colleges approved under Section 41 of the Children and Families Act 2014 (the Act) have the following specific statutory duties:

- **The duty to co-operate with the local authority on arrangements for children and young people with SEN**. This is a reciprocal duty. It means that, in carrying out their functions under this part of the Act, a local authority **must** co-operate with the named bodies who, in turn, **must** co-operate with the local authority.

- **The duty to admit a young person if the institution is named in an Education Health and Care (EHC) plan**. Young people have the right to request that an institution is named in their EHC plan, and local authorities have a duty to name that institution in the EHC plan unless, following consultation with the institution, the local authority determines that it is unsuitable for the young person's age, ability, aptitude or SEN, or that to place the young person there would be incompatible with the efficient use of resources or the efficient education of others.

- **The duty to have regard to this Code of Practice**

- **The duty to use their best endeavours to secure the special educational provision that the young person needs**. This duty applies to further education colleges, sixth form colleges and 16-19 academies. Its purpose is to ensure that providers give the right support to their students with SEN. It does not apply to independent specialist colleges or special schools, as their principal purpose is to provide for young people with SEN. They **must** fulfil this duty for students with SEN whether or not the students have EHC plans. This duty applies in respect of students with SEN up to age 25 in further education, including those aged between 14 and 16 recruited directly by colleges. The duty encompasses students on a wide variety of study programmes (including some on short programmes) and at every level from entry level upwards. It does not apply to any students on higher education courses, who can access the Disabled Students Allowance (DSA). Much of this section will also be relevant for independent specialist colleges.

7.4 A young person has SEN if he or she has a learning difficulty or disability which calls for special educational provision to be made for them. Special educational provision is support which is additional or different to support usually available to young people of the same age in mainstream colleges. For more detailed information on the definition of SEN, see the Introduction. Colleges should offer an inclusive approach to learning and teaching, with high quality teaching which is differentiated for individuals. This approach should be embedded in their provision in all subject areas and at all levels, and support the teaching of all students, including those with SEN.

7.5 Colleges should be ambitious for young people with SEN, whatever their needs and whatever their level of study. They should focus on supporting young people so they can progress and reach positive destinations in adult life. These destinations include higher education or further training or employment, independent living (which means having choice and control over the support received), good health and participating in the community. Further information on support for young people in preparing for adult life is set out in Chapter 8, Preparing for adulthood from the earliest years.

7.6 All students aged 16-19 (and students up to the age of 25 where they have an EHC plan) should follow a coherent study programme which provides stretch and progression and enables them to achieve the best possible outcomes in adult life. Further detail on study programmes and pathways to employment is given in Chapter 8, Preparing for adulthood from the earliest years, paragraphs 8.32 to 8.40. More detailed information on what constitutes good outcome setting is given in Chapter 9, Education, Health and Care needs assessments and plans, paragraphs 9.64 to 9.69). These principles should be applied to planning for all young people.

Equality Act 2010

7.7 FE colleges, sixth form colleges, 16-19 academies and independent special schools approved under Section 41 of the Children and Families Act 2014 have duties under the Equality Act 2010. In particular, they **must not** discriminate against, harass or victimise disabled children or young people and they **must** make reasonable adjustments to prevent them being placed at a substantial disadvantage. This duty is anticipatory – it requires thought to be given in advance to what disabled young people might require and what adjustments might need to be made to prevent that disadvantage.

7.8 Providers have wider duties to prevent discrimination, to promote equality of opportunity and to foster good relations. Chapter 1, Principles, provides further details on the disability discrimination duties in the Equality Act 2010. The guidance in this chapter should be read in the light of the principles in Chapter 1 which focus on inclusive practice and removing barriers to learning.

Careers guidance for young people

7.9 FE colleges and sixth form colleges are required through their funding agreements to secure access to independent careers guidance for all students up to and including age 18 and for 19- to 25-year-olds with EHC plans. Chapter 8 provides more information about careers guidance for children and young people.

Identifying SEN

7.10 Colleges should be involved in transition planning between school and college so that they can prepare to meet the student's needs and ensure a successful transition into college life. Chapter 8, paragraphs 8.22 to 8.28, gives guidance to schools and colleges on how they should work together to smooth that transition. Colleges should give all applicants an opportunity before or at entry and at subsequent points, to declare whether they have a learning need, a disability or a medical condition which will affect their learning. If a student makes a declaration the college should discuss with the student how they will provide support. Any screenings and assessments should be differentiated and proportionate to the likely level of SEN.

7.11 Some needs may emerge after a student has begun a programme. Teaching staff should work with specialist support to identify where a student may be having difficulty which may be because of SEN.

7.12 Students who fell behind at school, or who are studying below level 2, should have their needs identified and appropriate support should be provided. It should not be assumed that they have SEN just because they have lower attainment levels than the majority of their peers. They may do, but this should be identified specifically and supported. Equally it should not be assumed that students working on higher level courses do not have any learning difficulty or disability that may need special educational provision.

SEN support in college

7.13 Where a student has a learning difficulty or disability that calls for special educational provision, the college **must** use its best endeavours to put appropriate support in place. Young people should be supported to participate in discussions about their aspirations, their needs, and the support that they think will help them best. Support should be aimed at promoting student independence and enabling the young person to make good progress towards employment and/or higher education, independent living, good health and participating in the community. Chapter 8 provides guidance on preparing young people for adult life.

7.14 Support should be evidence based. This means that colleges should be aware of effective practice in the sector and elsewhere, and personalise it for the individual. They should keep the needs of students with SEN or disabilities under regular review. Colleges should take a cyclical approach to assessing need, planning and providing support, and reviewing and evaluating that support so that it can be adjusted where necessary. They should involve the student and, particularly for those aged 16 to 18, their parents, closely at all stages of the cycle, planning around the individual, and they should ensure that staff have the skills to do this effectively.

Assessing what support is needed

7.15 Where a student is identified as having SEN and needing SEN support, colleges should bring together all the relevant information from the school, from the student, from those working with the student and from any screening test or assessment the college has carried out. This information should be discussed with the student. The student should be offered support at this meeting and might be accompanied by a parent, advocate or other supporter. This discussion may identify the need for a more specialist assessment from within the college or beyond.

Planning the right support

7.16 Where the college decides a student needs SEN support, the college should discuss with the student their ambitions, the nature of the support to be put in place, the expected impact on progress and a date for reviewing the support. Plans should be developed with the student. The support and intervention provided should be selected to meet the student's aspirations, and should be based on reliable evidence of effectiveness and provided by practitioners with the relevant skills and knowledge.

7.17 Special educational support might include, for example:

- assistive technology
- personal care (or access to it)
- specialist tuition
- note takers
- interpreters
- one-to-one and small group learning support
- habilitation/independent living training
- accessible information such as symbol based materials
- access to therapies (for example, speech and language therapy)

Putting the provision in place

7.18 Colleges should ensure that the agreed support is put in place, and that appropriately qualified staff provide the support needed. The college should, in discussion with the student, assess the impact and success of the intervention.

Keeping support under review

7.19 The effectiveness of the support and its impact on the student's progress should be reviewed regularly, taking into account the student's progress and any changes to the student's own ambitions and aspirations, which may lead to changes in the type and level of their support. The college and the student together should plan any changes in support. Colleges should revisit this cycle of action, refining and revising their decisions about support as they gain a richer understanding of the student, and what is most effective in helping them secure good outcomes. Support for all students with SEN should be kept under review, whether or not a student has an EHC plan.

7.20 Where a student has an EHC plan, the local authority **must** review that plan as a minimum every twelve months, including a review of the student's support. The college **must** co-operate with the local authority in the review process. As part of the review, the local authority can ask the college to convene and hold the annual review meeting on its behalf. Further information about EHC plan reviews and the role of colleges is given in Chapter 9, Education, Health and Care needs assessments and plans. From the age of thirteen onwards, annual reviews focus on preparing for adulthood. Further information on pathways to employment and on support for young people in preparing for adult life is set out in Chapter 8, Preparing for adulthood from the earliest years.

7.21 Colleges should also keep under review the reasonable adjustments they make under the Equality Act 2010 to ensure they have removed all the barriers to learning that they reasonably can. Colleges should also ensure that students with SEN or disabilities know who to go to for support.

Expertise within and beyond the college

7.22 The governing bodies of colleges should ensure that all staff interact appropriately and inclusively with students who have SEN or a disability and should ensure that they have appropriate expertise within their workforce. They should also ensure that curriculum staff are able to develop their skills, are aware of effective practice and keep their knowledge up to date. Colleges should make sure they have access to specialist skills and expertise to support the learning of students with SEN. This can be through partnerships with other agencies such as adult social care or health services, or specialist organisations, and/or by employing practitioners directly. They should ensure that there is a named person in the college with oversight of SEN provision to ensure co-ordination of support, similar to the role of the SEN Co-ordinator (SENCO) in schools. This person should contribute to the strategic and operational management of the college. Curriculum and support staff in a college should know who to go to if they need help in identifying a student's SEN, are concerned about their progress or need further advice. In reviewing and managing support for students with SEN, colleges and 16-19 academies may find the broad areas of need and support outlined in Chapter 6 helpful (paragraph 6.28 onwards).

7.23 Colleges should ensure they have access to external specialist services and expertise. These can include, for example, educational psychologists, Child and Adolescent Mental Health Services (CAMHS), specialist teachers and support services, supported employment services and therapists. They can be involved at any point for help or advice on the best way to support a student with SEN or a disability. Specialist help should be involved where the student's needs are not being met by the strong, evidence-based support provided by the college. Where, despite the college having taken relevant and purposeful action to identify, assess and meet the needs of the student, the student is still not making the expected progress, the college or young person should consider requesting an EHC needs assessment (see Chapter 9).

7.24 More guidance on the advice and support colleges should give students with SEN or disabilities to enable them to prepare for adult life, including the transition out of college, is in Chapter 8, Preparing for adulthood from the earliest years.

Record keeping

7.25 Colleges should keep a student's profile and record of support up to date to inform discussions with the student about their progress and support. This should include accurate information to evidence the SEN support that has been provided over a student's time in college and its effectiveness. They should record details of what additional or different provision they make to meet a student's SEN and their progress towards specified outcomes. This should include information about the student's SEN, interventions and the support of specialists. The information should be used as part of regular discussions with the student and, where appropriate, the family, about the student's progress, the expected outcomes and planned next steps. For young people detained in custody, a Youth Offending Team will seek information from the college to support their initial assessments. The college should respond to such requests as soon as possible (see Chapter 10).

7.26 As with schools, colleges will determine their own approach to record keeping but should ensure that Individualised Learner Record (ILR) data is recorded accurately and in a timely manner in line with funding rules. Where students have EHC plans, colleges should provide the local authority with regular information about the progress that student is making towards the agreed outcomes set out in their EHC plan. Where a student has support from the local authority's high needs funding but does not have an EHC plan, colleges should also provide information on the student's progress to the local authority to inform its commissioning.

7.27 Further information on support to help children and young people prepare for adulthood, including pathways to employment and the transition to adult services, is in Chapter 8. Information about seeking needs assessments and about EHC plans is in Chapter 9.

Funding for SEN support

7.28 All school and academy sixth forms, sixth form colleges, further education colleges and 16-19 academies are provided with resources to support students with additional needs, including young people with SEN and disabilities.

7.29 These institutions receive an allocation based on a national funding formula for their core provision. They also have additional funding for students with additional needs, including those with SEN. This funding is not ring-fenced and is included in their main allocation in a 'single line' budget. Like mainstream schools, colleges are expected to provide appropriate, high quality SEN support using all available resources.

7.30 It is for colleges, as part of their normal budget planning, to determine their approach to using their resources to support the progress of young people with SEN. The principal or a senior leader should establish a clear picture of the resources available to the college and consider their strategic approach to meeting SEN in the context of the total resources available.

7.31 This will enable colleges to provide a clear description of the types of special educational provision they normally provide. This will help parents and others understand what they can normally expect the college to provide for young people with SEN.

7.32 Colleges are not expected to meet the full costs of more expensive support from their core and additional funding in their main allocation. They are expected to provide additional support which costs up to a nationally prescribed threshold per student per year. The responsible local authority, usually the authority where the young person lives, should provide additional top-up funding where the cost of the special educational provision required to meet the needs of an individual young person exceeds the nationally prescribed threshold. This should reflect the cost of providing the additional support that is in excess of the nationally prescribed threshold. There is no requirement for an EHC plan for a young person for whom a college receives additional top-up funding except in the case of a young person who is over 19. But where the local authority considers it is necessary for special educational provision to be made through an EHC plan it should carry out an EHC needs assessment. Local authorities should be transparent about how they will make decisions about high needs funding and education placements. They should share the principles and criteria which underpin those decisions with schools and colleges and with parents and young people.

7.33 It should be noted that colleges are funded by the Education Funding Agency (EFA) for all 16-18 year olds and for those aged 19-25 who have EHC plans, with support from the home local authority for students with high needs. Colleges **must not** charge tuition fees for these young people. Further information on funding can be found on the GOV.UK website – see the References section under Chapter 7 for a link.

7.34 Colleges are funded by the Skills Funding Agency (SFA) for all students aged 19 and over who do not have an EHC plan (including those who declare a learning difficulty or disability). Colleges are able to charge fees for these students. However, students who meet residency and eligibility criteria will have access to Government funding. Further information on funding eligibility is available on the SFA's website – see the References section under Chapter 7 for a link. Colleges also receive funding from HEFCE for their higher education (HE) students, but this Code does not apply to HE students.

7.35 Further information on funding places for 19-25 year olds is given in Chapter 8, Preparing for adulthood from the earliest years.

8 Preparing for adulthood from the earliest years

What this chapter covers

This chapter is relevant for everyone working with children and young people with SEN or disabilities and is particularly relevant for those working with children and young people aged 14 and over. It sets out how professionals across education (including early years, schools, colleges and 16-19 academies), health and social care should support children and young people with special educational needs (SEN) or disabilities to prepare for adult life, and help them go on to achieve the best outcomes in employment, independent living, health and community participation. The principles set out in this chapter apply to all young people with SEN or disabilities, except where it states they are for those with Education, Health and Care (EHC) plans only. The term 'colleges' in this chapter includes all post-16 institutions with duties under the Children and Families Act 2014 (further education (FE) colleges, sixth form colleges, 16-19 academies and independent specialist colleges approved under Section 41 of the Act).

High aspirations are crucial to success – discussions about longer term goals should start early and ideally well before Year 9 (age 13-14) at school. They should focus on the child or young person's strengths and capabilities and the outcomes they want to achieve. This chapter includes both the transition into post-16 education, and the transition from post-16 education into adult life. It covers:

- how local authorities and health services should plan strategically for the support children and young people will need to prepare for adult life
- how early years providers, schools and colleges should enable children and young people to have the information and skills they need to help them gain independence and prepare for adult life
- support from Year 9, including the content of preparing for adulthood reviews for children and young people with EHC plans
- planning the transition into post-16 education
- how post-16 institutions can design study programmes and create pathways to employment
- how young people should be supported to make decisions for themselves
- Packages of provision for children and young people with EHC plans across five days a week

- transition to higher education
- young people aged 19-25
- transition to adult health services
- transition to adult social care
- leaving education and training and progressing into employment

Relevant legislation

Primary

This chapter cross-references a wide range of duties under the Children and Families Act 2014 and regulations. Some, but not all, of the main duties are as follows:

- Local authority functions: supporting and involving children and young people, Section 19
- Joint commissioning arrangements: Section 26
- Duty to keep education and care provision under review: Section 27
- Co-operating generally: local authority functions: Section 28
- Co-operating generally: governing body functions: Section 29
- Local offer: Section 30
- Advice and information: Section 32
- Assessment of education, health and care needs: Section 36
- Preparation of EHC plans: draft plan: Section 38
- Personal Budgets and direct payments: Section 49
- Continuation of services under Section 17 of the Children Act 1989: Section 50
- Appeals: Section 51

Regulations

The Special Educational Needs and Disability Regulations 2014

The Special Educational Needs (Personal Budgets) Regulations 2014

Introduction

7.37 Being supported towards greater independence and employability can be life-transforming for children and young people with SEN. This support needs to start early, and should centre around the child or young person's own aspirations, interests and needs. All professionals working with them should share high aspirations and have a good understanding of what support is effective in enabling children and young people to achieve their ambitions.

7.38 Preparing for adulthood means preparing for:

- higher education and/or employment – this includes exploring different employment options, such as support for becoming self-employed and help from supported employment agencies
- independent living – this means young people having choice, control and freedom over their lives and the support they have, their accommodation and living arrangements, including supported living
- participating in society, including having friends and supportive relationships, and participating in, and contributing to, the local community
- being as healthy as possible in adult life

Strategic planning for the best outcomes in adult life

8.1 Local authorities **must** place children, young people and families at the centre of their planning, and work with them to develop co-ordinated approaches to securing better outcomes, as should clinical commissioning groups (CCGs). They should develop a shared vision and strategy which focuses on aspirations and outcomes, using information from EHC plans and other planning to anticipate the needs of children and young people with SEN and ensure there are pathways into employment, independent living, participation in society and good health. Where pathways need further development, local authorities and CCGs should set out clear responsibilities, timescales and funding arrangements for that work. This strategic planning will contribute to their

- joint commissioning
- Local Offer, which **must** include support in preparing for adulthood (see paragraphs 4.52 to 4.56 in Chapter 4, The Local Offer)
- preparation of EHC plans and support for children and young people to achieve the outcomes in their plan

8.2 This planning and support will bring enormous benefits to individuals. The National Audit Office report '*Oversight of special education for young people aged 16-25*' published in November 2011, estimates that supporting one person with a learning disability into employment could, in addition to improving their independence and self-esteem, increase that person's income by between 55 and 95 per cent. The National Audit Office also estimates that equipping a young person with the skills to live in semi-independent rather than fully supported housing could, in addition to quality of life improvements, reduce lifetime support costs to the public purse by around £1 million.

Duties on local authorities

8.3 Local authorities have a range of duties which are particularly relevant to this chapter. They are:

- when carrying out their functions, to support and involve the child and his or her parent, or the young person, and to have regard to their views, wishes and feelings (see Chapter 1, Principles). This includes their aspirations for adult life
- to offer advice and information directly to children and young people (see Chapter 2, Impartial information, advice and support). This includes information and advice which supports children and young people to prepare for adult life
- together with health services, to make joint commissioning arrangements about the education, health and care provision of children and young people to secure positive adult outcomes for young people with SEN (see Chapter 3, Working together across Education, Health and Care for joint outcomes)
- to keep education and care provision under review including the duty to consult young people directly, and to consult schools, colleges and other post-16 providers (see Chapter 3, Working together across Education, Health and Care for joint outcomes)
- to co-operate with FE colleges, sixth-form colleges, 16-19 academies and independent specialist colleges approved under Section 41 of the Children and Families Act 2014
- to include in the Local Offer provision which will help children and young people prepare for adulthood and independent living, to consult children and young people directly about the Local Offer and to publish those comments including details of any actions to be taken (Chapter 4, The Local Offer)

- to consider the need for EHC needs assessments, prepare EHC plans where needed, and maintain and review them, including the duty to ensure that all reviews of EHC plans from Year 9 (age 13-14) onwards include a focus on preparing for adulthood and, for 19-25 year olds, to have regard to whether educational or training outcomes specified in the EHC plan have been achieved
- to make young people aware through their Local Offer of the kind of support available to them in higher education and, where a higher education place has been confirmed for a young person with an EHC plan, to pass a copy of the EHC plan to the relevant institution and to the assessor for Disabled Students Allowance with the young person's permission

8.4 This is not a comprehensive list of local authority duties under the Children and Families Act 2014 or of regulations made under it. It is included to provide an overview, not detailed guidance on local authority duties.

Starting early

8.5 When a child is very young, or SEN is first identified, families need to know that the great majority of children and young people with SEN or disabilities, with the right support, can find work, be supported to live independently, and participate in their community. Health workers, social workers, early years providers and schools should encourage these ambitions right from the start. They should seek to understand the interests, strengths and motivations of children and young people and use this as a basis for planning support around them.

8.6 Early years providers and schools should support children and young people so that they are included in social groups and develop friendships. This is particularly important when children and young people are transferring from one phase of education to another (for example, from nursery to primary school). Maintained nurseries and schools **must** ensure that, subject to certain conditions, pupils with SEN engage in the activities of the nursery or school together with those who do not have SEN, and are encouraged to participate fully in the life of the nursery or school and in any wider community activity.

Support from Year 9 onwards (age 13-14)

8.7 High aspirations about employment, independent living and community participation should be developed through the curriculum and extra-curricular provision. Schools should seek partnerships with employment services, businesses, housing agencies, disability organisations and arts and sports groups, to help children understand what is available to them as they get older, and what it is possible for them to achieve. It can be particularly powerful to meet disabled adults who are successful in their work or who have made a significant contribution to their community. For children with EHC plans, Personal Budgets can be used to help children and young people with SEN to access activities that promote greater independence and learn important life skills. Local authorities **must** ensure that the relevant services they provide co-operate in helping children and young people to prepare for adulthood. This may include, for example, housing services, adult social care and economic regeneration.

8.8 For teenagers, preparation for adult life needs to be a more explicit element of their planning and support. Discussions about their future should focus on what they want to achieve and the best way to support them to achieve. Considering the right post-16 option is part of this planning. Chapter 9 includes more detail about the process of developing an EHC plan. Children and young people's aspirations and needs will not only vary according to individual circumstances, but will change over time as they get older and approach adult life.

Children and young people with EHC plans: preparing for adulthood reviews

8.9 Local authorities **must** ensure that the EHC plan review at Year 9, and every review thereafter, includes a focus on preparing for adulthood. It can be helpful for EHC plan reviews before Year 9 to have this focus too. Planning **must** be centred around the individual and explore the child or young person's aspirations and abilities, what they want to be able to do when they leave post-16 education or training and the support they need to achieve their ambition. Local authorities should ensure that children and young people have the support they need (for example, advocates) to participate fully in this planning and make decisions. Transition planning **must** be built into the revised EHC plan and should result in clear outcomes being agreed that are ambitious and stretching and which will prepare young people for adulthood.

8.10 Preparing for adulthood planning in the review of the EHC plan should include:

- support to prepare for higher education and/or employment. This should include identifying appropriate post-16 pathways that will lead to these outcomes. Training options such as supported internships, apprenticeships and traineeships should be discussed, or support for setting up your own business. The review should also cover support in finding a job, and learning how to do a job (for example, through work experience opportunities or the use of job coaches) and help in understanding any welfare benefits that might be available when in work

- support to prepare for independent living, including exploring what decisions young people want to take for themselves and planning their role in decision making as they become older. This should also include discussing where the child or young person wants to live in the future, who they want to live with and what support they will need. Local housing options, support in finding accommodation, housing benefits and social care support should be explained

- support in maintaining good health in adult life, including effective planning with health services of the transition from specialist paediatric services to adult health care. Helping children and young people understand which health professionals will work with them as adults, ensuring those professionals understand the young person's learning difficulties or disabilities and planning well-supported transitions is vital to ensure young people are as healthy as possible in adult life

- support in participating in society, including understanding mobility and transport support, and how to find out about social and community activities, and opportunities for engagement in local decision-making. This also includes support in developing and maintaining friendships and relationships

8.11 The review should identify the support the child or young person needs to achieve these aspirations and should also identify the components that should be included in their study programme to best prepare them for adult life. It should identify how the child or young person wants that support to be available and what action should be taken by whom to provide it. It should also identify the support a child or young person may need as they prepare to make more decisions for themselves.

8.12 Further guidance on preparing for the transition to post-16 education is given in paragraphs 8.22 to 8.28. Further guidance on transition to higher education is provided in paragraphs 8.45 to 8.50, and on leaving education and training in paragraphs 8.77 to 8.80.

Young people preparing to make their own decisions

8.13 As young people develop, and increasingly form their own views, they should be involved more and more closely in decisions about their own future. After compulsory school age (the end of the academic year in which they turn 16) the right to make requests and decisions under the Children and Families Act 2014 applies to them directly, rather than to their parents. Parents, or other family members, can continue to support young people in making decisions, or act on their behalf, provided that the young person is happy for them to do so, and it is likely that parents will remain closely involved in the great majority of cases.

8.14 The specific decision-making rights about EHC plans (see Chapter 9) which apply to young people directly from the end of compulsory school age are:

- the right to request an assessment for an EHC plan (which they can do at any time up to their 25th birthday)
- the right to make representations about the content of their EHC plan
- the right to request that a particular institution is named in their EHC plan
- the right to request a Personal Budget for elements of an EHC plan
- the right to appeal to the First-tier Tribunal (SEN and Disability) about decisions concerning their EHC plan

8.15 Local authorities, schools, colleges, health services and other agencies should continue to involve parents in discussions about the young person's future. In focusing discussions around the individual young person, they should support that young person to communicate their needs and aspirations and to make decisions which are most likely to lead to good outcomes for them, involving the family in most cases. A decision by a young person in respect of an EHC plan will typically involve discussion with their family and others, but the final decision rests with the young person.

8.16 A young person can ask a family member or friend to support them in any way they wish, including, for example, receiving correspondence on their behalf, filling in forms, attending meetings, making telephone calls and helping them to make decisions. Local authorities and other agencies working with young people should work flexibly to accommodate these arrangements. They should also be flexible about accommodating any changes in those arrangements over time, since the nature of the family's involvement may alter as the young person becomes older and more independent.

16- to 17-year-olds

8.17 Where a young person is under 18, the involvement of parents is particularly important and local authorities should continue to involve them in the vast majority of decisions. Schools and colleges normally involve the parents or family members of students under 18 where they have concerns about a young person's attendance, behaviour or welfare and they should continue to do so. They should also continue to involve parents or family members in discussions about the young person's studies where that is their usual policy. Child safeguarding law applies to children and young people up to the age of 18. The fact that the Children and Families Act 2014 gives rights directly to young people from the end of compulsory school age does not necessitate any change to a local authority's, school's or college's safeguarding or welfare policy.

Support for young people

8.18 Some young people will need support from an independent skilled supporter to ensure that their views are acknowledged and valued. They may need support in expressing views about their education, the future they want in adult life, and how they prepare for it, including their health, where they live, their relationships, control of their finances, how they will participate in the community and how they will achieve greater autonomy and independence. Local authorities should ensure young people who need it have access to this support.

The Mental Capacity Act

8.19 The right of young people to make a decision is subject to their capacity to do so as set out in the Mental Capacity Act 2005. The underlying principle of the Act is to ensure that those who lack capacity are empowered to make as many decisions for themselves as possible and that any decision made or action taken on their behalf is done so in their best interests. Decisions about mental capacity are made on an individual basis, and may vary according to the nature of the decision. Someone who may lack capacity to make a decision in one area of their life may be able to do so in another. There is further guidance on the Mental Capacity Act and how it applies both to parents and to young people in relation to the Act in Annex 1, Mental Capacity.

Planning the transition into post-16 education and training

8.20 Young people entering post-16 education and training should be accessing provision which supports them to build on their achievements at school and which helps them progress towards adulthood. Young people with EHC plans are likely to need more tailored post-16 pathways.

8.21 As children approach the transition point, schools and colleges should help children and their families with more detailed planning. For example, in Year 9, they should aim to help children explore their aspirations and how different post-16 education options can help them meet them. FE colleges and sixth form colleges can now recruit students directly from age 14, and so this will be an option in some cases. In Year 10 they should aim to support the child and their family to explore more specific courses or places to study (for example, through taster days and visits) so they can draw up provisional plans. In Year 11 they should aim to support the child and their family to firm up their plans for their post-16 options and familiarise themselves with the expected new setting. This should include contingency planning and the child and their family should know what to do if plans change (because of exam results for example).

8.22 It is important that information about previous SEN provision is shared with the further education or training provider. Schools should share information before the young person takes up their place, preferably in the spring term prior to the new course, so that the provider can develop a suitable study programme and prepare appropriate support. Where a change in education setting is planned, in the period leading up to that transition schools should work with children and young people and their families, and the new college or school, to ensure that their new setting has a good understanding of what the young person's aspirations are and how they would like to be supported. This will enable the new setting to plan support around the individual. Some children and young people will want a fresh start when leaving school to attend college and any sharing of information about their SEN should be sensitive to their concerns and done with their agreement.

8.23 Schools and colleges should work in partnership to provide opportunities such as taster courses, link programmes and mentoring which enable young people with SEN to familiarise themselves with the college environment and gain some experience of college life and study. This can include, for example, visits and taster days so that young people can become familiar with the size of the college, and how their studies will be structured, including how many days a week their programme covers. These will enable them to make more informed choices, and help them make a good transition into college life. Schools and colleges should agree a 'tell us once' approach so that families and young people do not have to repeat the same information unnecessarily.

8.24 For children and young people with EHC plans, discussions about post-16 options will be part of the preparing for adulthood focus of ECH plan reviews, which **must** be included as part of the review from Year 9 (age 13-14). The local authority **must** ensure these reviews take place, and schools and colleges **must** co-operate with the local authority in these reviews. If it is clear that a young person wants to attend a different school (sixth form) or a college, then that school or college **must** co-operate, so that it can help to shape the EHC plan, help to define the outcomes for that young person and start developing a post-16 study programme tailored to their needs.

8.25 Where SEN has been identified at school, colleges should use any information they have from the school about the young person. In some cases, SEN may have been identified at school, and information passed to the college in advance, and colleges should use this information, and seek clarification and further advice when needed from the school (or other agencies where relevant), to ensure they are ready to meet the needs of the student and that the student is ready for the move to college.

8.26 Under statutory guidance accompanying the Autism Strategy, SEN Co-ordinators (SENCOs) should inform young people with autism of their right to a community care assessment and their parents of the right to a carer's assessment. This should be built into preparing for adulthood review meetings for those with EHC plans. (See 8.61 to 8.66, Transition assessments for young people with EHC plans.)

Careers advice for children and young people

8.27 Maintained schools and pupil referral units (PRUs) have a statutory duty under section 42A of the Education Act 1997 to ensure pupils from Year 8 until Year 13 are provided with independent careers guidance. Academies, including 16-19 academies, and free schools are subject to this duty through their Funding Agreements. FE colleges also have equivalent requirements in their Funding Agreements – their duty applies for all students up to and including age 18 and will apply to 19- to 25-year-olds with EHC plans.

8.28 Schools and colleges should raise the career aspirations of their SEN students and broaden their employment horizons. They should use a wide range of imaginative approaches, such as taster opportunities, work experience, mentoring, exploring entrepreneurial options, role models and inspiring speakers.

8.29 Local authorities have a strategic leadership role in fulfilling their duties concerning the participation of young people in education and training. They should work with schools, colleges and other post-16 providers, as well as other agencies, to support young people to participate in education or training and to identify those in need of targeted support to help them make positive and well-informed choices. Statutory guidance for local authorities on the participation of young people in education, employment and training is available from the GOV.UK website – a link is given in the Reference section under Chapter 8.

High quality study programmes for students with SEN

8.30 All students aged 16 to 19 (and, where they will have an EHC plan, up to the age of 25) should follow a coherent study programme which provides stretch and progression and enables them to achieve the best possible outcomes in adult life. Schools and colleges are expected to design study programmes which enable students to progress to a higher level of study than their prior attainment, take rigorous, substantial qualifications, study English and maths, participate in meaningful work experience and non-qualification activity. They should not be repeating learning they have already completed successfully. For students who are not taking qualifications, their study programme should focus on high quality work experience, and on non-qualification activity which prepares them well for employment, independent living, being healthy adults and participating in society. Full guidance about study programmes is available on the GOV.UK website – a link is given in the Reference section under Chapter 8.

Pathways to employment

8.31 All young people should be helped to develop the skills and experience, and achieve the qualifications they need, to succeed in their careers. The vast majority of young people with SEN are capable of sustainable paid employment with the right preparation and support. All professionals working with them should share that presumption. Colleges that offer courses which are designed to provide pathways to employment should have a clear focus on preparing students with SEN for work. This includes identifying the skills that employers value, and helping young people to develop them.

8.32 One of the most effective ways to prepare young people with SEN for employment is to arrange work-based learning that enables them to have first-hand experience of work, such as:

- **Apprenticeships:** These are paid jobs that incorporate training, leading to nationally recognised qualifications. Apprentices earn as they learn and gain practical skills in the workplace. Many lead to highly skilled careers. Young people with EHC plans can retain their plan when on an apprenticeship.
- **Traineeships:** These are education and training programmes with work experience, focused on giving young people the skills and experience they need to help them compete for an apprenticeship or other jobs. Traineeships last a maximum of six months and include core components of work preparation training, English and maths (unless GCSE A*-C standard has already been achieved) and a high quality work experience placement. They are currently open to young people aged 16 to 24, including those with EHC plans. Young people with EHC plans can retain their plan when undertaking a traineeship.
- **Supported internships:** These are structured study programmes for young people with an EHC plan, based primarily at an employer. Internships normally last for a year and include extended unpaid work placements of at least six months. Wherever possible, they support the young person to move into paid employment at the end of the programme. Students complete a personalised study programme which includes the chance to study for relevant substantial qualifications, if suitable, and English and maths to an appropriate level. Young people with EHC plans will retain their plan when undertaking a supported internship.

8.33 When considering a work placement as part of a study programme, such as a supported internship, schools or colleges should match students carefully with the available placements. A thorough understanding of the student's potential, abilities, interests and areas they want to develop should inform honest conversations with potential employers. This is more likely to result in a positive experience for the student and the employer.

8.34 Schools and colleges should consider funding from Access to Work, available from the Department for Work and Pensions, as a potential source of practical support for people with disabilities or health (including mental health) conditions on entering work and apprenticeships, as well as the in-work elements of traineeships or supported internships. More information is available from the GOV.UK website and the Preparing for Adulthood website – links to both are given in the Reference section under Chapter 8.

8.35 In preparing young people for employment, local authorities, schools and colleges should be aware of the different employment options for disabled adults. This should include 'job-carving' – tailoring a job so it is suitable for a particular worker and their skills. This approach not only generates employment opportunities for young people with SEN, but can lead to improved productivity in the employer organisation.

8.36 Help to support young people with SEN into work is available from supported employment services. These can provide expert, individualised support to secure sustainable, paid work. This includes support in matching students to suitable work placements, searching for a suitable job and providing training (for example, from job coaches) in the workplace when a job has been secured. Local authorities should include supported employment services in their Local Offer (see Chapter 4, The Local Offer).

8.37 Education and training should include help for students who need it to develop skills which will prepare them for work, such as communication and social skills, using assistive technology, and independent travel training. It can also include support for students who may want to be self-employed, such as setting up a micro-enterprise.

8.38 It helps young people to know what support they may receive from adult services, when considering employment options. Where a young person may need support from adult services, local authorities should consider undertaking a transition assessment to aid discussions around pathways to employment (see paragraph 8.59 below under 'Transition to adult social care').

Packages of support across five days a week

8.39 Where young people have EHC plans, local authorities should consider the need to provide a full package of provision and support across education, health and care that covers five days a week, where that is appropriate to meet the young person's needs.

8.40 Five-day packages of provision and support do not have to be at one provider and could involve amounts of time at different providers and in different settings. It may include periods outside education institutions with appropriate support, including time and support for independent study. A package of provision can include non-educational activities such as:

- volunteering or community participation
- work experience
- opportunities that will equip young people with the skills they need to make a successful transition to adulthood, such as independent travel training, and/or skills for living in semi-supported or independent accommodation, and
- training to enable a young person to develop and maintain friendships and/or support them to access facilities in the local community.

It can also include health and care related activities such as physiotherapy. Full-time packages of provision and support set out in the EHC plan should include any time young people need to access support for their health and social care needs.

8.41 When commissioning provision, local authorities should have regard to how young people learn and the additional time and support they may need to undertake coursework and homework as well as time to socialise with their college peers within the college environment. In some cases, courses normally offered over three days may need to be spread over four or five days where that is likely to lead to better outcomes. Local authorities will need to work with providers and young people to ensure there is a range of opportunities that can be tailored to individual needs, including the use of Personal Budgets.

8.42 In making decisions about packages of support, local authorities should take into account the impact on the family and the effect this impact is likely to have on the young person's progress.

Transition to higher education

8.43 Securing a place in higher education is a positive outcome for many young people with SEN. Where a young person has this ambition, the right level of provision and support should be provided to help them to achieve that goal, wherever possible.

8.44 The local authority **must** make young people aware through their local offer of the support available to them in higher education and how to claim it, including the Disabled Students Allowance (DSA). DSAs are available to help students in higher education with the extra costs they may incur on their course because of a disability. This can include an ongoing health condition, mental health condition or specific learning difficulty such as dyslexia. Students need to make an application to Student Finance England (for students domiciled in England), providing accompanying medical evidence. A link to further information on DSAs is given in the Reference section under Chapter 7.

8.45 Applications for DSA can be made as soon as the student finance application service opens. This varies from year to year, but is generally at least six months before the start of the academic year in which a young person is expecting to take up a place in higher education. Local authorities should encourage young people to make an early claim for DSA so that support is in place when their course begins. Where a young person with an EHC plan makes a claim for DSA, the local authority **must** pass a copy of their plan to the relevant DSA assessor, to support and inform the application as soon as possible, where they are asked to do so by the young person. This should include relevant supporting diagnostic and medical information and assessments where the young person agrees.

8.46 Local authorities should plan a smooth transition to the higher education (and, where applicable, to the new local authority area) before ceasing to maintain a young person's EHC plan. Once the young person's place has been confirmed at a higher education institution, the local authority **must** pass a copy of their EHC plan to the relevant person in that institution at the earliest opportunity, where they are asked to do so by the young person.

8.47 The local authority should also plan how social care support will be maintained, where the young person continues to require it, and whether this will continue to be provided by the home local authority or by the authority in the area they are moving to. This should include consideration of how the student will be supported if they have a dual location, for example, if they live close to the higher education institution during term time and at home during vacations.

8.48 For most young people, their home local authority will continue to provide their care and support but this will depend on the circumstances of their case. The Ordinary Residence guidance published by the Department of Health provides a number of examples to help local authorities in making these decisions. The guidance is available on the GOV.UK website and a link is given in the Reference section under Chapter 8. Under the Care Act 2014, young people have the right to request transition assessments for adult care that will enable them to see whether they are likely to have eligible needs that will be met by adult services once they turn 18. Local authorities should use these assessments to help plan for support that will be provided by the local authority while a young person is in higher education.

Young people aged 19 to 25

8.49 Local authorities should be ambitious for children and young people with SEN, raising their aspirations and promoting high expectations about what they can achieve in school, college and beyond. Local authorities should ensure children and young people have access to the right support and opportunities that will prepare them successfully for adulthood by helping them achieve the agreed outcomes in their EHC plan. This will enable many more young people with SEN to complete their formal education.

8.50 Local authorities **must** set out in their Local Offer the support and provision that 19- to 25-year-olds with SEN can access regardless of whether they have an EHC plan (see Chapter 4, The Local Offer). Further education colleges **must** continue to use their best endeavours to secure the special educational provision needed by all young people aged 19 to 25 with SEN attending their institution. For guidance on EHC plans for young people aged 19 to 25, see Chapter 9.

Funding places for 19- to 25-year-olds

8.51 19- to 25-year-olds with EHC plans should have free access to further education in the same way as 16- to18-year-olds. Colleges or training providers **must not** charge young people tuition fees for such places as the funding will be provided by the local authority and the Education Funding Agency (EFA). Further information on funding is available from the EFA pages on GOV.UK – a link is provided in the References section under Chapter 7.

8.52 Apprentices aged 19 to 25 with EHC plans are fully funded on the same terms and funding rates as 16- to 18-year-old apprentices. The Local Offer should include apprenticeships for this age group and full details of apprenticeship funding are available from the Skills Funding Agency (SFA) website – a link is given in the References section under Chapter 7.

8.53 19- to 25-year-olds with SEN but without EHC plans can choose to remain in further education. Colleges are funded by the SFA for all students aged 19 and over who do not have an EHC plan (including those who declare a learning difficulty or disability). Colleges are able to charge fees for these students, but **must** use their best endeavours to secure the necessary special educational provision that they need. However, students who meet residency and eligibility criteria will have access to Government funding. Information on funding eligibility is available on the SFA's website – see the References section under Chapter 7 for a link. Local authorities are not responsible for securing or funding education and training opportunities for young people aged 19 to 25 who do not have EHC plans.

Transition to adult health services

8.54 Support to prepare young people for good health in adulthood should include supporting them to make the transition to adult health services. A child with significant health needs is usually under the care of a paediatrician. As an adult, they might be under the care of different consultants and teams. Health service and other professionals should work with the young person and, where appropriate, their family. They should gain a good understanding of the young person's individual needs, including their learning difficulties or disabilities, to co-ordinate health care around those needs and to ensure continuity and the best outcomes for the young person. This means working with the young person to develop a transition plan, which identifies who will take the lead in co-ordinating care and referrals to other services. The young person should know who is taking the lead and how to contact them.

8.55 For young people with EHC plans, the plan should be the basis for co-ordinating the integration of health with other services. Where young people are moving to adult health services, the local authority and health services **must** co-operate, working in partnership with each other and the young person to ensure that the EHC plan and the care plan for the treatment and management of the young person's health are aligned. The clinical commissioning group (CCG) **must** co-operate with the local authority in supporting the transition to adult services and **must** jointly commission services that will help meet the outcomes in the EHC plan.

8.56 In supporting the transition from Child and Adolescent Mental Health Services (CAMHS) to adult mental health services, clinical commissioning groups (CCGs) and local authorities should refer to *The Mental Health Action Plan, Closing the Gap: Priorities for essential change in mental health* (see References section under Chapter 8 for a link). This action plan identifies transition from CAMHS to adult services as a priority for action. CCGs and local authorities should have regard to any published service specification for transition from CAMHS. They should use the specification to build person-centred services that take into account the developmental needs of the young person as well as the need for age- appropriate services.

Transition to adult social care

8.57 Young people with SEN turning 18, or their carers, may become eligible for adult care services, regardless of whether they have an EHC plan or whether they have been receiving care services under section 17 of the Children Act 1989. Under the Care Act 2014, the local authority **must** carry out an adult care transition assessment where there is significant benefit to a young person or their carer in doing so and they are likely to have needs for care or support after turning 18. Transition assessments for adult care **must** take place at the right time for the individual. There is no set age when young people reach this point and as such transition assessments should take place when it is of 'significant benefit' to them.

8.58 The statutory guidance 'Transition Guidance for the Care Act 2014' explains 'likely need' and 'significant benefit' in more detail (see References section under Chapter 8 for a link). It also provides further information on local authorities' roles and responsibilities for carrying out transition assessments for those turning 18 and, where relevant, carers who may be eligible for adult assessments.

Transition assessments for young people with EHC plans

8.59 For a young person with an EHC plan, the local authority should ensure that the transition to adult care and support is well planned, is integrated with the annual reviews of the EHC plans and reflects existing special educational and health provision that is in place to help the young person prepare for adulthood.

8.60 As with EHC plan development in general, transition assessments for adult care and support **must** involve the young person and anyone else they want to involve in the assessment. They **must** also include the outcomes, views and wishes that matter to the young person – much of which will already be set out in their EHC plan.

8.61 Assessments for adult care or support **must** consider:

- current needs for care and support
- whether the young person is likely to have needs for care and support after they turn 18, and
- if so, what those needs are likely to be and which are likely to be eligible needs

8.62 Local authorities can meet their statutory duties around transition assessment through an annual review of a young person's EHC plan that includes the above elements. Indeed, EHC plans **must** include provision to assist in preparing for adulthood from Year 9 (age 13 to14).

8.63 Having carried out a transition assessment, the local authority **must** give an indication of which needs are likely to be regarded as eligible needs so the young person understands the care and support they are likely to receive once children's services cease. Where a young person's needs are not eligible for adult services, local authorities **must** provide information and advice about how those needs may be met and the provision and support that young people can access in their local area. Local authorities should ensure this information is incorporated into their Local Offer.

8.64 Statutory guidance accompanying the Autism Strategy places a duty on SENCOs in schools and a named person within a college with SEN oversight to inform young people with autism of their right to a community care assessment and their parents of a right to a carer's assessment. Where a young person has an EHC plan, this should be built into their preparing for adulthood reviews.

Continuity of provision

8.65 Under no circumstances should young people find themselves suddenly without support and care as they make the transition to adult services. Very few moves from children's to adult services will or should take place on the day of someone's 18th birthday. For the most part, transition to adult services for those with EHC plans should begin at an appropriate annual review and in many cases should be a staged process over several months or years.

8.66 Under the Care Act 2014 local authorities **must** continue to provide a young person with children's services until they reach a conclusion about their situation as an adult, so that there is no gap in provision. Reaching a conclusion means that, following a transition assessment, the local authority concludes that the young person:

- does not have needs for adult care and support, or
- does have such needs and begins to meet some or all of them, or
- does have such needs but decides it is not going to meet them (either because they are not eligible needs or because they are already being met)

8.67 The local authority can also decide to continue to provide care and support from children's services after the young person has turned 18. This can continue until the EHC plan is no longer maintained but when the EHC plan ceases or a decision is made that children's services are no longer appropriate, the local authority **must** continue the children's services until they have reached a conclusion about their need for support from adult services.

EHC plans and statutory care and support plans

8.68 Local authorities **must** put in place a statutory care and support plan for young people with eligible needs for adult care and support. Local authorities **must** meet the needs of the young person set out in their care and support plan.

8.69 Where young people aged 18 or over continue to have EHC plans, and are receiving care and support, this will be provided under the Care Act 2014. The statutory adult care and support plan should form the 'care' element of the young person's EHC plan. While the care part of the EHC plan **must** meet the requirements of the Care Act 2014 and a copy should be kept by adult services, it is the EHC plan that should be the overarching plan that is used with these young people to ensure they receive the support they need to enable them to achieve agreed outcomes.

8.70 Local authorities **must** set out in section H2 of the EHC plan any adult care and support that is reasonably required by the young person's learning difficulties or disabilities. For those over 18, this will be those elements of their statutory care and support plan that are directly related to their learning difficulties or disabilities. EHC plans may also specify other adult care and support in the young person's care and support plan where appropriate, but the elements directly related to learning difficulties and disabilities should always be included as they will be of particular relevance to the rest of the EHC plan.

8.71 Local authorities should ensure that local systems and processes for assessment and review of EHC plans and care and support plans are fully joined up for young people who will have both. Every effort should be made to ensure that young people with both EHC plans and care and support plans do not have to attend multiple reviews held by different services, provide duplicate information, or receive support that is not joined up and co-ordinated.

8.72 When a young person's EHC plan is due to come to an end, local authorities should put in place effective plans for the support the young person will be receiving across adult services. Where a care and support plan is in place, this will remain as the young person's statutory plan for care and support. Local authorities should review the provision of adult care and support at this point as the young person's circumstances will be changing significantly as they leave the formal education and training system.

8.73 Where a safeguarding issue arises for someone over 18 with an EHC plan, the matter should be dealt with as a matter of course by the adult safeguarding team. They should involve the local authority's child safeguarding colleagues where appropriate as well as any relevant partners (for example, the police or NHS) or other persons relevant to the case. The same approach should apply for complaints or appeals.

Personal Budgets

8.74 Where a transition assessment identifies needs that are likely to be eligible, local authorities should consider providing an indicative Personal Budget so that young people have an idea of how much their care and support will cost when they enter the adult system. This is particularly important if young people with EHC plans are already exercising their statutory right to a Personal Budget as any adult with eligible needs will have a care and support plan which **must** include a Personal Budget. Young people with EHC plans may also consider the transition to adult services a good opportunity to start exercising their right to start receiving their Personal Budget as a direct payment. Local authorities **must** follow the guidance on Personal Budgets set out in Chapter 9 of this Code of Practice and the Personal Budget Guidance for the Care Act 2014 (see References section under Chapter 8 for a link).

Leaving education or training

8.75 All young people with SEN should be supported to make the transition to life beyond school or college, whether or not they have an EHC plan. As well as preparing them for adulthood generally, schools and colleges should ensure that young people with SEN have the information they need to make the final steps in this transition. This includes information about local employers, further training, and where to go for further advice or support.

8.76 For young people with EHC plans, where it is known that a young person will soon be completing their time in education and training, the local authority should use the annual review prior to ceasing the EHC plan to agree the support and specific steps needed to help the young person to engage with the services and provision they will be accessing once they have left education.

8.77 Some young people will be moving into employment or going on to higher education. Others will primarily require ongoing health and/or care support and/or access to adult learning opportunities. They may be best supported by universal health services and adult social care and support, alongside learning opportunities in the adult skills sector. For those who have just completed an apprenticeship, traineeship or supported internship the best option may be for them to leave formal education or training and either begin some sort of paid employment resulting from their work placement, or to access further support and training available to help them secure a job through Jobcentre Plus.

8.78 This transition should be planned with timescales and clear responsibilities and the young person should know what will happen when their EHC plan ceases. During this planning process, the local authority **must** continue to maintain the young person's EHC plan as long as the young person needs it and remains in education or training.

9 Education, Health and Care needs assessments and plans

What the chapter covers

This chapter covers all the key stages in statutory assessment and planning and preparing the Education, Health and Care (EHC) plan, and guidance on related topics.

It includes:

- when a local authority **must** carry out an EHC needs assessment, including in response to a request
- who **must** be consulted and provide advice
- the statutory steps required by the process of EHC needs assessment and EHC plan development, including timescales
- how to write an EHC plan
- requesting a particular school, college or other institution
- requesting and agreeing Personal Budgets, including sources of funding
- finalising and maintaining an EHC plan
- transferring an EHC plan
- reviews and re-assessments of an EHC plan
- ceasing an EHC plan
- disclosing an EHC plan

Relevant legislation

Primary

Sections 36 – 50 of the Children and Families Act 2014

The Care Act 2014

Section 2 of the Chronically Sick and Disabled Persons Act 1970

Sections 17, 20 and 47 of the Children Act 1989

Regulations

The Special Educational Needs and Disability Regulations 2014

The Special Educational Needs (Personal Budgets) Regulations 2014

Special Educational Needs (Miscellaneous Amendments) Regulations 2014

The Community Care Services for Carers and Children's Services (Direct Payments) Regulations 2009

The National Health Service (Direct Payments) Regulations 2013

The Special Educational Needs and Disability (Detained Persons) Regulations 2015

Introduction

9.1 The majority of children and young people with SEN or disabilities will have their needs met within local mainstream early years settings, schools or colleges (as set out in the information on identification and support in Chapters 5, 6 and 7). Some children and young people may require an EHC needs assessment in order for the local authority to decide whether it is necessary for it to make provision in accordance with an EHC plan.

9.2 The purpose of an EHC plan is to make special educational provision to meet the special educational needs of the child or young person, to secure the best possible outcomes for them across education, health and social care and, as they get older, prepare them for adulthood. To achieve this, local authorities use the information from the assessment to:

- establish and record the views, interests and aspirations of the parents and child or young person
- provide a full description of the child or young person's special educational needs and any health and social care needs
- establish outcomes across education, health and social care based on the child or young person's needs and aspirations
- specify the provision required and how education, health and care services will work together to meet the child or young person's needs and support the achievement of the agreed outcomes

9.3 A local authority **must** conduct an assessment of education, health and care needs when it considers that it may be necessary for special educational provision to be made for the child or young person in accordance with an EHC plan. The factors a local authority should take into account in deciding whether it needs to undertake an EHC needs assessment are set out in paragraphs 9.14 to 9.15, and the factors a local authority should take into account in deciding whether an EHC plan is necessary are set out in paragraphs 9.53 to 9.56. The EHC needs assessment should not normally be the first step in the process, rather it should follow on from planning already undertaken with parents and young people in conjunction with an early years provider, school, post-16 institution or other provider. In a very small minority of cases children or young people may demonstrate such significant difficulties that a school or other provider may consider it impossible or inappropriate to carry out its full chosen assessment procedure. For example, where its concerns may have led to a further diagnostic assessment or examination which shows the child or young person to have severe sensory impairment or other impairment which, without immediate specialist intervention beyond the capacity of the school or other provider, would lead to increased learning difficulties.

9.4 During the transition period local authorities will transfer children and young people with statements onto the new system (see paragraphs x and xi of the Introduction and paragraph 1.17 in Chapter 1, Principles, for more information on transition and transfer of statements). No-one should lose their statement and not have it replaced with an EHC plan simply because the system is changing.

9.5 EHC plans should be forward-looking documents that help raise aspirations and outline the provision required to meet assessed needs to support the child or young person in achieving their ambitions. EHC plans should specify how services will be delivered as part of a whole package and explain how best to achieve the outcomes sought across education, health and social care for the child or young person.

9.6 An EHC needs assessment will not always lead to an EHC plan. The information gathered during an EHC needs assessment may indicate ways in which the school, college or other provider can meet the child or young person's needs without an EHC plan.

9.7 The statutory processes and timescales set out in this chapter **must** be followed by local authorities. Local authorities should conduct assessments and prepare and maintain EHC plans in the most efficient way possible, working collaboratively with children and young people and their parents. It should be possible to complete the process more quickly than the statutory timescales permit, except in more complex cases or where there is disagreement. It is vital that a timely process is supported by high quality engagement with the child and his or her parents or the young person throughout the assessment, planning and review process.

Requesting an EHC needs assessment

Relevant legislation: Section 36 of the Children and Families Act 2014

9.8 The following people have a specific right to ask a local authority to conduct an education, health and care needs assessment for a child or young person aged between 0 and 25:

- the child's parent
- a young person over the age of 16 but under the age of 25, and
- a person acting on behalf of a school or post-16 institution (this should ideally be with the knowledge and agreement of the parent or young person where possible)

9.9 In addition, anyone else can bring a child or young person who has (or may have) SEN to the attention of the local authority, particularly where they think an EHC needs assessment may be necessary. This could include, for example, foster carers, health and social care professionals, early years practitioners, youth offending teams or probation services, those responsible for education in custody, school or college staff or a family friend. Bringing a child or young person to the attention of the local authority will be undertaken on an individual basis where there are specific concerns. This should be done with the knowledge and, where possible, agreement of the child's parent or the young person.

9.10 Children and young people under 19 in youth custodial establishments also have the right to request an assessment for an EHC plan. The child's parent, the young person themselves or the professionals working with them can ask the home local authority to conduct an EHC needs assessment while they are still detained. The process and principles for considering and carrying out an EHC needs assessment and maintaining an EHC plan for children and young people in youth custody are set out in Chapter 10, Children and young people in specific circumstances.

Considering whether an EHC needs assessment is necessary

Relevant legislation: Section 36 of the Children and Families Act 2014 and Regulations 3, 4, and 5 of the SEND Regulations 2014

9.11 Following a request for an EHC needs assessment, or the child or young person having otherwise been brought to its attention, the local authority **must** determine whether an EHC needs assessment is necessary. The local authority **must** make a decision and communicate the decision to the child's parent or to the young person within 6 weeks of receiving the request. The local authority does not have to consider whether an EHC needs assessment is necessary where it has already undertaken an EHC needs assessment for the child or young person during the previous six months, although the local authority may choose to do so if it thinks it is appropriate.

9.12 The local authority **must** notify the child's parent or the young person that it is considering whether an EHC assessment is necessary, and **must** consult the child's parent or the young person as soon as practicable following a request for an EHC needs assessment (or having otherwise become responsible). This is particularly important where the request was not made by the child's parent or the young person, so they have sufficient time to provide their views. In considering whether an EHC needs assessment is necessary, local authorities **must** have regard to the views, wishes and feelings of the child and his or her parent, or the young person. At an early stage, the local authority should establish how the child and his or her parent or the young person can best be kept informed and supported to participate as fully as possible in decision-making. The local authority **must** arrange for the child and his or her parent or the young person to be provided with advice and information relevant to the child or young person's SEN, (for more information, see paragraph 9.21 and Chapter 2).

9.13 Where the local authority considers that special educational provision may need to be made in accordance with an EHC plan and is considering whether an EHC needs assessment is necessary, it **must** notify:

- the child's parent or the young person (and **must** inform them of their right to express written or oral views and submit evidence to the local authority)
- the health service (the relevant Clinical Commissioning Group (CCG) or NHS England where it has responsibility for a child or young person)
- local authority officers responsible for social care for children or young people with SEN
- where a child attends an early years setting, the manager of that setting
- where a child or young person is registered at a school, the head teacher (or equivalent)
- where the young person attends a post-16 institution, the principal (or equivalent)

9.14 In considering whether an EHC needs assessment is necessary, the local authority should consider whether there is evidence that despite the early years provider, school or post-16 institution having taken relevant and purposeful action to identify, assess and meet the special educational needs of the child or young person, the child or young person has not made expected progress. To inform their decision the local authority will need to take into account a wide range of evidence, and should pay particular attention to:

- evidence of the child or young person's academic attainment (or developmental milestones in younger children) and rate of progress

- information about the nature, extent and context of the child or young person's SEN
- evidence of the action already being taken by the early years provider, school or post-16 institution to meet the child or young person's SEN
- evidence that where progress has been made, it has only been as the result of much additional intervention and support over and above that which is usually provided
- evidence of the child or young person's physical, emotional and social development and health needs, drawing on relevant evidence from clinicians and other health professionals and what has been done to meet these by other agencies, and
- where a young person is aged over 18, the local authority **must** consider whether the young person requires additional time, in comparison to the majority of others of the same age who do not have special educational needs, to complete their education or training. Remaining in formal education or training should help young people to achieve education and training outcomes, building on what they have learned before and preparing them for adult life.

9.15 A young person who was well supported through the Local Offer while at school may move to a further education (FE) college where the same range or level of support is not available. An EHC plan may then be needed to ensure that support is provided and co-ordinated effectively in the new environment. It may also be the case that young people acquire SEN through illness or accident, or have an existing condition that requires increasing support as they get older.

9.16 Local authorities may develop criteria as guidelines to help them decide when it is necessary to carry out an EHC needs assessment (and following assessment, to decide whether it is necessary to issue an EHC plan). However, local authorities **must** be prepared to depart from those criteria where there is a compelling reason to do so in any particular case and demonstrate their willingness to do so where individual circumstances warrant such a departure. Local authorities **must not** apply a 'blanket' policy to particular groups of children or certain types of need, as this would prevent the consideration of a child's or young person's needs individually and on their merits.

9.17 The local authority **must** decide whether or not to proceed with an EHC needs assessment, and **must** inform the child's parent or the young person of their decision within a maximum of six weeks from receiving a request for an EHC needs assessment (or having otherwise become responsible). The local authority **must** give its reasons for this decision where it decides not to proceed. The local authority **must** also notify the other parties listed in section 9.13 above of its decision.

9.18 If the local authority intends to conduct an EHC needs assessment, it **must** ensure the child's parent or the young person is fully included from the start and made aware of opportunities to offer views and information.

9.19 If the local authority decides not to conduct an EHC needs assessment it **must** inform the child's parents or the young person of their right to appeal that decision and the time limit for doing so, of the requirement for them to consider mediation should they wish to appeal, and the availability of information, advice and support and disagreement resolution services. The local authority should also provide feedback collected during the process of considering whether an EHC needs assessment is necessary, including evidence from professionals, which the parent, young person, early years provider, school or post-16 institution may find useful.

Principles underpinning co-ordinated assessment and planning

Relevant legislation: Section 19 of the Children and Families Act 2014 and Regulations 7 and 9 of the SEND Regulations 2014

9.20 Children, young people and families should experience well co-ordinated assessment and planning leading to timely, well informed decisions. The following general principles underpin effective assessment and planning processes:

Involving children, young people and parents in decision-making

9.21 Local authorities **must** consult the child and the child's parent or the young person throughout the process of assessment and production of an EHC plan. They should also involve the child as far as possible in this process. The needs of the individual child and young person should sit at the heart of the assessment and planning process. Planning should start with the individual and local authorities **must** have regard to the views, wishes and feelings of the child, child's parent or young person, their aspirations, the outcomes they wish to seek and the support they need to achieve them. It should enable children, young people and parents to have more control over decisions about their support including the use of a Personal Budget for those with an EHC plan.

9.22 The assessment and planning process should:

- focus on the child or young person as an individual

- enable children and young people and their parents to express their views, wishes and feelings
- enable children and young people and their parents to be part of the decision-making process
- be easy for children, young people and their parents or carers to understand, and use clear ordinary language and images rather than professional jargon
- highlight the child or young person's strengths and capabilities
- enable the child or young person, and those that know them best to say what they have done, what they are interested in and what outcomes they are seeking in the future
- tailor support to the needs of the individual
- organise assessments to minimise demands on families
- bring together relevant professionals to discuss and agree together the overall approach, and
- deliver an outcomes-focused and co-ordinated plan for the child or young person and their parents

9.23 This approach is often referred to as a person-centred approach. By using this approach within a family context, professionals and local authorities can ensure that children, young people and parents are involved in all aspects of planning and decision-making.

9.24 Local authorities should support and encourage the involvement of children, young people and parents or carers by:

- providing them with access to the relevant information in accessible formats
- giving them time to prepare for discussions and meetings, and
- dedicating time in discussions and meetings to hear their views

9.25 In addition, some children and young people will require support from an advocate where necessary (this could be a family member or a professional) to ensure that their views are heard and acknowledged. They may need support in expressing views about their education, their health, the future and how to prepare for it, including where they will live, relationships, control of their finances, how they will participate in the community and how they will achieve greater autonomy and independence. Local authorities should ensure that children and young people who need it have access to this support.

9.26 Practitioners in all services involved in the assessment and planning process need to be skilled in working with children, parents and young people to help them make informed decisions. All practitioners should have access to training so they can do this effectively.

Support for children, young people and parents

9.27 Local authorities should have early discussions with parents or the young person about what the EHC needs assessment process and development of an EHC plan will involve, and the range of options that will be available, such as different types of educational institution and options for Personal Budgets and how these may differ depending on the type of educational institution for which the parents or young person express a preference.

9.28 Local authorities **must** work with parents and children and young people to understand how best to minimise disruption for them and their family life. For example, multiple appointments should be co-ordinated or combined where possible and appropriate.

9.29 Local authorities **must** provide all parents, children and young people with impartial information, advice and support in relation to SEN to enable them to take part effectively in the assessment and planning process. This will include the EHC needs assessment process, EHC plans and Personal Budgets (including the take-up and ongoing management of direct payments). This should include information on key working and independent supporters as appropriate. (See Chapter 2 for more information.)

Co-ordination

9.30 Local authorities are responsible for ensuring that there is effective co-ordination of the assessment and development process for an EHC plan. The co-ordination should include:

- planning the process to meet the needs of children, parents and young people
- timing meetings to minimise family disruption
- keeping the child's parent or young person informed through a single point of contact wherever possible and

- ensuring relevant professionals have sufficient notice to be able to contribute to the process

9.31 The EHC needs assessment and plan development process should be supported by senior leadership teams monitoring the quality and sufficiency of EHC needs assessments through robust quality assurance systems. Families should have confidence that those overseeing the assessment process will be impartial and act in their best interests.

Sharing information

9.32 Information sharing is vital to support an effective assessment and planning process which fully identifies needs and outcomes and the education, health and care provision needed by the child or young person. Local authorities with their partners should establish local protocols for the effective sharing of information which addresses confidentiality, consent and security of information (see the References section under Chapter 9 for a link to the DfE advice '*Information sharing for practitioners and managers*'). Agencies should work together to agree local protocols for information collection and management so as to inform planning of provision for children and young people with SEN or disabilities at both individual and strategic levels.

9.33 As far as possible, there should be a 'tell us once' approach to sharing information during the assessment and planning process so that families and young people do not have to repeat the same information to different agencies, or different practitioners and services within each agency.

9.34 Local authorities **must** discuss with the child and young person and their parents what information they are happy for the local authority to share with other agencies. A record should be made of what information can be shared and with whom. (See paragraphs 9.211 to 9.213 for further information on confidentiality and disclosing EHC plans.)

Timely provision of services

9.35 Where particular services are assessed as being needed, such as those resulting from statutory social care assessments under the Children Act 1989 or adult social care legislation, their provision should be delivered in line with the relevant statutory guidance and should not be delayed until the EHC plan is complete. For social care, help and support should be given to the child and family as soon as a need is identified and not wait until the completion of an EHC needs assessment.

Cross-agency working

9.36 Joint working between local authorities and CCGs in the development of an EHC plan supports the provision of effective services for children and young people with SEN. (See Chapter 3, Working together across Education, Health and Care for joint outcomes, for guidance on services working together, and the section later in this chapter on agreeing the health provision in EHC plans.)

9.37 Consideration should be given to:

- the range of professionals across education, health and care who need to be involved and their availability
- flexibility for professionals to engage in a range of ways and to plan their input as part of forward planning
- providing opportunities for professionals to feed back on the process, and its implementation, to support continuous improvement

Looked after children

9.38 Local authorities should be particularly aware of the need to avoid any delays for looked after children and carry out the EHC needs assessment in the shortest possible timescale. Addressing a looked after child's special educational needs will be a crucial part of avoiding breakdown in their care placement.

Timescales for EHC needs assessment and preparation of an EHC plan

Relevant legislation: Sections 36, 37, 38, 39 and 40 of the Children and Families Act 2014 and Regulations 4, 5, 8, 10, and 13 of the SEND Regulations 2014

9.39 The process of EHC needs assessment and EHC plan development **must** be carried out in a timely manner. The time limits set out below are the maximum time allowed. However, steps **must** be completed as soon as practicable. Local authorities should ensure that they have planned sufficient time for each step of the process, so that wherever possible, any issues or disagreements can be resolved within the statutory timescales. Where the child's parent or the young person agrees, it may be possible to carry out steps much more quickly and flexibly. For example, a child's parent or the young person might be happy to agree changes to an EHC plan following a review while at the review meeting, where all parties are content. Under no circumstances should the child's parent or the young person be put under pressure to agree things more quickly than they feel comfortable with, and where there is any doubt or the child's parent or the young person requests more time, local authorities **must** follow the steps and timescales set out in this guidance.

9.40 The whole process of EHC needs assessment and EHC plan development, from the point when an assessment is requested (or a child or young person is brought to the local authority's attention) until the final EHC plan is issued, **must** take no more than 20 weeks (subject to exemptions set out below).

9.41 The following specific requirements apply:

- Local authorities **must** give their decision in response to any request for an EHC needs assessment within a maximum of 6 weeks from when the request was received or the point at which a child or young person was brought to the local authority's attention

- When local authorities request information as part of the EHC needs assessment process, those supplying the information **must** respond in a timely manner and within a maximum of 6 weeks from the date of the request

- If a local authority decides, following an EHC needs assessment, not to issue an EHC plan, it **must** inform the child's parent or the young person within a maximum of 16 weeks from the request for a EHC needs assessment, and

- The child's parent or the young person **must** be given 15 calendar days to consider and provide views on a draft EHC plan and ask for a particular school or other institution to be named in it

9.42 Where there are exceptional circumstances, it may not be reasonable to expect local authorities and other partners to comply with the time limits above. The Special Educational Needs and Disability Regulations 2014 set out specific exemptions. These include where:

- appointments with people from whom the local authority has requested information are missed by the child or young person (this only applies to the duty on partners to comply with a request under the EHC needs assessment process within six weeks)

- the child or young person is absent from the area for a period of at least 4 weeks

- exceptional personal circumstances affect the child or his/her parent, or the young person, and

- the educational institution is closed for at least 4 weeks, which may delay the submission of information from the school or other institution (this does not apply to the duty on partners to comply with a request under the EHC needs assessment process within six weeks)

9.43 The child's parent or the young person should be informed if exemptions apply so that they are aware of, and understand, the reason for any delays. Local authorities should aim to keep delays to a minimum and as soon as the conditions that led to an exemption no longer apply the local authority should endeavour to complete the process as quickly as possible. All remaining elements of the process **must** be completed within their prescribed periods, regardless of whether exemptions have delayed earlier elements.

9.44 The diagram on the following page sets out the statutory timescales and decision points for the process of EHC needs assessment and EHC plan development that local authorities **must** adhere to, subject to the specific exemptions set out in paragraph 9.42. Throughout the statutory process for EHC needs assessment and EHC plan development, local authorities **must** work in partnership with the child and his or her parent or the young person. There is more information earlier in this chapter on the principles of working with parents and young people, and relevant statutory requirements.

Statutory timescales for EHC needs assessment and EHC plan development

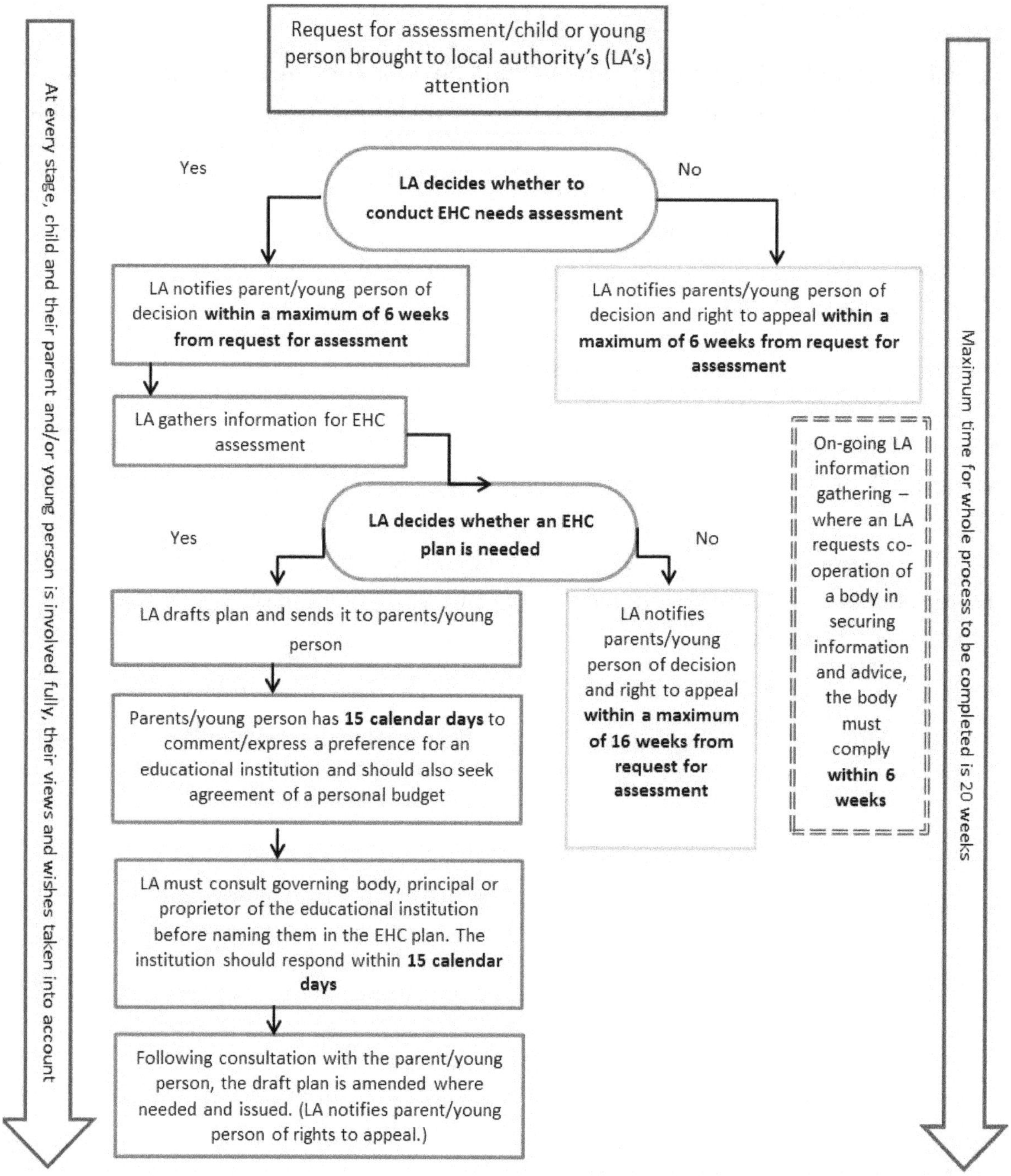

Advice and information for EHC needs assessments

Relevant legislation: Section 36 of the Children and Families Act 2014 and Regulations 6, 7, and 8 of the SEND Regulations 2014

9.45 When carrying out an EHC needs assessment the local authority should seek views and information from the child using appropriate methods, which might include observation for a very young child, or the use of different methods of communication such as the Picture Exchange Communication System.

9.46 The local authority **must** gather advice from relevant professionals about the child or young person's education, health and care needs, desired outcomes and special educational, health and care provision that may be required to meet identified needs and achieve desired outcomes.

9.47 The local authority should consider with the child's parent or the young person and the parties listed under paragraph 9.49 the range of advice required to enable a full EHC needs assessment to take place. The principle underpinning this is 'tell us once', avoiding the child's parent or the young person having to provide the same information multiple times. The child's parent or the young person should be supported to understand the range of assessments available so they can take an informed decision about whether existing advice is satisfactory. The local authority **must not** seek further advice if such advice has already been provided (for any purpose) and the person providing the advice, the local authority and the child's parent or the young person are all satisfied that it is sufficient for the assessment process. In making this decision, the local authority and the person providing the advice should ensure the advice remains current.

9.48 Decisions about the level of engagement and advice needed from different parties will be informed by knowledge of the child or young person held by the early years provider, school or post-16 institution they attend. For example, if the educational provider believes there are signs of safeguarding or welfare issues, a statutory social care assessment may be necessary. If there are signs of an underlying health difficulty, a specialist health assessment may be necessary.

9.49 In seeking advice and information, the local authority should consider with professionals what advice they can contribute to ensure the assessment covers all the relevant education, health and care needs of the child or young person. Advice and information **must** be sought as follows (subject to para 9.47 above):

- Advice and information from the child's parent or the young person. The local authority **must** take into account his or her views, wishes and feelings

- Educational advice and information from the manager, headteacher or principal of the early years setting, school or post-16 or other institution attended by the child or young person. Where this is not available the authority **must** seek advice from a person with experience of teaching children or young people with SEN, or knowledge of the provision which may meet the child's or young person's needs. Where advice from a person with relevant teaching experience or knowledge is not available and the child or young person does not attend an educational institution, the local authority **must** seek educational advice and information from a person responsible for educational provision for the child or young person

- If the child or young person is either vision or hearing impaired, or both, the educational advice and information **must** be given after consultation with a person who is qualified to teach pupils or students with these impairments

- Medical advice and information from health care professionals with a role in relation to the child's or young person's health (see the section later in this chapter on agreeing the health provision in EHC plans)

- Psychological advice and information from an educational psychologist who should normally be employed or commissioned by the local authority. The educational psychologist should consult any other psychologists known to be involved with the child or young person

- Social care advice and information from or on behalf of the local authority, including, if appropriate, children in need or child protection assessments, information from a looked after child's care plan, or adult social care assessments for young people over 18. In some cases, a child or young person may already have a statutory child in need or child protection plan, or an adult social care plan, from which information should be drawn for the EHC needs assessment

- From Year 9 onwards, advice and information related to provision to assist the child or young person in preparation for adulthood and independent living

- Advice and information from any person requested by the child's parent or young person, where the local authority considers it reasonable to do so. For example, they may suggest consulting a GP or other health professional

- Advice from a youth offending team, where the child or young person is detained in a Young Offender Institution. Where the young person is serving their sentence in the community the local authority should seek such advice where it considers it appropriate

- Any other advice and information which the local authority considers appropriate for a satisfactory assessment, for example:
    - Early Help Assessments
    - in the case of children of members of the Armed Forces, from the Children's Education Advisory Service
    - in the case of a looked after child, from the Virtual School Head in the authority that looks after the child and the child's Designated Teacher and the Designated Doctor or Nurse for looked after children

9.50 The local authority **must** give to those providing advice copies of any representations made by the child's parent or the young person, and any evidence submitted by or at the request of the child's parent or the young person.

9.51 The evidence and advice submitted by those providing it should be clear, accessible and specific. They should provide advice about outcomes relevant for the child or young person's age and phase of education and strategies for their achievement. The local authority may provide guidance about the structure and format of advice and information to be provided. Professionals should limit their advice to areas in which they have expertise. They may comment on the amount of provision they consider a child or young person requires and local authorities should not have blanket policies which prevent them from doing so.

9.52 Advice and information requested by the local authority **must** be provided within six weeks of the request, and should be provided more quickly wherever possible, to enable a timely process. (This is subject to the exemptions set out in paragraph 9.42.)

Deciding whether to issue an EHC plan

Relevant legislation: Sections 36 and 37 of the Children and Families Act 2014

9.53 Where, in the light of an EHC needs assessment, it is necessary for special educational provision to be made in accordance with an EHC plan, the local authority **must** prepare a plan. Where a local authority decides it is necessary to issue an EHC plan, it **must** notify the child's parent or the young person and give the reasons for its decision. The local authority should ensure it allows enough time to prepare the draft plan and complete the remaining steps in the process within the 20-week overall time limit within which it **must** issue the finalised EHC plan.

9.54 In deciding whether to make special educational provision in accordance with an EHC plan, the local authority should consider all the information gathered during the EHC needs assessment and set it alongside that available to the local authority prior to the assessment. Local authorities should consider both the child or young person's SEN and the special educational provision made for the child or young person and whether:

- the information from the EHC needs assessment confirms the information available on the nature and extent of the child or young person's SEN prior to the EHC needs assessment, and whether

- the special educational provision made prior to the EHC needs assessment was well matched to the SEN of the child or young person

9.55 Where, despite appropriate assessment and provision, the child or young person is not progressing, or not progressing sufficiently well, the local authority should consider what further provision may be needed. The local authority should take into account:

- whether the special educational provision required to meet the child or young person's needs can reasonably be provided from within the resources normally available to mainstream early years providers, schools and post-16 institutions, or

- whether it may be necessary for the local authority to make special educational provision in accordance with an EHC plan

9.56 Where a local authority carries out an EHC needs assessment for a child or young person and

- their circumstances have changed significantly, or

- the child or young person has recently been placed in a new setting, or

- their special educational needs were identified shortly before the EHC needs assessment,

and no comparable special educational provision was being made for the child or young person prior to the EHC needs assessment, then the local authority should consider what new special educational provision is needed, taking into account the points in 9.55 above.

Decision not to issue an EHC plan

Relevant legislation: Section 36 of the Children and Families Act 2014 and Regulation 10 of the SEND Regulations 2014

9.57 Following the completion of an EHC needs assessment, if the local authority decides that an EHC plan is not necessary, it **must** notify the child's parent or the young person, the early years provider, school or post-16 institution currently attended, and the health service and give the reasons for its decision. This notification **must** take place as soon as practicable and at the latest within 16 weeks of the initial request or of the child or young person having otherwise been brought to the local authority's attention. The local authority **must** also inform the child's parent or the young person of their right to appeal that decision and the time limit for doing so, of the requirement for them to consider mediation should they wish to appeal, and the availability of information, advice and support and disagreement resolution services.

9.58 The local authority should ensure that the child's parent or the young person are aware of the resources available to meet SEN within mainstream provision and other support set out in the Local Offer.

9.59 The local authority should provide written feedback collected during the EHC needs assessment process, which the child's parent, the young person, early years provider, school or post-16 institution can understand and may find useful, including evidence and reports from professionals. This information can then inform how the outcomes sought for the child or young person can be achieved through special educational provision made by the early years provider, school or post-16 institution and co-ordinated support from other agencies.

Transparent and consistent decision-making

9.60 It is helpful for local authorities to set up moderating groups to support transparency in decision-making. Such groups can improve the consistency of decision-making about whether to carry out an EHC needs assessment and whether to issue an EHC plan. Through sampling and retrospective comparison, moderating groups can also help local authority practice to become more robust and clearly understood by schools, early years settings, post-16 institutions, young people and parents.

Writing the EHC plan

Relevant legislation: Section 37 of the Children and Families Act 2014 and Regulations 11 and 12 of the SEND Regulations 2014

9.61 The following principles and requirements apply to local authorities and those contributing to the preparation of an EHC plan:

- Decisions about the content of EHC plans should be made openly and collaboratively with parents, children and young people. It should be clear how the child or young person has contributed to the plan and how their views are reflected in it

- EHC plans should describe positively what the child or young person can do and has achieved

- EHC plans should be clear, concise, understandable and accessible to parents, children, young people, providers and practitioners. They should be written so they can be understood by professionals in any local authority

- In preparing the EHC plan the local authority **must** consider how best to achieve the outcomes sought for the child or young person. The local authority **must** take into account the evidence received as part of the EHC needs assessment

- EHC plans **must** specify the outcomes sought for the child or young person. Outcomes in EHC plans should be SMART (specific, measurable, achievable, realistic, time-bound). See the section on 'Outcomes' (paragraph 9.64 onwards) for detailed guidance on outcomes.

- Where a young person or parent is seeking an innovative or alternative way to receive their support services – particularly through a Personal Budget, but not exclusively so – then the planning process should include the consideration of those solutions with support and advice available to assist the parent or young person in deciding how best to receive their support

- EHC plans should show how education, health and care provision will be co-ordinated wherever possible to support the child or young person to achieve their outcomes. The plan should also show how the different types of provision contribute to specific outcomes

- EHC plans should be forward looking – for example, anticipating, planning and commissioning for important transition points in a child or young person's life, including planning and preparing for their transition to adult life

- EHC plans should describe how informal (family and community) support as well as formal support from statutory agencies can help in achieving agreed outcomes
- EHC plans should have a review date (which should link to other regular reviews, including the child in need plan or child protection plan reviews if appropriate)

Content of EHC plans

Relevant legislation: Section 37 of the Children and Families Act 2014 and Regulation 12 of the SEND Regulations 2014

9.62 The format of an EHC plan will be agreed locally, and it is expected that the plan will reflect the principles set out in Chapter 1 of this document. However, as a statutory minimum, EHC plans **must** include the following sections, which **must** be separately labelled from each other using the letters below. The sections do not have to be in the order below and local authorities may use an action plan in tabular format to include different sections and demonstrate how provision will be integrated, as long as the sections are separately labelled.

Section A: The views, interests and aspirations of the child and his or her parents or the young person.

Section B: The child or young person's special educational needs.

Section C: The child or young person's health needs which are related to their SEN.

Section D: The child or young person's social care needs which are related to their SEN or to a disability.

Section E: The outcomes sought for the child or the young person. This should include outcomes for adult life. The EHC plan should also identify the arrangements for the setting of shorter term targets by the early years provider, school, college or other education or training provider.

Section F: The special educational provision required by the child or the young person.

Section G: Any health provision reasonably required by the learning difficulties or disabilities which result in the child or young person having SEN. Where an Individual Health Care Plan is made for them, that plan should be included.

Section H1: Any social care provision which **must** be made for a child or young person under 18 resulting from section 2 of the Chronically Sick and Disabled Persons Act 1970.

Section H2: Any other social care provision reasonably required by the learning difficulties or disabilities which result in the child or young person having SEN. This will include any adult social care provision being provided to meet a young person's eligible needs (through a statutory care and support plan) under the Care Act 2014.

Section I: The name and type of the school, maintained nursery school, post-16 institution or other institution to be attended by the child or young person and the type of that institution (or, where the name of a school or other institution is not specified in the EHC plan, the type of school or other institution to be attended by the child or young person).

Section J: Where there is a Personal Budget, the details of how the Personal Budget will support particular outcomes, the provision it will be used for including any flexibility in its usage and the arrangements for any direct payments for education, health and social care. The special educational needs and outcomes that are to be met by any direct payment **must** be specified.

Section K: The advice and information gathered during the EHC needs assessment **must** be attached (in appendices). There should be a list of this advice and information.

9.63 In addition, where the child or young person is in or beyond Year 9, the EHC plan **must** include (in sections F, G, H1 or H2 as appropriate) the provision required by the child or young person to assist in preparation for adulthood and independent living, for example, support for finding employment, housing or for participation in society.

Outcomes

Relevant legislation: Section 37 of the Children and Families Act 2014 and Regulations 11 and 12 of the SEND Regulations 2014

9.64 EHC plans **must** specify the outcomes sought for the child or young person in Section E. EHC plans should be focused on education and training, health and care outcomes that will enable children and young people to progress in their learning and, as they get older, to be well prepared for adulthood. EHC plans can also include wider outcomes such as positive social relationships and emotional resilience and stability. Outcomes should always enable children and young people to move towards the long-term aspirations of employment or higher education, independent living and community participation. (See Chapter 8 for more details on preparing for adulthood.)

9.65 Long-term aspirations are not outcomes in themselves – aspirations **must** be specified in Section A of the EHC plan. A local authority cannot be held accountable for the aspirations of a child or young person. For example, a local authority cannot be required to continue to maintain an EHC plan until a young person secures employment. However, the EHC plan should continue to be maintained where the young person wants to remain in education and clear evidence shows that special educational provision is needed to enable them to achieve the education and training outcomes required for a course or programme that moves them closer to employment. For example, by accessing a supported internship or apprenticeship.

9.66 An outcome can be defined as the benefit or difference made to an individual as a result of an intervention. It should be personal and not expressed from a service perspective; it should be something that those involved have control and influence over, and while it does not always have to be formal or accredited, it should be specific, measurable, achievable, realistic and time bound (SMART). When an outcome is focused on education or training, it will describe what the expected benefit will be to the individual as a result of the educational or training intervention provided. Outcomes are not a description of the service being provided – for example the provision of three hours of speech and language therapy is not an outcome. In this case, the outcome is what it is intended that the speech and language therapy will help the individual to do that they cannot do now and by when this will be achieved.

9.67 When agreeing outcomes, it is important to consider both what is important *to* the child or young person – what they themselves want to be able to achieve – and what is important *for* them as judged by others with the child or young person's best interests at heart. In the case of speech and language needs, what is important to the child may be that they want to be able to talk to their friends and join in their games at playtime. What is important for them is that their behaviour improves because they no longer get frustrated at not being understood.

9.68 Outcomes underpin and inform the detail of EHC plans. Outcomes will usually set out what needs to be achieved by the end of a phase or stage of education in order to enable the child or young person to progress successfully to the next phase or stage. An outcome for a child of secondary school age might be, for example, to make sufficient progress or achieve a qualification to enable him or her to attend a specific course at college. Other outcomes in the EHC plan may then describe what needs to be achieved by the end of each intervening year to enable him or her to achieve the college place. From Year 9 onwards, the nature of the outcomes will reflect the need to ensure young people are preparing for adulthood. In all cases,

EHC plans **must** specify the special educational provision required to meet each of the child or young person's special educational needs. The provision should enable the outcomes to be achieved.

9.69 The EHC plan should also specify the arrangements for setting shorter term targets at the level of the school or other institution where the child or young person is placed. Professionals working with children and young people during the EHC needs assessment and EHC plan development process may agree shorter term targets that are not part of the EHC plan. These can be reviewed and, if necessary, amended regularly to ensure that the individual remains on track to achieve the outcomes specified in their EHC plan. Professionals should, wherever possible, append these shorter term plans and targets to the EHC plan so that regular progress monitoring is always considered in the light of the longer term outcomes and aspirations that the child or young person wants to achieve. In some exceptional cases, progress against these targets may well lead to an individual outcome within the EHC plan being amended at times other than following the annual review.

What to include in each section of the EHC plan

Section	Information to include
(A) The views, interests and aspirations of the child and their parents, or of the young person	• Details about the child or young person's aspirations and goals for the future (but not details of outcomes to be achieved – see section above on outcomes for guidance). When agreeing the aspirations, consideration should be given to the child or young person's aspirations for paid employment, independent living and community participation • Details about play, health, schooling, independence, friendships, further education and future plans including employment (where practical) • A summary of how to communicate with the child or young person and engage them in decision-making. • The child or young person's history • If written in the first person, the plan should make clear whether the child or young person is being quoted directly, or if the views of parents or professionals are being represented
(B) The child or young person's special educational needs (SEN)	• All of the child or young person's identified special educational needs **must** be specified • SEN may include needs for health and social care provision that are treated as special educational provision

Section	Information to include
	because they educate or train the child or young person (see paragraphs 9.73 onwards)
(C) The child or young person's health needs which relate to their SEN	• The EHC plan **must** specify any health needs identified through the EHC needs assessment which relate to the child or young person's SEN. Some health care needs, such as routine dental health needs, are unlikely to be related • The Clinical Commissioning Group (CCG) may also choose to specify other health care needs which are not related to the child or young person's SEN (for example, a long-term condition which might need management in a special educational setting)
(D) The child or young person's social care needs which relate to their SEN	• The EHC plan **must** specify any social care needs identified through the EHC needs assessment which relate to the child or young person's SEN or which require provision for a child or young person under 18 under section 2 of the Chronically Sick and Disabled Persons Act 1970 • The local authority may also choose to specify other social care needs which are not linked to the child or young person's SEN or to a disability. This could include reference to any child in need or child protection plan which a child may have relating to other family issues such as neglect. Such an approach could help the child and their parents manage the different plans and bring greater co-ordination of services. Inclusion **must** only be with the consent of the child and their parents
(E) The outcomes sought for the child or the young person	• A range of outcomes over varying timescales, covering education, health and care as appropriate but recognising that it is the education and training outcomes only that will help determine when a plan is ceased for young people aged over 18. Therefore, for young people aged over 17, the EHC plan should identify clearly which outcomes are education and training outcomes. See paragraph 9.64 onwards for more detail on outcomes • A clear distinction between outcomes and provision. The provision should help the child or young person achieve an outcome, it is not an outcome in itself • Steps towards meeting the outcomes • The arrangements for monitoring progress, including review and transition review arrangements and the arrangements for setting and monitoring shorter term

Section	Information to include
	targets by the early years provider, school, college or other education or training provider • Forward plans for key changes in a child or young person's life, such as changing schools, moving from children's to adult care and/or from paediatric services to adult health, or moving on from further education to adulthood • For children and young people preparing for the transition to adulthood, the outcomes that will prepare them well for adulthood and are clearly linked to the achievement of the aspirations in section A

(F) The special educational provision required by the child or the young person	• Provision **must** be detailed and specific and should normally be quantified, for example, in terms of the type, hours and frequency of support and level of expertise, including where this support is secured through a Personal Budget
	• Provision **must** be specified for each and every need specified in section B. It should be clear how the provision will support achievement of the outcomes
	• Where health or social care provision educates or trains a child or young person, it **must** appear in this section (see paragraph 9.73)
	• There should be clarity as to how advice and information gathered has informed the provision specified. Where the local authority has departed from that advice, they should say so and give reasons for it
	• In some cases, flexibility will be required to meet the changing needs of the child or young person including flexibility in the use of a Personal Budget
	• The plan should specify:
	    o any appropriate facilities and equipment, staffing arrangements and curriculum
	    o any appropriate modifications to the application of the National Curriculum, where relevant
	    o any appropriate exclusions from the application of the National Curriculum or the course being studied in a post-16 setting, in detail, and the provision which it is proposed to substitute for any such exclusions in order to maintain a balanced and broadly based curriculum
	    o where residential accommodation is appropriate,

Section	Information to include
	that fact ◦ where there is a Personal Budget, the outcomes to which it is intended to contribute (detail of the arrangements for a Personal Budget, including any direct payment, **must** be included in the plan and these should be set out in section J) • See paragraph 9.131 onwards for details of duties on the local authority to maintain the special educational provision in the EHC plan
(G) Any health provision reasonably required by the learning difficulties or disabilities which result in the child or young person having SEN	• Provision should be detailed and specific and should normally be quantified, for example, in terms of the type of support and who will provide it • It should be clear how the provision will support achievement of the outcomes, including the health needs to be met and the outcomes to be achieved through provision secured through a personal (health) budget • Clarity as to how advice and information gathered has informed the provision specified • Health care provision reasonably required may include specialist support and therapies, such as medical treatments and delivery of medications, occupational therapy and physiotherapy, a range of nursing support, specialist equipment, wheelchairs and continence supplies. It could include highly specialist services needed by only a small number of children which are commissioned centrally by NHS England (for example therapeutic provision for young offenders in the secure estate) • The local authority and CCG may also choose to specify other health care provision reasonably required by the child or young person, which is not linked to their learning difficulties or disabilities, but which should sensibly be co-ordinated with other services in the plan • See paragraph 9.141 for details of duties on the health service to maintain the health care provision in the EHC plan
(H1) Any social care provision which must be made for a child or young person under 18 resulting from	• Provision should be detailed and specific and should normally be quantified, for example, in terms of the type of support and who will provide it (including where this is to be secured through a social care direct payment) • It should be clear how the provision will support achievement of the outcomes, including any provision

<table>
<tr><th>Section</th><th>Information to include</th></tr>
<tr><td>section 2 of the Chronically Sick and Disabled Persons Act 1970 (CSDPA)</td><td>secured through a Personal Budget. There should be clarity as to how advice and information gathered has informed the provision specified
<ul>
<li>Section H1 of the EHC plan must specify all services assessed as being needed for a disabled child or young person under 18, under section 2 of the CSDPA. These services include:
<ul>
<li>practical assistance in the home</li>
<li>provision or assistance in obtaining recreational and educational facilities at home and outside the home</li>
<li>assistance in travelling to facilities</li>
<li>adaptations to the home</li>
<li>facilitating the taking of holidays</li>
<li>provision of meals at home or elsewhere</li>
<li>provision or assistance in obtaining a telephone and any special equipment necessary</li>
<li>non-residential short breaks (included in Section H1 on the basis that the child as well as his or her parent will benefit from the short break)</li>
</ul></li>
<li>This may include services to be provided for parent carers of disabled children, including following an assessment of their needs under sections 17ZD-17ZF of the Children Act 1989</li>
<li>See paragraph 9.137 onwards for details of duties on local authorities to maintain the social care provision in the EHC plan</li>
</ul></td></tr>
<tr><td>(H2) Any other social care provision reasonably required by the learning difficulties or disabilities which result in the child or young person having SEN</td><td><ul>
<li>Social care provision reasonably required may include provision identified through early help and children in need assessments and safeguarding assessments for children. Section H2 must only include services which are not provided under Section 2 of the CSDPA. For children and young people under 18 this includes residential short breaks and services provided to children arising from their SEN but unrelated to a disability. This should include any provision secured through a social care direct payment. See chapter 10 for more information on children's social care assessments</li>
<li>Social care provision reasonably required will include any adult social care provision to meet eligible needs for</li>
</ul></td></tr>
</table>

Section	Information to include
	young people over 18 (set out in an adult care and support plan) under the Care Act 2014. See Chapter 8 for further detail on adult care and EHC plans • The local authority may also choose to specify in section H2 other social care provision reasonably required by the child or young person, which is not linked to their learning difficulties or disabilities. This will enable the local authority to include in the EHC plan social care provision such as child in need or child protection plans, or provision meeting eligible needs set out in an adult care plan where it is unrelated to the SEN but appropriate to include in the EHC plan • See paragraph 9.137 onwards for details of duties on local authorities to maintain the social care provision in the EHC plan
(I) Placement	• The name *and* type of the school, maintained nursery school, post-16 institution or other institution to be attended by the child or young person and the type of that institution (or, where the name of a school or other institution is not specified in the EHC plan, the type of school or other institution to be attended by the child or young person) • These details **must** be included only in the final EHC plan, *not* the draft EHC plan sent to the child's parent or to the young person • See paragraph 9.78 onwards for more details
(J) Personal Budget (including arrangements for direct payments)	• This section should provide detailed information on any Personal Budget that will be used to secure provision in the EHC plan • It should set out the arrangements in relation to direct payments as required by education, health and social care regulations • The special educational needs and outcomes that are to be met by any direct payment **must** be specified
(K) Advice and information	• The advice and information gathered during the EHC needs assessment **must** be set out in appendices to the EHC plan. There should be a list of this advice and information

Agreeing the health provision in EHC plans

Relevant legislation: Sections 26 and 37 of the Children and Families Act 2014 and Regulation 12 of the SEND Regulations 2014

9.70 Each CCG will determine which services it will commission to meet the reasonable health needs of the children and young people with SEN or disabilities for whom it is responsible. These services should be described in the Local Offer. Relevant local clinicians, such as community paediatricians, will participate in the development of the child's or young person's EHC plan, advising on the child's needs and the provision appropriate to meet them. CCGs **must** ensure that commissioned services are mobilised to participate in the development of EHC plans. The CCG as commissioner will often have a limited involvement in the process (as this will be led by clinicians from the services they commission) but **must** ensure that there is sufficient oversight to provide assurance that the needs of children with SEN are being met in line with their statutory responsibility. The CCG will have a more direct role in considering the commissioning of a service that does not appear in the Local Offer to meet the complex needs of a specific individual, or in agreeing a Personal Budget.

9.71 The health care provision specified in section G of the EHC plan **must** be agreed by the CCG (or where relevant, NHS England) and any health care provision should be agreed in time to be included in the draft EHC plan sent to the child's parent or to the young person. As part of the joint commissioning arrangements, partners **must** have clear disagreement resolution procedures where there is disagreement on the services to be included in an EHC plan.

9.72 For children and young people in youth custody, the arrangements for carrying out the health part of EHC needs assessments and arranging for the health provision in EHC plans to be made will be slightly different and further guidance for CCGs and relevant health commissioners is set out in Chapter 10.

Responsibility for provision

Relevant legislation: Section 21 of the Children and Families Act 2014

9.73 Health or social care provision which educates or trains a child or young person **must** be treated as special educational provision and included in Section F of the EHC plan.

9.74 Decisions about whether health care provision or social care provision should be treated as special educational provision **must** be made on an individual basis. Speech and language therapy and other therapy provision can be regarded as either education or health care provision, or both. It could therefore be included in an EHC plan as either educational or health provision. However, since communication is so fundamental in education, addressing speech and language impairment should normally be recorded as special educational provision unless there are exceptional reasons for not doing so.

9.75 Agreement should be reached between the local authority and health and social care partners about where provision will be specified in an EHC plan.

9.76 In cases where health care provision or social care provision is to be treated as special educational provision, ultimate responsibility for ensuring that the provision is made rests with the local authority (unless the child's parent has made suitable arrangements) and the child's parent or the young person will have the right to appeal to the First-tier Tribunal (SEN and Disability) where they disagree with the provision specified.

The draft EHC plan

Relevant legislation: Section 38 of the Children and Families Act 2014 and Regulation 13 of the SEND Regulations 2014

9.77 The local authority **must** send the draft EHC plan (including the appendices containing the advice and information gathered during the EHC needs assessment) to the child's parent or to the young person and give them at least 15 days to give views and make representations on the content. During this period, the local authority **must** make its officers available for a meeting with the child's parent or the young person on request if they wish to discuss the content of the draft EHC plan. When the local authority sends the draft EHC plan to the child's parent or the young person the following apply:

- The local authority **must** notify the child's parent or the young person that during this period they can request that a particular school or other institution, or type of school or other institution, be named in the plan. The draft plan **must not** contain the name of the school, maintained nursery school, post-16 institution or other institution or the type of school or other institution to be attended by the child or young person (see below)

- The local authority **must** advise the child's parent or the young person where they can find information about the schools and colleges that are available for the child or young person to attend, for example through the Local Offer

- The local authority should also seek agreement of any Personal Budget specified in the draft plan (see paragraph 9.95 onwards for more information on Personal Budgets)

Requests for a particular school, college or other institution

Relevant legislation: Sections 33 and 39 of the Children and Families Act 2014

9.78 The child's parent or the young person has the right to request a particular school, college or other institution of the following type to be named in their EHC plan:

- maintained nursery school
- maintained school and any form of academy or free school (mainstream or special)
- non-maintained special school
- further education or sixth form college
- independent school or independent specialist colleges (where they have been approved for this purpose by the Secretary of State and published in a list available to all parents and young people)

9.79 If a child's parent or a young person makes a request for a particular nursery, school or post-16 institution in these groups the local authority **must** comply with that preference and name the school or college in the EHC plan unless:

- it would be unsuitable for the age, ability, aptitude or SEN of the child or young person, or
- the attendance of the child or young person there would be incompatible with the efficient education of others, or the efficient use of resources

Efficient education means providing for each child or young person a suitable, appropriate education in terms of their age, ability, aptitude and any special educational needs they may have. Where a local authority is considering the appropriateness of an individual institution, 'others' is intended to mean the children and young people with whom the child or young person with an EHC plan will directly come into contact on a regular day-to-day basis.

9.80 The local authority **must** consult the governing body, principal or proprietor of the school or college concerned and consider their comments very carefully before deciding whether to name it in the child or young person's EHC plan, sending the school or college a copy of the draft plan. If another local authority maintains the school, they too **must** be consulted.

9.81 The local authority **must** also seek the agreement of the nursery, school or post-16 institution where the draft plan sets out any provision to be delivered on their premises which is secured through a direct payment. (See paragraph 9.119 onwards for more information on direct payments). Where this includes a direct payment for SEN provision, it **must** include formal written notice of the proposal specifying:

- the name of the child or young person in respect of whom direct payments are to be made
- the qualifying goods and services which are to be secured by direct payments
- the proposed amount of direct payments
- any conditions on how the direct payments may be spent
- the dates for payments into a bank account approved by the local authority, and
- any conditions of receipt that recipients **must** agree to before any direct payment can be made

9.82 Advice from schools, colleges and other education or training providers will contribute to the development of an EHC plan to ensure that it meets the child or young person's needs, the outcomes they want to achieve and the aspirations they are aiming for.

9.83 The nursery, school or college and, where relevant, the other local authority, should respond within 15 days. Where a nursery, school or college identified at 9.78 above is named on an EHC plan they **must** admit the child or young person.

9.84 The child's parent or the young person may also make representations for places in non-maintained early years provision or at independent schools or independent specialist colleges or other post-16 providers that are not on the list mentioned at 9.78 above and the local authority **must** consider their request. The local authority is not under the same conditional duty to name the provider but **must** have regard to the general principle in section 9 of the Education Act 1996 that children should be educated in accordance with their parents' wishes, so long as this is compatible with the provision of efficient instruction and training and does not mean unreasonable public expenditure. The local authority should be satisfied that the institution would admit the child or young person before naming it in a plan since these providers are not subject to the duty to admit a child or young person even if named in their plan.

9.85 Children with EHC plans can attend more than one school under a dual placement. Dual placements enable children to have support from a mainstream and a special school. This can help to prepare children for mainstream education and enable mainstream and special schools to share and develop their expertise in supporting children with different types of SEN. In order for a child with SEN who is being supported by a dual placement to be deemed as being educated at a mainstream school they should spend the majority of their time there.

9.86 Where appropriate, a young person with an EHC plan can attend a dual placement at an institution within the further education sector and a special post-16 institution. The local authority should work with the young person, post-16 provider and independent specialist college to commission such a placement where that will achieve the best possible outcome for the young person. To be deemed as being educated in a mainstream further education institution, young people should spend the majority of their time there.

9.87 The local authority should consider very carefully a request from a parent for a denominational school, but denominational considerations cannot override the requirements of the Children and Families Act 2014.

Where no request is made for a particular school or college or a request for a particular school or college has not been met

Relevant legislation: Sections 33 and 40 of the Children and Families Act 2014

9.88 Where a parent or young person does not make a request for a particular nursery, school or college, or does so and their request is not met, the local authority **must** specify mainstream provision in the EHC plan unless it would be:

- against the wishes of the parent or young person, or
- incompatible with the efficient education of others

9.89 Mainstream education cannot be refused by a local authority on the grounds that it is not suitable. A local authority can rely on the exception of incompatibility with the efficient education of others in relation to maintained nursery schools, mainstream schools or mainstream post-16 institutions taken as a whole only if it can show that there are no reasonable steps it could take to prevent that incompatibility. Where a parent's or young person's request for a particular mainstream school or mainstream post-16 institution has not been met, the school or post-16 institution in question becomes a possible candidate for consideration by the local authority according to the conditions in the above paragraph.

9.90 Where the local authority considers a particular mainstream place to be incompatible with the efficient education of others it **must** demonstrate, in relation to maintained nursery schools, mainstream schools or mainstream post-16 institutions in its area taken as a whole, that there are no reasonable steps that it, or the school or college, could take to prevent that incompatibility. Efficient education means providing for each child or young person a suitable, appropriate education in terms of their age, ability, aptitude and any special educational needs they may have. Where a local authority is considering whether mainstream education is appropriate (as opposed to considering the appropriateness of an individual institution) the term 'others' means the children or young people with whom the child or young person with an EHC plan would be likely to come into contact on a regular day-to-day basis. Where a parent or young person wants mainstream education and it would not be incompatible with the efficient education of others, the local authority has a duty to secure that provision.

Reasonable steps

9.91 What constitutes a reasonable step will depend on all the circumstances of the individual case. The following are some of the factors that may be taken into account:

- Whether taking the step would be effective in removing the incompatibility
- The extent to which it is practical for the early years provider, school, college or local authority to take the step
- The extent to which steps have already been taken in relation to a particular child or young person and their effectiveness
- The financial and other resource implications of taking the step, and
- The extent of any disruption that taking the step would cause

9.92 The following are examples of reasonable steps that might be taken in different circumstances:

- Reasonable steps to ensure that the inclusion of a child with challenging behaviour in a mainstream primary school setting is not incompatible with the efficient education of others may include:
    - addressing factors within the class that may exacerbate the problem, for example using circle time to discuss difficult relationships and identify constructive responses
    - teaching the child alternative behaviour, for example by taking quiet time in a specially designated area at times of stress

- providing the child with a channel of communication, for example use of peer support
- using a carefully designed system of behaviour targets drawn up with the child and linked to a reward system which, wherever possible, involves parents or carers
- ensuring that all staff coming into contact with the child are briefed on potential triggers for outbursts and effective ways of heading off trouble at an early stage
- drawing up a contingency plan if there is an outburst in class, for example, identifying with the child a key helper who can be called to remove the child from the situation, and
- ensuring that if there is any possibility that positive handling may need to be used to prevent injury to the child, young person or others or damage to property, relevant staff have had training in appropriate techniques, that these have been carefully explained to the child and that the circumstances in which they will be used are recorded in a written plan agreed with and signed by the child and their parents or carers

- Reasonable steps taken to ensure that the inclusion of a child with autistic spectrum disorder who is distracting and constantly moves around in a mainstream secondary school is not incompatible with the efficient education of others may include:
    - ensuring all possible steps are taken to provide structure and predictability to the child's day, for example by the use of visual timetables, careful prior explanation of changes to routines and clear instructions for tasks
    - ensuring that the child is taught a means of communicating wants and needs using sign, symbol or spoken language
    - working with a member of staff on a structured programme of activities designed to prepare him or her for joining in class or group activities, for example by using 'social scripts' to rehearse appropriate behaviour
    - having an individual workstation within a teaching space where distractions can be kept to a minimum and everything needed for the work to be done can be organised in sequence, and

- ensuring that all staff are briefed on the warning signs which may indicate potential behaviour challenge and on a range of activities which provide effective distraction if used sufficiently early

- Reasonable steps taken to ensure that the inclusion of a young person with a learning disability who does not use verbal communication in a mainstream course at a further education college is not incompatible with the efficient education of others may include:
  - the involvement of staff from the college's learning support team in the school-based transition reviews
  - an orientation period during the summer holidays, to enable the student to find his or her way around the college campus and meet the learning support staff
  - opportunities to practise travelling to and from college
  - the development of an individual learning programme outlining longer term outcomes covering all aspects of learning and development, with shorter term targets to meet the outcomes
  - supported access to taster sessions over a first year in college
  - a more detailed assessment of the young person's needs and wishes provided by learning support tutors during a 'taster' year
  - staff development to ensure an understanding of the student's particular method of communication
  - use of expertise in access technology to identify appropriate switches or communication boards to facilitate the student's involvement in an entry-level course, and
  - courses normally covered in one year planned over two years to meet the young person's learning needs

9.93 There may be a range of reasons why it may not always be possible to take reasonable steps to prevent a mainstream place from being incompatible with the efficient education of others – for example, where the child or young person's behaviour systematically, persistently or significantly threatens the safety and/or impedes the learning of others.

9.94 A decision not to educate a child or young person in a mainstream setting against the wishes of the child's parent or the young person should not be taken lightly. It is important that all decisions are taken on the basis of the circumstances of each case and in consultation with the parents or young person, taking account of the child or young person's views. Local authorities should consider reasonable steps that can be taken for mainstream schools and mainstream post-16 institutions generally to provide for children and young people with SEN and disabled children and young people.

Requesting a Personal Budget

Relevant legislation: Section 49 of the Children and Families Act 2014, the Special Educational Needs (Personal Budgets) Regulations 2014, the Community Care, services for Carers and Children's Services (Direct Payments) Regulations 2009 (the 2009 regulations will be replaced by those made under the Care Act 2014), and the National Health Service (Direct Payments) Regulations 2013

9.95 A Personal Budget is an amount of money identified by the local authority to deliver provision set out in an EHC plan where the parent or young person is involved in securing that provision (see 'Mechanisms for delivery of a Personal Budget' below).

9.96 Local authorities **must** provide information on Personal Budgets as part of the Local Offer. This should include a policy on Personal Budgets that sets out a description of the services across education, health and social care that currently lend themselves to the use of Personal Budgets, how that funding will be made available, and clear and simple statements of eligibility criteria and the decision-making processes.

9.97 Personal Budgets are optional for the child's parent or the young person but local authorities are under a duty to prepare a budget when requested. Local authorities **must** provide information about organisations that may be able to provide advice and assistance to help parents and young people to make informed decisions about Personal Budgets. Local authorities should use the information on Personal Budgets set out in the Local Offer to introduce the idea of Personal Budgets to parents and young people within the person-centred approach described in paragraphs 9.21 to 9.26.

9.98 The child's parent or the young person has a right to request a Personal Budget, when the local authority has completed an EHC needs assessment and confirmed that it will prepare an EHC plan. They may also request a Personal Budget during a statutory review of an existing EHC plan.

9.99 Personal Budgets should reflect the holistic nature of an EHC plan and can include funding for special educational, health and social care provision. They should be focused to secure the provision agreed in the EHC plan and should be designed to secure the outcomes specified in the EHC plan.

9.100 Further resources on Personal Budgets are available through the DfE-funded 'Making it Personal' project. This includes guidance for parents, commissioners and suppliers and is available on the Kids website – a link is provided in the References section under Chapter 3.

Mechanisms for delivery of a Personal Budget

9.101 There are four ways in which the child's parent and/or the young person can be involved in securing provision:

- Direct payments – where individuals receive the cash to contract, purchase and manage services themselves
- An arrangement – whereby the local authority, school or college holds the funds and commissions the support specified in the plan (these are sometimes called notional budgets)
- Third party arrangements – where funds (direct payments) are paid to and managed by an individual or organisation on behalf of the child's parent or the young person
- A combination of the above

Setting and agreeing the Personal Budget

9.102 The child's parent or the young person should be given an indication of the level of funding that is likely to be required to make the provision specified, or proposed to be specified in the EHC plan. An indicative figure can be identified through a resource allocation or banded funding system. As part of a person-centred approach to the development of the EHC plan, the local authority should agree the provision to be made in the plan and help the parent or young person to decide whether they want to take up a Personal Budget. Local authorities should be clear that any figure discussed at this stage is indicative and is a tool to support the planning process including the development of the draft EHC plan. The final allocation of funding budget **must** be sufficient to secure the agreed provision specified in the EHC plan and **must** be set out as part of that provision.

9.103 Details of the proposed Personal Budget should be included in section J of the draft EHC plan and, where the proposed budget includes direct payments for special educational provision, this section must include the SEN and outcomes to be met by the payment. Local authorities must also provide written notice of the conditions for receipt of any direct payment for special educational provision and can do this alongside the draft EHC plan. The child's parent or the young person should confirm their decision and agreement of the budget. Where appropriate, this **must** include their agreement, in writing, of the conditions for receipt of the direct payment, alongside any request for a particular school, college or other institution to be named in the EHC plan. Where the child's parent or the young person has nominated a person to receive payments on their behalf, the agreement must come from the proposed recipient.

9.104 Where a direct payment is proposed for special educational provision, local authorities **must** secure the agreement of the early years setting, school or college, if any of the provision is to be delivered on that institution's premises. Local authorities should usually do this when they consult the institution about naming it on the child or young person's EHC plan. The local authority should also seek assurance from the child's parent, young person or nominee that any person employed by the child's parent or young person, but working on early years, school or college premises, will conform to the policies and procedures of that institution and may write such an assurance into the conditions for receipt of the direct payment.

9.105 Where agreement cannot be reached with the early years setting, school or college, the local authority **must not** go ahead with the direct payment. However, they should continue to work with the child's parent or the young person and the school, college or early years setting to explore other opportunities for the personalisation of provision in the EHC plan. Local authorities may wish to discuss the potential for arrangements whereby the local authority, the early years setting, school or college, holds a notional budget with a view to involving the child's parent or the young person in securing the provision. The broader purpose of such arrangements is to increase the participation of children, their parents and young people in decision-making in relation to special educational provision

9.106 Local authorities **must** consider each request for a Personal Budget on its individual merits and prepare a Personal Budget in each case unless the sum is part of a larger amount and disaggregation of the funds for the Personal Budget:

- would have an adverse impact on services provided or arranged by the local authority for other EHC plan holders, or
- where it should not be an efficient use of the local authority's resources

In these circumstances, the local authority should inform the child's parent or the young person of the reasons it is unable to identify a sum of money and work with them to ensure that services are personalised through other means. Demand from parents and young people for funds that cannot, at present, be disaggregated should inform joint commissioning arrangements for greater choice and control (see Chapter 3, Working together across education, health and care for joint outcomes, paragraphs 3.38 and 3.39).

9.107 If the local authority refuses a request for a direct payment for special educational provision on the grounds set out in regulations (see paragraphs 9.119 to 9.124 below) the local authority **must** set out their reasons in writing and inform the child's parent or the young person of their right to request a formal review of the decision. The local authority **must** consider any subsequent representation made by the child's parent or the young person and notify them of the outcome, in writing, setting out the reasons for their decision.

9.108 Where the disagreement relates to the special educational provision to be secured through a Personal Budget the child's parent or the young person can appeal to the First-tier Tribunal (SEN and Disability), as with any other disagreement about provision to be specified in an EHC plan.

9.109 Decisions in relation to the health element (Personal Health Budget) remain the responsibility of the CCG or other health commissioning bodies and where they decline a request for a direct payment, they **must** set out the reasons in writing and provide the opportunity for a formal review. Where more than one body is unable to meet a request for a direct payment, the local authority and partners should consider sending a single letter setting out the reasons for the decisions.

Scope of Personal Budgets

9.110 The Personal Budget can include funding from education, health and social care. However, the scope of that budget will vary depending on the needs of the individual, the eligibility criteria for the different components and the mechanism for delivery. It will reflect local circumstances, commissioning arrangements and school preference. The scope of Personal Budgets should increase over time as local joint commissioning arrangements provide greater opportunity for choice and control over local provision.

9.111 Local authority commissioners and their partners should seek to align funding streams for inclusion in Personal Budgets and are encouraged to establish arrangements that will allow the development of a single integrated fund from which a single Personal Budget, covering all three areas of additional and individual support, can be made available. EHC plans can then set out how this budget is to be used including the provision to be secured, the outcomes it will deliver and how health, education and social care needs will be met.

Education

9.112 The special educational provision specified in an EHC plan can include provision funded from the school's budget share (or in colleges from their formula funding) and more specialist provision funded wholly or partly from the local authority's high needs funding. It is this latter funding that is used for Personal Budgets, although schools and colleges should be encouraged to personalise the support they provide and they can choose to contribute their own funding to a Personal Budget (this will usually be an organised arrangement managed by the setting, but some schools and colleges, including specialist settings, have made innovative arrangements with young people, giving them direct (cash) payments).

9.113 High needs funding can also be used to commission services from schools and colleges, including from special schools. In practice, this will mean the funding from the local authority's high needs budget for the SEN element of a Personal Budget will vary depending on how services are commissioned locally and what schools and colleges are expected to provide as part of the Local Offer. The child's parent or the young person should be made aware that the scope for a Personal Budget varies depending on their school preference. For example, as part of their core provision, special schools and colleges make some specialist provision available that is not normally available at mainstream schools and colleges. The particular choice of a special school, with integrated specialist provision, might reduce the scope for a Personal Budget, whereas the choice of a place in a mainstream school that does not make that particular provision could increase the opportunity for a Personal Budget.

Health

9.114 Personal Health Budgets for healthcare are not appropriate for all of the aspects of NHS care an individual may require. Full details of excluded services are set out in guidance provided by NHS England and include primary medical (i.e. GP services) and emergency services.

9.115 In principle, other than excluded services a Personal Health Budget could be given to anyone who needs to receive healthcare funded by the NHS where the benefits of having the budget for healthcare outweigh any additional costs associated with having one.

9.116 Since April 2014, everyone receiving NHS Continuing Healthcare (including children's continuing care) has had the right to ask for a Personal Health Budget, including a direct payment. From October 2014 this group will benefit from 'a right to have' a Personal Health Budget.

9.117 The mandate to NHS England sets an objective that from April 2015 Personal Health Budgets including direct payments should be an option for people with long-term health needs who could benefit from one. This includes people who use NHS services outside NHS Continuing Healthcare.

Social Care

9.118 The Care Act 2014 mandates, for the first time in law, a Personal Budget as part of the care and support plan for people over 18 with eligible care and support needs, or where the local authority decides to meet needs. The Act also clarifies people's right to request a direct payment to meet some or all of their care and support needs, and covers people with and without capacity to request a direct payment. For children and young people under 18, local authorities are under a duty to offer direct payments (see paragraph 9.123 below) for services which the local authority may provide to children with disabilities, or their families, under section 17 of the Children Act 1989.

Use of direct payments

9.119 Direct payments are cash payments made directly to the child's parent, the young person or their nominee, allowing them to arrange provision themselves. They **must** be set at a level that will secure the provision specified in the EHC plan. If a direct payment is not set at a suitable level, it **must** be reviewed and adjusted. Local authorities **must not** make direct payments for the purpose of funding a school place or post-16 institution.

9.120 Local authority and health commissioning body duties to secure or arrange the provision specified in EHC plans are discharged through a direct payment only when the provision has been acquired for, or on behalf of, the child's parent or the young person and this has been done in keeping with regulations. Funding **must** be set at a level to secure the agreed provision in the EHC plan and meet health needs agreed in the Personal Health Budget Care Plan (see paragraph 9.124 below for the additional information that needs to be included in an EHC plan to meet the requirements for a Care Plan).

9.121 Direct payments for special educational provision, health care and social care provision are subject to separate regulations. These are:

- The Community Care, services for Carers and Children's Services (Direct Payments) Regulations 2009 (the 2009 regulations will be replaced by those made under the Care Act 2014)
- The National Health Service (Direct Payments) Regulations 2013
- The Special Educational Needs (Personal Budgets) Regulations 2014

9.122 The regulations have many common requirements including those covering consent, use of nominees, conditions for receipt, monitoring and review of direct payments and persons to whom direct payments **must not** be made (such as those subject to certain rehabilitation orders). Detailed arrangements for direct payments should be set out in section J of the EHC plan.

9.123 Local authorities **must** offer direct payments for social care services. For both education and social care the local authority **must** be satisfied that the person who receives the direct payments will use them in an appropriate way and that they will act in the best interests of the child or young person. Regulations governing the use of direct payments for special educational provision place a number of additional requirements on both local authorities and parents before a direct payment can be agreed. These include requirements to consider the impact on other service users and value for money and to seek agreement from educational establishments where a service funded by a direct payment is delivered on their premises.

9.124 Direct payments for health require the agreement of a Care Plan between the CCG and the recipient. This requirement can be fulfilled by sections G and J of the EHC plan as long as it includes the following information:

- the health needs to be met and the outcomes to be achieved through the provision in the plan
- the things that the direct payment will be used to purchase, the size of the direct payment, and how often it will be paid
- the name of the care co-ordinator responsible for managing the Care Plan
- who will be responsible for monitoring the health condition of the person receiving care
- the anticipated date of the first review, and how it is to be carried out
- the period of notice that will apply if the CCG decides to reduce the amount of the direct payment
- where necessary, an agreed procedure for discussing and managing any significant risk, and
- where people lack capacity or are more vulnerable, the plan should consider safeguarding, promoting liberty and where appropriate set out any restraint procedures

Finalising and maintaining the EHC plan

Relevant legislation: Sections 39, 40 and 43 of the Children and Families Act 2014 and Regulations 13 and 14 of the SEND Regulations 2014

9.125 When changes are suggested to the draft EHC plan by the child's parent or the young person and agreed by the local authority, the draft plan should be amended and issued as the final EHC plan as quickly as possible. The final EHC plan can differ from the draft EHC plan only as a result of any representations made by the child's parent or the young person (including a request for a Personal Budget) and decisions made about the school or other institution (or type of school or other institution) to be named in the EHC plan. The local authority **must not** make any other changes – if the local authority wishes to make other changes it **must** re-issue the draft EHC plan to the child's parent or the young person (see paragraph 9.77). The final EHC plan should be signed and dated by the local authority officer responsible for signing off the final plan.

9.126 Where changes suggested by the child's parent or the young person are not agreed, the local authority may still proceed to issue the final EHC plan. In either case the local authority **must** notify the child's parent or the young person of their right to appeal to the Tribunal and the time limit for doing so, of the requirement for them to consider mediation should they wish to appeal, and the availability of information, advice and support and disagreement resolution services. The local authority should also notify the child's parent or the young person how they can appeal the health and social care provision in the EHC plan.

9.127 The child's parent or the young person may appeal to the Tribunal against the description of SEN in the EHC plan, the special educational provision, and the school or other provider named, or the fact that no school or other provider is named.

9.128 Mediation and appeals for children and young people whose EHC plans are finalised while they remain in custody are covered in Chapter 10.

9.129 As well as the child's parent or the young person, the final EHC plan **must** also be issued to the governing body, proprietor or principal of any school, college or other institution named in the EHC plan, and to the relevant CCG (or where relevant, NHS England).

9.130 Where a nursery, school or college (of a type identified in paragraph 9.78) is named in an EHC plan, they **must** admit the child or young person. The headteacher or principal of the school, college or other institution named in the EHC plan should ensure that those teaching or working with the child or young person are aware of their needs and have arrangements in place to meet them. Institutions should also ensure that teachers and lecturers monitor and review the child or young person's progress during the course of a year. Formal reviews of the EHC plan **must** take place at least annually. If a child or young person's SEN change, the local authority should hold a review as soon as possible to ensure that provision specified in the EHC plan is appropriate.

Maintaining special educational provision in EHC plans

Relevant legislation: Section 42 of the Children and Families Act 2014

9.131 When an EHC plan is maintained for a child or young person the local authority **must** secure the special educational provision specified in the plan. If a local authority names an independent school or independent college in the plan as special educational provision it **must** also meet the costs of the fees, including any boarding and lodging where relevant.

9.132 The local authority is relieved of its duty to secure the special educational provision in the EHC plan, including securing a place in a school or college named in the plan, if the child's parent or the young person has made suitable alternative arrangements for special educational provision to be made, say in an independent school or college or at home.

9.133 Where the child's parent or the young person makes alternative arrangements, the local authority **must** satisfy itself that those arrangements are suitable before it is relieved of its duty to secure the provision. It can conclude that those arrangements are suitable only if there is a realistic possibility of them being funded for a reasonable period of time. If it is satisfied, the authority need not name its nominated school or college in the EHC plan and may specify only the type of provision. This is to avoid the school or other institution having to keep a place free that the child's parent or the young person has no intention of taking up.

9.134 If the local authority is not satisfied that the alternative arrangements made by the child's parent or the young person are suitable, it could either conclude that the arrangements are not suitable and name another appropriate school or college, or it could choose to assist the child's parent or the young person in making their arrangements suitable, including through a financial contribution. But the local authority would be under no obligation to meet the costs of those arrangements.

9.135 Where the child's parent or the young person makes suitable alternative arrangements for educational provision the health commissioning body is still responsible for arranging the health care specified in the child or young person's EHC plan. If the child's parent or the young person makes alternative arrangements for health care provision then the health commissioning body would need to satisfy itself that those arrangements are suitable. If the arrangements are not suitable the health commissioning body would arrange the provision specified in the plan or, if they felt it appropriate, assist the child's parent or the young person in making their own arrangements suitable.

9.136 These arrangements ensure that local authorities meet their fundamental responsibility to ensure that children and young people with EHC plans get the support they need whilst enabling flexibility to accommodate alternative arrangements made by the child's parent or the young person.

Maintaining social care provision in EHC plans

9.137 For social care provision specified in the plan, existing duties on social care services to assess and provide for the needs of disabled children and young people under the Children Act 1989 continue to apply. Where the local authority decides it is necessary to make provision for a disabled child or young person under 18 pursuant to Section 2 of the Chronically Sick and Disabled Person Act (CSDPA) 1970, the local authority **must** identify which provision is made under section 2 of the CSDPA. The local authority **must** specify that provision in section H1 of the EHC plan. It **must** secure that provision because under Section 2 of the CSDPA there is a duty to provide the services assessed by the local authority as being needed.

9.138 Where the young person is over 18, the care element of the EHC plan will usually be provided by adult services. Under the Care Act 2014, local authorities **must** meet eligible needs set out in an adult care and support plan (as set out in the Care Act 2014). Local authorities should explain how the adult care and support system works, and support young people in making the transition to adult services. Local authorities should have in place arrangements to ensure that young people with social care needs have every opportunity to lead as independent a life as possible and that they are not disadvantaged by the move from children's to adult services.

9.139 However, where it will benefit a young person with an EHC plan, local authorities have the power to continue to provide children's services past a young person's 18th birthday for as long as is deemed necessary. This will enable the move to adult services to take place at a time that avoids other key changes in the young person's life such as the move from special school sixth form to college.

9.140 The Care Act 2014 requires local authorities to ensure there is no gap in support while an individual makes the transition from children's to adult services on or after their 18th birthday. Children's services **must** be maintained until a decision on adult provision is reached and where it is agreed that adult services will be provided, children's services **must** continue until the adult support begins. Young people will also be able to request an assessment for adult care in advance of their 18th birthday so they can plan ahead knowing what support will be received. See Chapter 8 for further details on young adults over 18 with social care needs, and Chapter 10 for further details on children and young people with social care needs.

Maintaining health provision in EHC plans

Relevant legislation: Section 42 of the Children and Families Act 2014

9.141 For health care provision specified in the EHC plan, the CCG (or where relevant NHS England) **must** ensure that it is made available to the child or young person. The joint arrangements underpinning the plan will include agreement between the partners of their respective responsibilities for funding the arrangements, to ensure that the services specified are commissioned. CCGs will need therefore to satisfy themselves that the arrangements they have in place for participating in the development of EHC plans include a mechanism for agreeing the health provision, which would usually be delegated to the relevant health professionals commissioned by the CCG. CCGs may however wish to have more formal oversight arrangements for all EHC plans to which they are a party.

Specific age ranges

All children under compulsory school age

9.142 Children under compulsory school age are considered to have SEN if they have a learning difficulty or disability which calls for special educational provision to be made and when they reach compulsory school age are likely to have greater difficulty in learning than their peers, or have a disability which prevents or hinders them from making use of the facilities that are generally provided. There is an additional precautionary consideration, that they are considered to have a learning difficulty or disability if they would be likely to have a learning difficulty or disability when they are of compulsory school age if no special educational provision were made for them. The majority of children with SEN are likely to receive special educational provision through the services set out in the Local Offer. A local authority **must** conduct an EHC needs assessment for a child under compulsory school age when it considers it may need to make special educational provision in accordance with an EHC plan (see paragraphs 9.11 to 9.19 for details of the process for deciding whether to undertake an EHC needs assessment). Where an EHC plan may be needed, the local authority should involve fully the child's parent and any early years or school setting attended by the child in making decisions about undertaking an EHC needs assessment and whether provision may need to be made in accordance with an EHC plan.

Children aged under 2

9.143 Parents, health services, childcare settings, Sure Start Children's Centres or others may identify young children as having or possibly having SEN. For most children under two whose SEN are identified early, their needs are likely to be best met from locally available services, particularly the health service, and for disabled children, social care services provided under Section 17 of the Children Act 1989. The Local

Offer should set out how agencies will work together to provide integrated support for young children with SEN, and how services will be planned and commissioned jointly to meet local needs.

9.144 For very young children local authorities should consider commissioning the provision of home-based programmes such as Portage, or peripatetic services for children with hearing or vision impairment. Parents should be fully involved in making decisions about the nature of the help and support that they would like to receive – some may prefer to attend a centre or to combine home-based with centre-based support. Children and their parents may also benefit from Early Support, which provides materials and resources on co-ordinated support. Further information about the programme can be found on the GOV.UK website – a link is given in the References section under Chapter 2.

9.145 Special educational provision for a child aged under two means educational provision of any kind. Children aged under two are likely to need special educational provision in accordance with an EHC plan where they have particularly complex needs affecting learning, development and health and are likely to require a high level of special educational provision which would not normally be available in mainstream settings. A decision to issue an EHC plan may be made in order to allow access to a particular specialist service that cannot otherwise be obtained, such as home-based teaching. The factors a local authority should take into account in deciding whether an EHC plan is necessary are set out in paragraphs 9.53 to 9.56.

Children aged 2 to 5

9.146 Where young children are attending an early years setting, the local authority should seek advice from the setting in making decisions about undertaking an EHC needs assessment and preparing an EHC plan. Local authorities should consider whether the child's current early years setting can support the child's SEN, or whether they need to offer additional support through an EHC plan, which may include a placement in an alternative early years setting. Chapter 5 sets out more detail on SEN support for children in early years settings.

9.147 Where a child is not attending an early years setting the local authority should collect as much information as possible before deciding whether to assess. The local authority will then consider the evidence and decide whether the child's difficulties or developmental delays are likely to require special educational provision through an EHC plan. The local authority **must** decide this in consultation with the child's parent, taking account of the potential for special educational provision made early to prevent or reduce later need.

9.148 Following an assessment, the local authority **must** decide whether to make special educational provision in accordance with an EHC plan. For children within one to two years of starting compulsory education who are likely to need an EHC plan in primary school, it will often be appropriate to prepare an EHC plan during this period so the EHC plan is in place to support the transition to primary school.

9.149 Parents of children under compulsory school age can ask for a particular maintained nursery school to be named in their child's plan. The local authority **must** name the school unless it would be unsuitable for the age, ability, aptitude or SEN of the child, or the attendance of the child there would be incompatible with the efficient education of others or the efficient use of resources. The child's parents may also make representations in favour of an independent, private or voluntary early years setting for their child. If the local authority considers such provision appropriate, it is entitled to specify this in the plan and if it does, it **must** fund the provision. However, it cannot require an independent, private or voluntary setting to admit a child, unless the setting agrees. The local authority should ensure that parents have full information on the range of provision available within the authority's area and may wish to offer parents the opportunity to visit such provision.

Young people aged 19 to 25

9.150 It is important to ensure young people are prepared effectively for adulthood and the decision to provide or continue an EHC plan should take this into account, including the need to be ambitious for young people (see paragraph 8.51). The outcomes specified in the EHC plan should reflect the need to be ambitious, showing how they will enable the young person to make progress towards their aspirations. The local authority, in collaboration with the young person, his or her parent where appropriate, and relevant professionals should use the annual review process to consider whether special educational provision provided through an EHC plan will continue to enable young people to progress towards agreed outcomes that will prepare them for adulthood and help them meet their aspirations.

Young people turning 19 who have EHC plans

9.151 In line with preparing young people for adulthood, a local authority **must** not cease an EHC plan simply because a young person is aged 19 or over. Young people with EHC plans may need longer in education or training in order to achieve their outcomes and make an effective transition into adulthood. However, this position does not mean that there is an automatic entitlement to continued support at age 19 or an expectation that those with an EHC plan should all remain in education until age 25. A local authority may cease a plan for a 19- to 25-year-old if it decides that it is no longer necessary for the EHC plan to be maintained. Such circumstances include where the young person no longer requires the special educational provision specified in their EHC plan. In deciding that the special educational provision is no longer required, the local authority **must** have regard to whether the educational or training outcomes specified in the plan have been achieved (see the section on Outcomes, paragraphs 9.64 to 9.69).

9.152 The local authority should also consider whether remaining in education or training would enable the young person to progress and achieve those outcomes, and whether the young person wants to remain in education or training so they can complete or consolidate their learning. In both cases, this should include consideration of access to provision that will help them prepare for adulthood. Young people who no longer need to remain in formal education or training will not require special educational provision to be made for them through an EHC plan.

Reviewing and re-assessing EHC plans

9.153 Where an EHC plan will still be maintained for a young person aged 19 or over, it **must** continue to be reviewed at least annually. The plan **must** continue to contain outcomes which should enable the young person to complete their education and training successfully and so move on to the next stage of their lives, including employment or higher education and independent living. This will happen at different stages for individual young people and EHC plans extended beyond age 19 will not all need to remain in place until age 25.

9.154 Local authorities should ensure that young people are given clear information about what support they can receive, including information about continuing study in adult or higher education, and support for health and social care, when their plan ceases. See paragraphs 9.199 to 9.210 for guidance on the process for ceasing an EHC plan.

New requests for EHC needs assessments for 19- to 25-year-olds

9.155 Young people who do not already have an EHC plan continue to have the right to request an assessment of their SEN at any point prior to their 25th birthday (unless an assessment has been carried out in the previous six months).

9.156 Where such a request is made, or the young person is otherwise brought to the attention of the local authority as being someone who may have SEN, the local authority **must** follow the guidance earlier in this chapter for carrying out EHC needs assessments. In addition, when making decisions about whether a plan needs to be made for a 19- to 25-year-old, local authorities **must** consider whether the young person requires additional time, in comparison to the majority of others of the same age who do not have SEN, to complete his or her education or training.

Transfer of EHC plans

Relevant legislation: Section 47 of the Children and Families Act 2014 and Regulations 15 and 16 of the SEND Regulations 2014

Transfers between local authorities

9.157 Where a child or young person moves to another local authority, the 'old' authority **must** transfer the EHC plan to the 'new' authority. The old authority **must** transfer the EHC plan to the new authority on the day of the move, unless the following condition applies. Where the old authority has not been provided with 15 working days' notice of the move, the old authority **must** transfer the EHC plan within 15 working days beginning with the day on which it did become aware.

9.158 The old authority should also transfer any opinion they have received under the Disabled Persons (Services, Consultation and Representation) Act 1986 that the child or young person is disabled. Upon the transfer of the EHC plan, the new authority becomes responsible for maintaining the plan and for securing the special educational provision specified in it.

9.159 The requirement for the child or young person to attend the educational institution specified in the EHC plan continues after the transfer. However, where attendance would be impractical, the new authority **must** place the child or young person temporarily at an appropriate educational institution other than that specified – for example, where the distance between the child or young person's new home and the educational institution would be too great – until the EHC plan is formally amended. The new authority may not decline to pay the fees or otherwise maintain the child at an independent or non-maintained special school or a boarding school named in an EHC plan unless and until they have amended the EHC plan.

9.160 The new authority may, on the transfer of the EHC plan, bring forward the arrangements for the review of the plan, and may conduct a new EHC needs assessment regardless of when the previous EHC needs assessment took place. This will be particularly important where the plan includes provision that is secured through the use of a direct payment, where local variations may mean that arrangements in the original EHC plan are no longer appropriate. The new authority **must** tell the child's parent or the young person, within six weeks of the date of transfer, when they will review the plan (as below) and whether they propose to make an EHC needs assessment.

9.161 The new authority **must** review the plan before one of the following deadlines, whichever is the later:

- within 12 months of the plan being made or being previously reviewed by the old authority, or
- within 3 months of the plan being transferred

9.162 Some children and young people will move between local authority areas while they are being assessed for a plan. The new authority in such cases should decide whether it needs to carry out an EHC needs assessment themselves and it **must** decide whether to undertake an EHC needs assessment if it receives a request from the child's parent or the young person. The new authority should take account of the fact that the old authority decided to carry out an EHC needs assessment when making its decision. If it decides to do so then it should use the information already gathered as part of its own EHC needs assessment. Depending on how far the assessment had progressed, this information should help the new authority complete the assessment more quickly than it would otherwise have done.

Transfers between clinical commissioning groups

9.163 Where the child or young person's move between local authority areas also results in a new CCG becoming responsible for the child or young person, the old CCG **must** notify the new CCG on the day of the move or, where it has not become aware of the move at least 15 working days prior to that move, within 15 working days beginning on the day on which it did become aware. Where for any other reason a new CCG becomes responsible for the child or young person, for example on a change of GP or a move within the local authority's area, the old CCG **must** notify the new CCG within 15 working days of becoming aware of the move. Where it is not practicable for the new CCG to secure the health provision specified in the EHC plan, the new CCG **must**, within 15 working days of becoming aware of the change of CCG, request the (new) local authority to make an EHC needs assessment or review the EHC plan. The (new) local authority **must** comply with any request.

9.164 For looked after children moving between local authorities, the old CCG retains responsibility for provision in the new local authority – for example, commissioning the provision from the new CCG as required.

9.165 Where a child or young person with an EHC plan moves to Northern Ireland, Wales or Scotland, the old authority should send a copy of the child or young person's EHC plan to the new authority or board, although there will be no obligation on the new authority or board to continue to maintain it.

Reviewing an EHC plan

Relevant legislation: Section 44 of the Children and Families Act 2014 and Regulations 2, 18, 19, 20, and 21 of the SEND Regulations 2014

9.166 EHC plans should be used to actively monitor children and young people's progress towards their outcomes and longer term aspirations. They **must** be reviewed by the local authority as a minimum every 12 months. Reviews **must** focus on the child or young person's progress towards achieving the outcomes specified in the EHC plan. The review **must** also consider whether these outcomes and supporting targets remain appropriate.

9.167 Reviews should also:

- gather and assess information so that it can be used by early years settings, schools or colleges to support the child or young person's progress and their access to teaching and learning
- review the special educational provision made for the child or young person to ensure it is being effective in ensuring access to teaching and learning and good progress
- review the health and social care provision made for the child or young person and its effectiveness in ensuring good progress towards outcomes
- consider the continuing appropriateness of the EHC plan in the light of the child or young person's progress during the previous year or changed circumstances and whether changes are required including any changes to outcomes, enhanced provision, change of educational establishment or whether the EHC plan should be discontinued
- set new interim targets for the coming year and where appropriate, agree new outcomes
- review any interim targets set by the early years provider, school or college or other education provider

9.168 Reviews **must** be undertaken in partnership with the child and their parent or the young person, and **must** take account of their views, wishes and feelings, including their right to request a Personal Budget.

9.169 The first review **must** be held within 12 months of the date when the EHC plan was issued, and then within 12 months of any previous review, and the local authority's decision following the review meeting **must** be notified to the child's parent or the young person within four weeks of the review meeting (and within 12 months of the date of issue of the EHC plan or previous review). Professionals across education, health and care **must** co-operate with local authorities during reviews. The review of the EHC plan should include the review of any existing Personal Budget arrangements including the statutory requirement to review any arrangements for direct payments. For looked after children the annual review should, if possible and appropriate, coincide with one of the reviews in their Care Plan and in particular the personal education plan (PEP) element of the Care Plan.

9.170 Local authorities **must** also review and maintain an EHC plan when a child or young person has been released from custody. The responsible local authority **must** involve the child's parent or the young person in reviewing whether the EHC plan still reflects their needs accurately and should involve the youth offending team in agreeing appropriate support and opportunities.

9.171 When reviewing an EHC plan for a young person aged over 18, the local authority **must** have regard to whether the educational or training outcomes specified in the EHC plan have been achieved.

9.172 The local authority should provide a list of children and young people who will require a review of their EHC plan that term to all headteachers and principals of schools, colleges and other institutions attended by children or young people with EHC plans, at least two weeks before the start of each term. The local authority should also provide a list of all children and young people with EHC plan reviews in the forthcoming term to the CCG (or, where relevant, NHS England) and local authority officers responsible for social care for children and young people with SEN or disabilities. This will enable professionals to plan attendance at review meetings and/or provide advice or information about the child or young person where necessary. These lists should also indicate which reviews **must** be focused on transition and preparation for adulthood.

Reviews where a child or young person attends a school or other institution

9.173 As part of the review, the local authority and the school, further education college or section 41 approved institution attended by the child or young person **must** co-operate to ensure a review meeting takes place. This includes attending the review when requested to do so. The local authority can require the following types of school to convene and hold the meeting on the local authority's behalf:

- maintained schools
- maintained nursery schools
- academy schools

- alternative provision academies
- pupil referral units
- non-maintained special schools
- independent educational institutions approved under Section 41 of the Children and Families Act 2014

9.174 Local authorities can request (but not require) that the early years setting, further education college or other post-16 institution convene and hold the meeting on their behalf. There may be a requirement on the post-16 institution to do so as part of the contractual arrangements agreed when the local authority commissioned and funded the placement.

9.175 In most cases, reviews should normally be held at the educational institution attended by the child or young person. Reviews are generally most effective when led by the educational institution. They know the child or young person best, will have the closest contact with them and their family and will have the clearest information about progress and next steps. Reviews led by the educational institution will engender the greatest confidence amongst the child, young person and their family. There may be exceptional circumstances where it will be appropriate for the review meeting to be held by the local authority in a different location, for example where a young person attends programmes of study at more than one institution.

9.176 The following requirements apply to reviews where a child or young person attends a school or other institution:

- The child's parents or young person, a representative of the school or other institution attended, a local authority SEN officer, a health service representative and a local authority social care representative **must** be invited and given at least two weeks' notice of the date of the meeting. Other individuals relevant to the review should also be invited, including youth offending teams and job coaches where relevant
- The school (or, for children and young people attending another institution, the local authority) **must** seek advice and information about the child or young person prior to the meeting from all parties invited, and send any advice and information gathered to all those invited at least two weeks before the meeting
- The meeting **must** focus on the child or young person's progress towards achieving the outcomes specified in the EHC plan, and on what changes might need to be made to the support that is provided to help them achieve

those outcomes, or whether changes are needed to the outcomes themselves. Children, parents and young people should be supported to engage fully in the review meeting

- The school (or, for children and young people attending another institution, the local authority) **must** prepare and send a report of the meeting to everyone invited within two weeks of the meeting. The report **must** set out recommendations on any amendments required to the EHC plan, and should refer to any difference between the school or other institution's recommendations and those of others attending the meeting

- Within four weeks of the review meeting, the local authority **must** decide whether it proposes to keep the EHC plan as it is, amend the plan, or cease to maintain the plan, and notify the child's parent or the young person and the school or other institution attended

- If the plan needs to be amended, the local authority should start the process of amendment without delay (see paragraph 9.193 onwards)

- If the local authority decides not to amend the plan or decides to cease to maintain it, they **must** notify the child's parent or the young person of their right to appeal that decision and the time limits for doing so, of the requirements for them to consider mediation should they wish to appeal, and the availability of information, advice and support and disagreement resolution services

Reviews where a child or young person does not attend a school or other institution

9.177 The following requirements apply to review meetings where a child or young person does not attend a school or other institution:

- The child's parent or the young person, a local authority SEN officer, a health service representative and a local authority social care representative **must** be invited and given at least two weeks' notice of the date of the meeting. Other individuals relevant to the review should also be invited, including youth offending teams and job coaches where relevant, and any other person whose attendance the local authority considers appropriate

- The local authority **must** seek advice and information about the child or young person prior to the meeting from all parties invited and send any advice and information gathered to all those invited at least two weeks before the meeting

- The meeting **must** focus on the child or young person's progress towards achieving the outcomes specified in the EHC plan, and on what changes might need to be made to the support provided to help them achieve those outcomes, or whether changes are needed to the outcomes themselves. Children, parents and young people should be supported to engage fully in the review meeting

- The local authority **must** prepare and send a report of the meeting to everyone invited within two weeks of the meeting. The report **must** set out recommendations on any amendments required to the EHC plan, and should refer to any difference between the local authority's recommendations, and those of others attending the meeting

- Within four weeks of the review meeting, the local authority **must** decide whether it proposes to keep the plan as it is, amend the plan, or cease to maintain the plan, and notify the child's parent or the young person

- If the plan needs to be amended, the local authority should start the process of amendment without delay (see paragraph 9.193 onwards)

- If the local authority decides not to amend the plan or decides to cease to maintain it, they **must** notify the child's parent or young person of their right to appeal that decision and the time limit for doing so, of the requirement for them to consider mediation should they wish to appeal, and the availability of information, advice and support, and disagreement resolution services

Reviews of EHC plans for children aged 0 to 5

9.178 Local authorities should consider reviewing an EHC plan for a child under five at least every three to six months to ensure that the provision continues to be appropriate. Such reviews would complement the duty to carry out a review at least annually but may be streamlined and not necessarily require the attendance of the full range of professionals, depending on the needs of the child. The child's parent **must** be fully consulted on any proposed changes to the EHC plan and made aware of their right to appeal to the Tribunal.

Transfer between phases of education

9.179 An EHC plan **must** be reviewed and amended in sufficient time prior to a child or young person moving between key phases of education, to allow for planning for and, where necessary, commissioning of support and provision at the new institution.

The review and any amendments **must** be completed by 15 February in the calendar year of the transfer at the latest for transfers into or between schools. The key transfers are:

- early years provider to school
- infant school to junior school
- primary school to middle school
- primary school to secondary school, and
- middle school to secondary school

9.180 For young people moving from secondary school to a post-16 institution or apprenticeship, the review and any amendments to the EHC plan – including specifying the post-16 provision and naming the institution – **must** be completed by the 31 March in the calendar year of the transfer.

9.181 For young people moving between post-16 institutions, the review process should normally be completed by 31 March where a young person is expected to transfer to a new institution in the new academic year. However, transfers between post-16 institutions may take place at different times of the year and the review process should take account of this. In all cases, where it is proposed that a young person is to transfer between one post-16 institution and another within the following 12 months, the local authority **must** review and amend, where necessary, the young person's EHC plan at least five months before the transfer takes place.

9.182 In some cases, young people may not meet the entry requirements for their chosen course or change their minds about what they want to do after the 31 March or five-month deadline. Where this is the case, local authorities should review the EHC plan with the young person as soon as possible, to ensure that alternative options are agreed and new arrangements are in place as far in advance of the start date as practicable.

9.183 Note: For those moving from secondary school to a post-16 institution or apprenticeship starting in September 2015, any amendments to the EHC plan – including specifying the post-16 provision and naming the institution – **must** be completed by 31 May 2015. For those moving between post-16 institutions at other times of year prior to March 2016, these amendments must be made three months before the transfer takes place. Thereafter, the deadlines set out above **must** be adhered to in all cases.

Preparing for adulthood in reviews

9.184 All reviews taking place from Year 9 at the latest and onwards **must** include a focus on preparing for adulthood, including employment, independent living and participation in society. This transition planning **must** be built into the EHC plan and where relevant should include effective planning for young people moving from children's to adult care and health services. It is particularly important in these reviews to seek and to record the views, wishes and feelings of the child or young person. The review meeting organiser should invite representatives of post-16 institutions to these review meetings, particularly where the child or young person has expressed a desire to attend a particular institution. Review meetings taking place in Year 9 should have a particular focus on considering options and choices for the next phase of education.

9.185 As the young person is nearing the end of their time in formal education and the plan is likely to be ceased within the next 12 months, the annual review should consider good exit planning. Support, provision and outcomes should be agreed that will ensure the young person is supported to make a smooth transition to whatever they will be doing next – for example, moving on to higher education, employment, independent living or adult care. For further guidance on preparing for adulthood reviews, see Chapter 8, Preparing for adulthood from the earliest years.

Re-assessments of EHC plans

Relevant legislation: Section 44 of the Children and Families Act 2014 and Regulations 23, 24, 25, 26 and 27 of the SEND Regulations 2014

9.186 The review process will enable changes to be made to an EHC plan so it remains relevant to the needs of the child or young person and the desired outcomes. There may be occasions when a re-assessment becomes appropriate, particularly when a child or young person's needs change significantly.

Requesting a re-assessment

9.187 Local authorities **must** conduct a re-assessment of a child or young person's EHC plan if a request is made by the child's parent or the young person, or the governing body, proprietor or principal of the educational institution attended by the child or young person, or the CCG (or NHS England where relevant). A local authority may also decide to initiate a re-assessment without a request if it thinks one is necessary. A re-assessment may be necessary when a young person with care support specified in their EHC plan turns 18. Adult care services will need to carry out an assessment to identify what support adult services may need to provide, and ensure the assessment is timely so that services are in place when needed.

9.188 A local authority can refuse a request for a re-assessment (from the child's parent, young person or educational institution attended) if less than 6 months have passed since the last EHC needs assessment was conducted. However the local authority can re-assess sooner than this if they think it is necessary. A local authority may also decide to refuse a request for re-assessment (from the child's parent, young person or educational institution attended) if it thinks that a further EHC needs assessment is not necessary, for example because it considers the child or young person's needs have not changed significantly.

9.189 When deciding whether to re-assess an EHC plan for a young person aged 19 or over, the local authority **must** have regard to whether the educational or training outcomes specified in the EHC plan have been achieved.

9.190 The local authority **must** notify the child's parent or the young person of its decision as to whether or not it will undertake a re-assessment within 15 calendar days of receiving the request to re-assess. If the local authority decides not to re-assess, it **must** notify the child's parent or the young person of their right to appeal that decision and the time limit for doing so, of the requirement for them to consider mediation should they wish to appeal and the availability of information, advice and support and disagreement resolution services.

The re-assessment process

9.191 The process for re-assessment will be the same as the process for a first assessment (once the decision to carry out an assessment has been taken). Re-assessments **must** follow the same process as for the first EHC needs assessment and drawing up of the EHC plan, set out earlier in this chapter, with the same timescales and rights of appeal for the child's parent or the young person.

9.192 The overall maximum timescale for a re-assessment is 14 weeks from the decision to re-assess to the issuing of the final EHC plan, subject to the exemptions set out in paragraph 9.42. However, the local authority **must** aim to complete the process as soon as practicable. Following a re-assessment, the EHC plan **must** be reviewed within 12 months of the date that the finalised EHC plan is sent to the child's parent or the young person and subsequently reviewed every twelve months from the date the EHC plan was last reviewed.

Amending an existing plan

Relevant legislation: Sections 37 and 44 of the Children and Families Act 2014 and Regulations 22 and 28 of the SEND Regulations 2014

9.193 This section applies to amendments to an existing EHC plan following a review, or at any other time a local authority proposes to amend an EHC plan other than as part of a re-assessment. EHC plans are not expected to be amended on a very frequent basis. However, an EHC plan may need to be amended at other times where, for example, there are changes in health or social care provision resulting from minor or specific changes in the child or young person's circumstances, but where a full review or re-assessment is not necessary.

9.194 Where the local authority proposes to amend an EHC plan, it **must** send the child's parent or the young person a copy of the existing (non-amended) plan and an accompanying notice providing details of the proposed amendments, including copies of any evidence to support the proposed changes. The child's parent or the young person should be informed that they may request a meeting with the local authority to discuss the proposed changes.

9.195 The parent or young person **must** be given at least 15 calendar days to comment and make representations on the proposed changes, including requesting a particular school or other institution be named in the EHC plan, in accordance with paragraphs 9.78 to 9.94 of this chapter.

9.196 Following representations from the child's parent or the young person, if the local authority decides to continue to make amendments, it **must** issue the amended EHC plan as quickly as possible and within 8 weeks of the original amendment notice. If the local authority decides not to make the amendments, it **must** notify the child's parent or the young person, explaining why, within the same time limit.

9.197 When the EHC plan is amended, the new plan should state that it is an amended version of the EHC plan and the date on which it was amended, as well as the date of the original plan. Additional advice and information, such as the minutes of a review meeting and accompanying reports which contributed to the decision to amend the plan, should be appended in the same way as advice received during the original EHC needs assessment. The amended EHC plan should make clear which parts have been amended. Where an EHC plan is amended, the following review **must** be held within 12 months of the date of issue of the original EHC plan or previous review (not 12 months from the date the amended EHC plan is issued).

9.198 When sending the final amended EHC plan, the local authority **must** notify the child's parent or the young person of their right to appeal and the time limit for doing so, of the requirement for them to consider mediation should they wish to appeal, and the availability of information, advice and support and disagreement resolution services.

Ceasing an EHC plan

Relevant legislation: Section 45 of the Children and Families Act 2014 and Regulations 29, 30 and 31 of the SEND Regulations 2014

9.199 A local authority may cease to maintain an EHC plan only if it determines that it is no longer necessary for the plan to be maintained, or if it is no longer responsible for the child or young person. As set out in the Introduction (paragraph xi.), the legal definition of when a child or young person requires an EHC plan remains the same as that for a statement under the Education Act 1996. The circumstances in which a statement can be ceased or not replaced with an EHC plan during the transition period are the same as that for ceasing an EHC plan.

9.200 The circumstances where a local authority may determine that it is no longer necessary for the EHC plan to be maintained include where the child or young person no longer requires the special educational provision specified in the EHC plan. When deciding whether a young person aged 19 or over no longer needs the special educational provision specified in the EHC plan, a local authority **must** take account of whether the education or training outcomes specified in the EHC plan have been achieved. Local authorities **must not** cease to maintain the EHC plan simply because the young person is aged 19 or over.

9.201 The circumstances where a local authority is no longer responsible for the child or young person include where any of the following conditions apply (subject to paragraphs 9.202 and 9.203 below:

- A young person aged 16 or over leaves education to take up paid employment (including employment with training but excluding apprenticeships)
- The young person enters higher education
- A young person aged 18 or over leaves education and no longer wishes to engage in further learning
- The child or young person has moved to another local authority area

9.202 Where a young person of compulsory school or participation age – i.e. under the age of 18 – is excluded from their education or training setting or leaves voluntarily, the local authority **must not** cease their EHC plan, unless it decides that it is no longer necessary for special educational provision to be made for the child or young person in accordance with an EHC plan. The focus of support should be to re-engage the young person in education or training as soon as possible and the local authority **must** review the EHC plan and amend it as appropriate to ensure that the young person continues to receive education or training.

9.203 Where a young person aged 18 or over leaves education or training before the end of their course, the local authority **must not** cease to maintain the EHC plan unless it has reviewed the young person's EHC plan to determine whether the young person wishes to return to education or training, either at the educational institution specified in the EHC plan or somewhere else. If the young person does wish to return to education or training, and the local authority thinks it is appropriate, then the local authority **must** amend the EHC plan as necessary and it **must** maintain the plan.

The local authority should seek to re-engage the young person in education or training as soon as possible.

9.204 A local authority will not be able to cease an EHC plan because a child or young person has been given a custodial sentence. The local authority will have to keep the plan while the child or young person is in custody. Details of the local authority's duties in those circumstances are set out in Chapter 10, Children and young people in specific circumstances.

9.205 Where a local authority is considering ceasing to maintain a child or young person's EHC plan it **must**:

- inform the child's parent or the young person that it is considering this
- consult the child's parent or the young person
- consult the school or other institution that is named in the EHC plan

9.206 Where, following the consultation, the local authority decides to cease to maintain the child or young person's EHC plan, it **must** notify the child's parent or the young person, the institution named in the child or young person's EHC plan and the responsible CCG of that decision. The local authority **must** also notify the child's parent or the young person of their right to appeal that decision and the time limit for doing so, of the requirement for them to consider mediation should they wish to appeal, and the availability of information, advice and support, and disagreement resolution services.

9.207 Support should generally cease at the end of the academic year, to allow young people to complete their programme of study. In the case of a young person who reaches their 25th birthday before their course has ended, the EHC plan can be maintained until the end of the academic year in which they turn 25 (or the day the apprenticeship or course ends, or the day before their 26th birthday if later). It is important that a child or young person's exit from an EHC plan is planned carefully, to support smooth transitions and effective preparation for adulthood. See paragraphs 8.77 to 8.80 of Chapter 8 on 'Leaving education or training' for more information.

9.208 Where a young person aged 18 or over is in receipt of adult services, the local authority should ensure that adult services are involved in and made aware of the decision to cease the young person's EHC plan.

9.209 Where the child's parent or the young person disagrees with the local authority's decision to cease their EHC plan, they may appeal to the Tribunal. Local authorities

must continue to maintain the EHC plan until the time has passed for bringing an appeal or, when an appeal has been registered, until it has been concluded.

9.210 Where the care part of an EHC plan is provided by adult services under the Care Act 2014 because the person is 18 or over, the Care Plan will remain in place when the other elements of the EHC plan cease. There will be no requirement for the young person to be re-assessed at this point, unless there is reason to re-assess him or her for health and social care because their circumstances have changed.

Disclosure of an EHC plan

Relevant legislation: Regulations 17 and 47 of the SEND Regulations 2014

9.211 A child or young person's EHC plan **must** be kept securely so that unauthorised persons do not have access to it, so far as reasonably practicable (this includes any representations, evidence, advice or information related to the EHC plan). An EHC plan **must not** be disclosed without the consent of the child or the young person, except for specified purposes or in the interests of the child or young person. If a child does not have sufficient age or understanding to allow him or her to consent to such disclosure, the child's parent may give consent on the child's behalf. The specified purposes include:

- disclosure to the Tribunal when the child's parent or the young person appeals, and to the Secretary of State if a complaint is made to him or her under the 1996 Act
- disclosure on the order of any court or for the purpose of any criminal proceedings
- disclosure for the purposes of investigations of maladministration under the Local Government Act 1974
- disclosure to enable any authority to perform duties arising from the Disabled Persons (Services, Consultation and Representation) Act 1986, or from the Children Act 1989 relating to safeguarding and promoting the welfare of children
- disclosure to Ofsted inspection teams as part of their inspections of schools or other educational institutions and local authorities
- disclosure to any person in connection with the young person's application for a Disabled Students Allowance in advance of taking up a place in higher education, when requested to do so by the young person

- disclosure to the principal (or equivalent position) of the institution at which the young person is intending to start higher education, when requested to do so by the young person, and
- disclosure to persons engaged in research on SEN on the condition that the researchers do not publish anything derived from, or contained in, the plan which would identify any individual, particularly the child, young person or child's parent. Disclosure in the interests of research should be in accordance with the Data Protection Act 1998 and wherever possible should be with the knowledge and consent of the child and his or her parent or the young person

9.212 The interests of the child or young person include the provision of information to the child or young person's educational institution. It is important that teachers or other educational professionals working closely with the child or young person should have full knowledge of the child or young person's EHC plan. School governing bodies should have access to a child or young person's EHC plan. Disclosure in the interests of the child or young person also includes disclosure to any agencies other than the local authority which may be referred to in the plan as making educational, health or social care provision.

9.213 Disclosure of the EHC plan, where the local authority considers this necessary in the interests of the child or young person, can be in whole or in part. Local authorities should consider carefully when disclosing an EHC plan whether there are parts of the EHC plan that do not need to be disclosed in the interests of the child or young person, for example sensitive health or social care information. All those who have access to the EHC plan should always bear in mind the need to maintain confidentiality about the child or young person in question.

Transport costs for children and young people with EHC plans

Relevant legislation: Section 30 of the Children and Families Act 2014 and Schedule 2(14) of the SEND Regulations 2014

9.214 The parents' or young person's preferred school or college might be further away from their home than the nearest school or college that can meet the child or young person's SEN. In such a case, the local authority can name the nearer school or college if it considers it to be appropriate for meeting the child or young person's SEN. If the parents prefer the school or college that is further away, the local authority may agree to this but is able to ask the parents to provide some or all of the transport funding.

9.215 Transport should be recorded in the EHC plan only in exceptional cases where the child has particular transport needs. Local authorities **must** have clear general arrangements and policies relating to transport for children and young people with SEN or disabilities that **must** be made available to parents and young people, and these should be included in the Local Offer. Such policies **must** set out the transport arrangements which are over and above those required by section 508B of the Education Act 1996.

9.216 Where the local authority names a residential provision at some distance from the family's home, the local authority **must** provide reasonable transport or travel assistance. The latter might be reimbursement of public transport costs, petrol costs or provision of a travel pass.

9.217 Transport costs may be provided as part of a Personal Budget where one is agreed and included in the EHC plan as part of the special educational provision.

10 Children and young people in specific circumstances

What this chapter covers

This chapter highlights particular groups of children and young people whose specific circumstances require additional consideration by those who work with them and support their special educational needs (SEN). It sets out information about managing their circumstances in order to achieve effective joined-up service provision that can help achieve good outcomes for them.

These groups include:

- looked after children
- care leavers
- children and young people with SEN and social care needs, including children in need
- children and young people educated out of area
- children and young people with SEN who are educated at home
- children and young people in alternative provision
- children and young people who have SEN and are in hospital
- children of service personnel
- children and young people in youth custody

Relevant legislation

Primary

The Children and Families Act 2014

The Chronically Sick and Disabled Persons Act 1970

The Children Act 1989

The Education Act 1996

The Crime and Disorder Act 1998

Section 20 of the Children and Young Persons Act 2008

The Apprenticeship, Skills and Learning Act 2009

The Equality Act 2010

The National Health Service Act 2006

Regulations

The Children Act 1989 – Guidance and Regulations Volume 3: Planning Transitions to Adulthood for Care Leavers

Education (Pupil Information) Regulations 2005

The Designated Teacher (Looked after Pupils etc) Regulations 2009

The Special Educational Needs and Disability (Detained Persons) Regulations 2015

The National Health Service Commissioning Board and Clinical Commissioning Groups (Responsibilities and Standing Rules) Regulations 2012

Looked-after children

10.1 Children who are being accommodated, or who have been taken into care, by a local authority (i.e. under Section 20, or Sections 31 or 38 of the Children Act 1989) are legally defined as being 'looked after' by the local authority. Around 70% of looked after children have some form of SEN, and it is likely that a significant proportion of them will have an Education, Health and Care (EHC) plan. Children and young people on remand to youth detention accommodation are treated as looked after by their designated local authority under the terms of the Legal Aid, Sentencing and Punishment of Offenders Act 2012 (section 104(1)). Further information is provided in paragraphs 10.142 to 10.145.

10.2 Local authorities will have particular responsibilities for these children and will act as a 'corporate parent'. The local authority **must** safeguard and promote the welfare of all children they are looking after.

10.3 All maintained schools and academies and free schools **must** appoint a Designated Teacher for looked after children. Where that role is carried out by a person other than the SEN Co-ordinator (SENCO), Designated Teachers should work closely with the SENCO to ensure that the implications of a child being both looked after and having SEN are fully understood by relevant school staff.

10.4 Local authorities **must** promote the educational achievement of the children they look after, regardless of where they are placed. The Children and Families Act 2014 requires every local authority to appoint an officer who is an employee of that or another authority to discharge that duty. This officer, often known as a Virtual School Head (VSH), will lead a virtual school team which tracks the progress of children looked after by the authority as if they attended a single school. Special Educational Needs and Disabilities departments should work closely with the VSH as well as social workers to ensure that local authorities have effective and joined-up processes for meeting the SEN of looked after children.

10.5 Local authorities are required to act under care planning statutory guidance issued by the Secretary of State when exercising their social services functions with regard to the children they look after. This is set out in volume 2 of the Children Act 1989 guidance.

10.6 This means that a considerable amount of planning will be done around the care, health and education needs of looked after children. They will have a Care Plan, which sets out how the local authority will meet the care needs of the child, addressing all important dimensions of a child's developmental needs. These include health, education, emotional and behavioural development, identity, family and social relationships, social presentation and self-care skills. The Care Plan will specifically include a Personal Education Plan (PEP) and a Health Plan (both are a statutory requirement) which will particularly assess and set out the child's education and health needs. It may be through making these assessments that a child's SEN will be identified.

10.7 Where a looked after child is being assessed for SEN it is vital to take account of information set out in the Care Plan. SEN professionals **must** work closely with other relevant professionals involved in the child's life as a consequence of his/her being looked after. These include the social worker, Designated Doctor or Nurse, Independent Reviewing Officer (IRO), VSH and Designated Teacher in school. This will ensure that the child's EHC plan works in harmony with his/her Care Plan and adds to, but does not duplicate, information about how education, health and care needs will be met. It is essential to involve the child, their carers and, where appropriate, their parents in the planning process. When referencing information contained within the Care Plan only information relevant to meeting the child's SEN should be included in the EHC plan. If in any doubt SEN professionals should discuss this with the social worker and, where appropriate, the child and their carers.

10.8 A significant proportion of looked after children live with foster carers or in a children's home and attend schools in a different local authority area to the local authority that looks after them. Local authorities who place looked after children in another authority need to be aware of that authority's Local Offer if the children have SEN. Where an assessment for an EHC plan has been triggered, the authority that carries out the assessment is determined by Section 24 of the Children and Families Act 2014. This means that the assessment **must** be carried out by the authority where the child lives (i.e. is ordinarily resident), which may not be the same as the authority that looks after the child. If a disagreement arises, the authority that looks after the child, will act as the 'corporate parent' in any disagreement resolution, as described in Chapter 11.

10.9 It is the looked after child's social worker (in close consultation with the VSH in the authority that looks after the child) that will ultimately make any educational decision on the child's behalf. However, the day-to-day responsibility for taking these decisions should be delegated to the carer who will advocate for the looked after child and make appeals to the First-tier Tribunal (SEN and Disability) as necessary.

10.10 For a child in a stable, long-term foster placement it may well be appropriate for the carer to take on the responsibility of managing a Personal Budget but this will need careful case-by-case consideration. (See Chapter 9).

10.11 The Care Planning Regulations specify the frequency with which Care Plans are reviewed. It is important to ensure the annual review of an EHC plan coincides with one of the child's Care Plan reviews. This could be done as part of the review of a child's PEP which feeds into the review of the wider Care Plan. Social workers and SEN teams will need to work closely together to ensure that transitions from being looked after to returning home are managed effectively, to ensure continuing provision.

Care leavers

10.12 Some children will cease to be looked after at 16 or 17 and others will continue to be looked after until their 18th birthday. (Some care leavers will remain living with their former foster carers past their 18th birthday in 'Staying Put' arrangements, but they are no longer looked after). Local authorities continue to have responsibilities to provide a Personal Adviser and to prepare a Pathway Plan. The Personal Adviser is there to ensure that care leavers are provided with the right kind of personal support, for example by signposting them to services and providing advice. The Pathway Plan plots transition from care to adulthood for care leavers up to the age of 25 if they remain in education and/or training or are not in employment, education or training and plan to return to education and/or training. In reviewing their arrangements for EHC needs assessment and EHC plan development local authorities should ensure good advanced planning involving the young person and Personal Adviser.

SEN and social care needs, including children in need

Children's social care

10.13 There is a statutory duty, under Section 17 of the Children Act 1989, for local authorities to safeguard and promote the welfare of 'children in need' in their area, including disabled children, by providing appropriate services to them. Services for disabled children provided under Section 17 will typically include short breaks for parent carers, equipment or adaptations to the home, and support for parents from social workers, for example in support of parenting capacity. If a local authority determines that a disabled child needs support under Section 17, it **must** consider whether such support is of the type outlined in Section 2 of the Chronically Sick and Disabled Persons Act (CSDPA) 1970. Where it is, the local authority **must** provide that support. Where an EHC plan is being prepared for a disabled child or young person under the age of 18, any services to be provided under Section 2 of the CSDPA must be included in section H1 of the EHC plan. All other social care services, including services provided under Section 17 of the Children Act but not under Section 2 of the CSDPA must be included in Section H2 of the EHC plan. Chapter 9 gives further details on what to include in Sections H1 and H2 of the EHC plan, in the table after paragraph 9.69.

10.14 Following acceptance of a referral by the local authority children's social care service, a social worker should lead a multi-agency assessment under section 17 of the Children Act 1989. Local authorities have a duty to ascertain the child's wishes and feelings and take account of them when planning the provision of services.

10.15 The purposes of social care assessments are:

- to gather important information about a child and family
- to analyse their needs and/or the nature and level of any risk or harm being suffered by a child
- to decide whether the child is a child in need (Section 17 of the Children Act 1989) and/or is suffering significant harm (Section 47 of the Children Act 1989), and
- to provide support to address those needs to improve the child's outcomes

10.16 A good social care assessment supports professionals to understand whether a child has needs relating to their care or a disability and/or is suffering or likely to suffer significant harm. *Working Together to Safeguard Children 2013* sets out the process for managing individual cases which are referred to and accepted by children's social care. All assessments should be child centred, focused on outcomes, transparent, timely and proportionate to the needs of each child. The maximum timeframe for a social care assessment to conclude that a decision can be taken on next steps is 45 working days from the point of referral.

10.17 Local authorities with their partners should develop and publish local protocols for assessment which should set out how the needs of disabled children will be addressed in the assessment process and clarify how statutory social care assessments will be informed by and inform other specialist assessments including EHC needs assessments leading to an EHC plan.

10.18 Where there is an EHC needs assessment, it should be an holistic assessment of the child or young person's education, health and social care needs. EHC needs assessments should be combined with social care assessments under Section 17 of the Children Act 1989 where appropriate. This is explicit in *Working Together to Safeguard Children 2013*, which can be found on the GOV.UK website – a link is given in the References section under Introduction, and a webtext version is also available.

10.19 For all children who have social care plans the social worker should co-ordinate any outward facing plan with other professionals. Where there are specific child protection concerns resulting in action under Section 47 of the Children Act, careful consideration should be given to how closely the assessment processes across education, health and care can be integrated, in order to ensure that the needs of vulnerable children are put first.

10.20 EHC plan reviews should be synchronised with social care plan reviews, and **must** always meet the needs of the individual child.

Power to continue children's social care services to those aged 18 to 25

10.21 Where a local authority has been providing children's social care services to a young person under the age of 18, and they have an EHC plan in place, local authorities can continue to provide these services on the same basis after the age of 18.

10.22 The local authority retains discretion over how long it chooses to provide these services, so long as an EHC plan remains in place. Where the young person no longer has an EHC plan, the local authority no longer has the power to extend the provision of these services to young people over 18.

10.23 This will enable local authorities to agree with young people when the most appropriate time for transition to adult services will be, avoiding key pressure points such as exams or a move from school to college. Poorly timed and planned transition to adult services will have a detrimental effect on achievement of outcomes and may result in young people requiring far longer to complete their education or leaving education altogether. This can have a negative impact on their health and care needs and it is essential that the transition between children's and adult's services is managed and planned carefully.

10.24 As part of transition planning, the needs of carers should also be assessed or reviewed to explore the impact of changing circumstances on the carer. More guidance on planning the transition from children's to adult services can be found in Chapter 8, Preparing for adulthood from the earliest years.

10.25 Information on adult social care can be found in Chapters 8 and 9. Further information about preparing for transition can be found in the Preparing for Adulthood factsheet 'The Links Between the Children and Families Act 2014 and the Care Act'. A web link for this is given in the References section under Chapter 10.

Children and young people educated out of area

10.26 Where a child or young person being educated out of the local authority's area is brought to the local authority's attention as potentially having SEN, the home local authority (where the child normally lives) should decide whether to assess the child or young person and decide whether an EHC plan is required.

10.27 Where a child or young person being educated out of area has an EHC plan, the home local authority **must** ensure that the special educational provision set out in the plan is being made. They **must** review the EHC plan annually. Local authorities can make reciprocal arrangements to carry out these duties on each other's behalf.

10.28 If the child or young person is placed by a local authority at an independent special school, non-maintained special school or independent specialist provider, the local authority **must** pay the appropriate costs.

10.29 If it is a residential placement, so far as reasonably practicable, those placing the child or young person should try to secure a placement that is near to the child's home. However, in making this decision they **must** have regard for the views, wishes and feelings of the child or young person and their families about the placement. Where the local authority names a residential provision at some distance from the family's home the local authority **must** provide reasonable transport or travel assistance. The latter might be reimbursement of public transport costs, petrol costs or provision of a travel pass.

Children and young people with SEN educated at home

10.30 Under Section 7 of the Education Act 1996 parents have the right to educate children, including children with SEN, at home. Home education **must** be suitable to the child's age, ability, aptitude and SEN. Local authorities should work in partnership with, and support, parents to ensure that the SEN of these children are met where the local authority already knows the children have SEN or the parents have drawn the children's special needs to the authority's attention. Local authorities do not have a duty under section 22 of the Children and Families Act 2014 to assess every home educated child to see whether or not they have SEN. The high needs block of the Dedicated Schools Grant is intended to fund provision for all relevant children and young people in the authority's area, including home-educated children. Local authorities should fund the SEN needs of home-educated children where it is appropriate to do so. Guidance is available to local authorities from the Department for Education on funding provision for home-educated children.

10.31 In cases where local authorities and parents agree that home education is the right provision for a child or young person with an EHC plan, the plan should make clear that the child or young person will be educated at home. If it does then the local authority, under Section 42(2) of the Children and Families Act 2014, **must** arrange the special educational provision set out in the plan, working with the parents. Under Section 19 of the Act, a local authority **must** have regard to the views, wishes and feelings of the child and his or her parents, or the young person.

10.32 In cases where the EHC plan gives the name of a school or type of school where the child will be educated and the parents decide to educate at home, the local authority is not under a duty to make the special educational provision set out in the plan provided it is satisfied that the arrangements made by the parents are suitable. The local authority **must** review the plan annually to assure itself that the provision set out in it continues to be appropriate and that the child's SEN continue to be met (see Chapter 9). Where the local authority has decided that the provision is appropriate, it should amend the plan to name the type of school that would be suitable but state that parents have made their own arrangements under Section 7 of the Education Act 1996.

10.33 Where a child or young person is a registered pupil and the parent decides to home educate, the parent **must** notify the school in writing that the child or young person is receiving education otherwise than at school and the school **must** then remove the pupil's name from the admission register. If the school is a special school, the local authority **must** give consent for the child's name to be removed, but this should not be a lengthy or complex process. There is no provision in law for a 'trial period' of home education.

10.34 Local authorities do not have the right of entry to the family home to check that the provision being made by the parents is appropriate and may only enter the home at the invitation of the parents. Parents should be encouraged to see this process as part of the authority's overall approach to home education of pupils with SEN, including the provision of appropriate support, rather than an attempt to undermine the parents' right to home educate.

10.35 Local authorities should not assume that because the provision being made by parents is different from that which was being made or would have been made in school that the provision is necessarily unsuitable. Local authorities should also consider using their power to help parents make suitable provision.

10.36 In some cases a local authority will conclude that, even after considering its power to provide support to home-educating parents, the provision that is or could be made for a child or young person with an EHC plan does not meet the child or young person's needs. The local authority is required to intervene through the school attendance order framework 'if it appears…that a child of compulsory school age is not receiving suitable education'. The serving of a school attendance order is a last resort if all attempts to improve provision are unsuccessful. 'Suitable education' means efficient full-time education suitable to the child or young person's age, ability and aptitude and to any SEN he or she may have.

10.37 Parents may also home educate children who have SEN but do not have EHC plans. As with children and young people with EHC plans, local authorities should work with parents and consider whether to provide support in the home to help the parents make suitable provision. Information about the right to request an EHC needs assessment and the right to appeal should be available to all parents including those who are considering home education because they feel that the special educational support being provided in the school is insufficient to meet the child or young person's needs.

10.38 Young people may also be educated at home in order to meet the requirement to participate in education and training until the age of 18. Local authorities should involve parents, as appropriate, in the reviews of EHC plans of home-educated young people who are over compulsory school age.

Children with SEN who are in alternative provision

10.39 Local authorities **must** make arrangements where, for any reason, a child of compulsory school age would not otherwise receive suitable education. Suitable education means efficient education suitable to a child or young person's age, ability and aptitude and to any SEN he or she may have. This education **must** be full time, unless the local authority determines that, for reasons relating to the physical or mental health of the child, a reduced level of education would be in the child's best interests.

10.40 Where this education is arranged elsewhere than at a school it is commonly referred to as alternative provision. Alternative provision includes pupil referral units, alternative provision academies and alternative provision free schools. Local authorities **must** have regard to statutory guidance on alternative provision and on the education of children unable to attend school because of health needs. This guidance specifies that the education provided should be on a par with mainstream schools. The guidance is available on the GOV.UK website – see the References section under Chapter 10 for a link.

10.41 Local authorities, schools and post-16 education providers may commission alternative provision for other children and young people who face barriers to participation in mainstream education or training.

10.42 Alternative provision **must** be arranged in line with a child or young person's EHC plan. Local authorities may need to amend a plan where, for example, a child or young person is no longer attending the institution named on it. They should also consider whether the EHC plan needs to be reviewed to ensure that the child or young person's SEN will be appropriately supported. Where alternative provision is specified in a child or young person's EHC plan the local authority **must** arrange that provision.

10.43 Where a child or young person in alternative provision has SEN that are not specified in an EHC plan then the alternative provider should employ a graduated response to these needs, as set out in Chapter 6.

10.44 The support that will be provided for children and young people with SEN, with or without an EHC plan, should be agreed as part of the commissioning process. To allow for continuity of support, mainstream and alternative providers should promptly share appropriate information on a child or young person's SEN. Commissioners of alternative provision should ensure that there is a clear plan for pupils' progression and keep the arrangements under regular review so that they can be adapted in response to the needs of the child or young person. Where an alternative provider has concerns that a child or young person may have SEN that are not being appropriately supported then they should raise their concerns with the commissioner and agree how these potential needs will be assessed and supported.

10.45 Alternative provision includes providers of online learning. Whilst it will not be appropriate in every case, online learning can offer certain benefits where there are significant barriers to a child or young person physically attending an educational institution. For example, online learning can provide for real-time teaching support, allow access to a broader curriculum and offer opportunities for students to interact with each other. Decisions on whether to arrange online learning are for the local authority or institution commissioning the provision to make, although they should take into account the views of professionals, parents or carers and the child or young person.

10.46 In making this decision, commissioners should give particular consideration to the support that will be provided for children or young people's SEN, as well as their social, emotional and physical development. Where feasible, online learning should be accompanied by opportunities for face-to-face contact with peers. Any decision to use online learning from a child or young person's own home should include an assessment of his or her suitability for independent learning and home circumstances.

Children and young people in alternative provision because of health needs

10.47 In line with local authorities' duty to arrange suitable education as set out above, children and young people who are in hospital or placed in other forms of alternative provision because of their health needs should have access to education that is on a par with that of mainstream provision, including appropriate support to meet the needs of those with SEN. The education they receive should be good quality and prevent them from slipping behind their peers. It should involve suitably qualified staff who can help pupils progress and enable them to successfully reintegrate back into school as soon as possible. This includes children and young people admitted to hospital under Section 2 of the Mental Health Act 2007.

10.48 Young people with health needs who are over the school leaving age should also be encouraged to continue learning. Under Raising the Participation Age legislation, local authorities have duties to promote effective participation in education or training for 16- and 17-year-olds. Useful information on Raising the Participation Age can be found on the GOV.UK website – a link is given in the References section under Chapter 10.

10.49 When a child or young person with an EHC plan is admitted to hospital, the local authority that maintains the plan should be informed so that they can ensure the provision set out in the plan continues to be provided. If necessary, the EHC plan may be reviewed and amended to ensure it remains appropriate and the child's SEN continue to be met.

10.50 Where children or young people with health needs are returning to mainstream education then the local authority should work with them, their family, the current education provider and the new school or post-16 provider to produce a reintegration plan. This will help ensure that their educational, health and social care needs continue to be met. Where relevant, a reintegration plan should be linked to a child or young person's EHC plan or individual healthcare plan.

10.51 It is important that medical commissioners and local authorities work together to minimise the disruption to children and young people's education. In order for local authorities to meet their duties, medical commissioners should notify them as soon as possible about any need to arrange education, ideally in advance of the hospital placement. For example, where a child of compulsory school age is normally resident in a local authority but is receiving medical treatment elsewhere, it is still the duty of the 'home' local authority to arrange suitable education if it would not otherwise be received.

10.52 In certain circumstances, local authorities' duties may require them to commission independent educational provision. Such providers would need to be funded directly by the home local authority. Local authorities' duties do not specifically require them to commission a particular educational provider. Medical commissioners should, therefore, avoid making commitments to fund education without the local authority's agreement. Decisions about educational provision should not, however, unnecessarily disrupt a child or young person's education or treatment.

Children of Service personnel

10.53 The Children's Education Advisory Service (CEAS) within the Ministry of Defence provides advice and guidance to Service parents, educational establishments and local authorities on educational issues relating to Service children, including issues relating to SEN. Service Children's Education (SCE) provides mainstream education for Service children in some overseas locations. As the education, health and social care resources available overseas are different from the UK, MoD services complete an MoD Assessment of Supportability Overseas (MASO) for all Service children with complex needs before an overseas posting is agreed. Personal Budgets agreed in the UK cannot be transferred to SCE locations overseas.

10.54 Children whose parent(s) are Service personnel may face difficulties that are unique to the nature of their serving parent's employment. These needs may arise from:

- **service induced mobility:** Service personnel may relocate more often than the rest of the population and, sometimes, at short notice. Such transitions should be well managed to avoid Service children with SEN experiencing delays in having their needs assessed and met
- the **deployment** of serving parents to operational arenas, while not constituting SEN in itself, may result in a Service child experiencing anxiety, dips in educational performance and/or emotional difficulties. Children may also be affected similarly by siblings' deployment

Action to take in respect of Service children with SEN

10.55 In having regard to this Code of Practice and in meeting the aspirations of the Armed Forces Covenant, which attempts to eliminate or mitigate some of the potential disadvantages faced by Service families, all those with statutory responsibilities towards Service children with SEN should ensure that the impact of their policies, administrative processes and patterns of provision do not disadvantage such children because of their Service-related lifestyle.

10.56 In respect of Service children, schools and other education providers should:

- ensure that mechanisms are in place to enable effective and timely receipt and dispatch of all relevant records for Service children with SEN moving between schools in the UK and overseas, to enable effective planning, ideally in advance of the child's arrival in school. Maintained schools **must** transfer information, including SEN information, about pupils to other schools in the UK (maintained or independent) in accordance with the Education (Pupil Information) Regulations 2005. To support the transfer of information on Service children with SEN the MoD has developed the Pupil Information Profile for Service children, which includes details of a child's SEN. It is available for use by schools across the UK and overseas and is available from the Children's Education Advisory Service (CEAS) on the GOV.UK website (see the References section under Chapter 10 for a link)

- ensure that all reviews for Service children with SEN explicitly consider those Service-related issues (for example, Service-induced mobility) relevant to the outcomes of those reviews

- ensure that access to appropriate assessments, interventions and provision is determined solely on the nature, severity and complexity of the needs presented by Service children with SEN and not related to the amount of time they have left in a particular school

- consider how any funds received through the Service Pupils' Premium might be used to improve their overall approaches to meeting the SEN of Service children

10.57 Local authorities should:

- when commissioning services for children and young people with SEN, take account, with their partners (for example, Health and Social Care), of the particular needs of any Service communities within their boundaries for a Service child with SEN, consider the likely impact on the child's needs and the provision made to meet them of any relevant Service-related issue. When carrying out an assessment of a Service child's needs or making an EHC plan, local authorities **must** seek advice from CEAS, acting on behalf of the Secretary of State for Defence

- when children move home across local authority boundaries, transfer the EHC plan from the 'old' local authority to the 'new' local authority within 15 days from when they first become aware of the move. The new local authority will have to tell the parents within 6 weeks of the transfer of the EHC plan whether the authority will bring forward the annual review of the plan and whether it intends to reassess the child. From the transfer of the plan the new local authority **must** arrange the special educational provision set out in it, although a child may have to be placed in a school other than the one named on the plan if the distance of the move makes it impractical to send the child to the named school

- work with each other, particularly those which have bases within their areas, and CEAS, so that special educational provision can be made as soon as a child arrives in the new authority. Anticipated moves should not be used to delay the provision of appropriate support for children or the carrying out of needs assessments

- when considering provision for Service children with SEN or disabilities, use all relevant evidence, including statements made for Service children in Wales and Northern Ireland, as well as Co-ordinated Support Plans made for them in Scotland and the Service Children's Assessment of Need (SCAN) completed for them by SCE

- when Personal Budgets are agreed with mobile Service parents, work with sending/receiving local authorities and the parents concerned to ensure that adequate, appropriate and timely arrangements are made in the receiving authority to ensure continuity of those elements of the overall provision purchased for Service children with SEN by the Personal Budgets allocated

First-tier Tribunal (SEN and Disability)

10.58 In reaching decisions about appeals from Service parents, the First-tier Tribunal (SEN and Disability) should consider, on the basis of the evidence available to them, the extent to which Service-induced mobility has had, is having and will have an impact on the appropriateness and effectiveness of the provision offered by local authorities and that requested by the parents.

Further information

10.59 Further information and advice about the education of Service children with SEN, in England or elsewhere in the world, including the public funds available for boarding placements and the services available in SCE schools overseas, is available from the Children's Education Advisory Service (CEAS) information page on the GOV.UK website – see the References section under Chapter 10 for a link.

Children and young people with SEN who are in youth custody

Relevant legislation

Primary

Sections 70-75 of the Children and Families Act 2014, together with sections 28, 31, and 77

The National Health Service Act 2006

The Equality Act 2010

Section 2 of the Chronically Sick and Disabled Persons Act 1970

Section 17 of the Children Act 1989

Section 39A of the Crime and Disorder Act 1998

Section 562B of the Education Act 1996

Regulations

The Special Educational Needs and Disability (Detained Persons) Regulations 2015

The Special Education Needs and Disability Regulations 2014

The National Health Service Commissioning Board and Clinical Commissioning Groups (Responsibilities and Standing Rules) Regulations 2012 (Part 3 and Schedule 3)

What this section covers

10.60 This section outlines roles and responsibilities in relation to children and young people aged 18 and under who have been remanded or sentenced by the Courts to relevant youth accommodation in England. Relevant Youth Accommodation refers to a Young Offender Institution, Secure Training Centre, Secure Children's Home or Secure College. The term 'detained person' is used throughout to describe these children and young people and includes those who are voluntarily detained in a Secure Children's Home. The term 'appropriate person' is used throughout this section to describe either the detained person's parent, where the detained person is a child, or the young person, where the detained person is a young person. 'Parent' includes any person who is not a parent of the child but has parental responsibility or who cares for him or her (see Glossary).

10.61 This section does not apply to children and young people serving their sentence in the community, to persons detained in a Young Offenders Institution for 18- to 21-year-olds or to persons detained in the adult estate.

10.62 Unless otherwise stated a reference to 'a local authority' means the home local authority. For a detained person with an EHC plan this is the local authority which maintained their EHC plan when they were in the community. In custody a request for an assessment of post-detention EHC needs **must** be made to the home local authority, meaning where the detained person is 'ordinarily resident'.

10.63 'The person in charge of the relevant youth accommodation' includes the Governor, Director or Principal in charge of the accommodation.

Introduction

10.64 Local authorities, Youth Offending Teams (YOTs), health commissioners and those in charge of the relevant youth accommodation **must** have regard to this Code of Practice and this section should be read alongside the guidance in other chapters.

10.65 The principles underpinning the Code (see Chapter 1) are relevant when supporting detained persons to achieve the best possible educational and other outcomes and to prepare for adulthood and independent living. They support:

- the participation of the detained person and the child's parents in decisions relating to their individual support. Local authorities **must** have regard to their views, wishes and feelings and **must** provide them with information, advice and support to enable them to participate

- the timely identification and assessment of special educational needs and provision of high quality support at the earliest opportunity whether they have an EHC plan or not

- greater collaboration between education, health and social care with a focus on continuity of provision both when a detained person enters custody and after their release. Custodial sentences are often short, it is therefore important for decisions to be made as soon as possible to ensure appropriate provision is put in place without delay

Summary of statutory requirements

10.66 The statutory requirements relating to children and young people detained in youth custody are:

- Local authorities **must not** cease an EHC plan when a child or young person enters custody. They **must** keep it while the detained person is detained and they **must** maintain and review it when the detained person is released (see paragraphs 10.121 to 10.122 and paragraph 10.136)

- If a detained person has an EHC plan before being detained (or one is completed while the detained person is in the relevant youth accommodation) the local authority **must** arrange appropriate special educational provision for the detained person while he or she is detained (see paragraphs 10.123 to 10.127)

- If the EHC plan for a detained person specifies health care provision, the health services commissioner for the relevant youth accommodation **must** arrange appropriate health care provision for the detained person (see paragraph 10.128 to 10.131). (The NHS Commissioning Board and Clinical Commissioning Groups (Responsibilities and Standing Rules) Regulations confer responsibility on the NHS Commissioning Board (NHS England) for commissioning health services in prisons and custodial establishments.)

10.67 For a detained person with an EHC plan, appropriate special educational and health care provision is the provision specified in the plan. If it is not practicable to arrange the provision specified in the EHC plan, special educational and health provision corresponding as closely as possible to that in the EHC plan **must** be arranged. If it appears to the local authority that the special educational provision in the EHC plan is no longer appropriate, the local authority **must** arrange provision it considers appropriate. Likewise, if it appears to the health care commissioner for the relevant youth accommodation that the health care provision in the EHC plan is no longer appropriate, that commissioner **must** arrange health care provision that appears appropriate to it. Local authorities should also consider whether any social care needs identified in the EHC plan will remain while the detained person is in custody and provide appropriate provision if necessary. For example, if a detained child is looked after, the existing relationship with their social worker should continue and the detained child should continue to access specific services and support where needed.

10.68 Where a detained person does not have an EHC plan, the appropriate person or the person in charge of the relevant youth accommodation can request an assessment of the detained person's post-detention EHC needs from the local authority. The appropriate person can appeal to the First-tier Tribunal (SEN and Disability) if they disagree with the decisions of the local authority about certain matters.

10.69 Anyone else, including YOTs and the education provider in custody, has a right to bring the detained person to the notice of the local authority as someone who may have special educational needs and the local authority **must** consider whether an assessment of their post-detention EHC needs is necessary.

10.70 YOTs and those in charge of the relevant youth accommodation **must** co-operate with the local authority to ensure that these duties can be fulfilled and **must** have regard to this Code of Practice.

Sharing information

10.71 All detained persons entering the youth justice system are assessed by the YOT using the approved Youth Justice Board (YJB) assessment tool. As part of the assessment process, YOTs will seek information from a number of sources, including local authorities, education institutions and health providers. The local authority, education institution and health provider should respond to this request as soon as possible.

10.72 The YOT **must** notify the local authority when a child or young person aged 18 and under is detained. If the detained person has an EHC plan the local authority **must** send it to the YOT, the person in charge of the relevant youth accommodation and the detained person's health commissioner within five working days of becoming aware of the detention. Information from the EHC plan will feed into the YOT assessment. The information sharing protocols described in the section in Chapter 9 (9.32 to 9.34), on 'Sharing information' and the protocols on disclosure of EHC plans (9.211 to 9.213) apply in the same way to EHC plans which are kept for detained persons (under Regulation 17 of the Special Educational Needs and Disability (Detained Persons) Regulations 2012).

10.73 If a detained person has SEN and this is known to the local authority, the local authority should provide all available information to the YOT, including details of any assessments the detained person has had and any needs which have been identified. The YOT will then share this information with the detained person's custodial case manager (using the established information sharing process via the YJB's placements team) to inform the work of key personnel (such as the health provider or SENCO for the relevant youth accommodation) who will be involved in delivering the detained person's sentence plan. Information about a detained person's educational history, including any SEN, should be reflected in the pre-sentence report if deemed relevant to the court case. The court may ask for sight of the detained person's EHC plan.

Education for children and young people in youth custody

10.74 The local authority **must** promote the fulfilment of the detained person's learning potential while they are in custody and on their release, whether they have an EHC plan or not.

10.75 The detained person's YOT will remain the key point of contact between the person in charge of the relevant youth accommodation and the local authority, although the local authority may also need to discuss the provision directly with the person in charge of the relevant youth accommodation (as well as the education provider).

10.76 Each detained person entering custody will undergo an educational assessment, including an assessment of literacy, numeracy and, where necessary, a screening to identify whether further assessments to identify SEN are required. This assessment also relies on information from the local authority provided by the YOT and will include any current EHC plan for the detained person (which the local authority **must** send to both the YOT and to the person in charge of the relevant youth accommodation). The results of assessments should enable the education provider to develop an individual learning plan for the delivery of education for each detained person.

10.77 Special educational provision should be put in place as soon as possible. Providers in relevant youth accommodation should:

- meet the educational needs of all detained persons, including those with SEN, whether they have an EHC plan or not
- ensure SEN provision, identification and support of SEN follows the model (for schools and colleges) set out in Chapters 6 and 7 of this Code
- have staff who are suitably qualified to support this (such as SENCOs), and make referrals to other specialist support where this is appropriate
- liaise and co-operate with the local authority where a detained person has an EHC plan

Healthcare for children and young people in youth custody

10.78 NHS England is the commissioner of healthcare services in prisons and custodial establishments (with the exception of some emergency care, ambulance, out of hours and 111 services) and manages contracts with healthcare providers to ensure the delivery of agreed services for detained persons.

10.79 Standards for the healthcare of detained persons in secure settings are available from the website of the Royal College of Paediatrics and Child Health (see the References section under Chapter 10 for a link). These standards include guidance on entry and assessment, care planning, physical and mental health, transfer and continuity of care and multi-agency working. The relevant NHS England provider/secure establishment is expected to consider these standards when organising health care for those under 18 years old in secure settings.

10.80 All children and young people entering custody will be screened and assessed using the Comprehensive Health Assessment Tool (CHAT) which includes a screening for speech, language and communication needs. If a detained person has an EHC plan when they enter custody, the information in the plan as well as information from the local authority provided by the YOT, should inform or supplement this assessment. This should lead to an individual health care plan for each detained person.

Requesting an EHC needs assessment for a detained person

10.81 Appropriate support after release will help the resettlement process. Therefore, if the detained person has SEN, the appropriate person, or the person in charge of the relevant youth accommodation, has a right to ask the local authority to arrange an assessment of the detained person's post-detention education, health and care needs.

10.82 In addition, anyone can bring a detained person to the attention of their local authority if they are concerned that the detained person has or may have SEN and the local authority **must** determine whether an assessment of their post-detention needs is necessary. This could include, for example, carers, health and social care professionals, YOTs and those responsible for education in custody. YOTs, for example, should consider bringing a detained person to the attention of the local authority if the approved YJB assessment tool raises concerns about a detained person who may have SEN. This should be done with the knowledge and, where possible, the agreement of the appropriate person.

10.83 The purpose of assessing a detained person's post-detention education, health and care needs is to consider whether they may need support from an EHC plan on their release from custody. EHC needs assessments can take up to 20 weeks to complete, so enabling the assessment to begin in custody will help ensure that appropriate support is in place as soon as possible after the detained person has been released, in addition to ensuring support is in place in custody if the EHC plan is finalised while they are detained.

Considering whether an assessment of post-detention education, health and care needs is necessary

10.84 Following a request for an assessment of post-detention education, health and care needs, or if the detained person has been brought to its attention, the local authority **must** determine whether an assessment is necessary. When considering a request the local authority **must** consult the appropriate person and the person in charge of the relevant youth accommodation.

10.85 Where a local authority considers that the detained person may have SEN and is considering whether an assessment of their post-detention EHC needs is necessary, it **must** notify:

- the appropriate person (and **must** inform them of their right to express written or oral views and submit evidence to the local authority)
- the person in charge of the relevant youth accommodation (informing them of their right to express written or oral views and submit evidence to the local authority, including evidence from the education provider)
- the home Clinical Commissioning Group (CCG) (with responsibility for commissioning the detained person's health services before he or she entered the relevant youth accommodation)
- NHS England (since it has commissioning responsibility for health services for detained persons while they are in the relevant youth accommodation)
- local authority officers responsible for social care for children or young people with SEN
- where a detained person is registered at a school, the headteacher (or equivalent)
- where the detained young person is registered at a post-16 institution, the principal (or equivalent)
- where a detained person is registered at a Pupil Referral Unit, the principal (or equivalent)
- the YOT responsible for the detained person

10.86 The local authority **must** secure an assessment of post-detention needs if the detained person has or may have SEN and it may be necessary for special educational provision to be made in accordance with an EHC plan on their release from detention.

10.87 To inform their decision the local authority will need to take into account a wide range of evidence, and should pay particular attention to:

- evidence of the detained person's academic attainment, rate of progress and engagement with education (such as exclusions and absence)
- information about the nature, extent and context of the detained person's SEN
- evidence of the action already being taken by the school or post-16 institution the detained person was attending prior to detention to meet their SEN

- evidence that where progress has been made, it has only been as the result of much additional intervention and support over and above that which is usually provided, and

- evidence of the detained person's physical, emotional and social development and health needs, drawing on relevant evidence from clinicians and other health professionals and what has been done to meet these by other agencies including healthcare professionals in the relevant youth accommodation

10.88 Local authorities may develop criteria to guide them in deciding whether it is necessary to carry out an assessment of post-detention EHC needs and following this whether to issue an EHC plan. However, local authorities **must not** apply a 'blanket' policy, for example, refusing to assess where a detained person has a relatively long sentence or where they have not been engaged in education for a number of years. The local authority **must** consider cases individually and be prepared to depart from any local criteria where it is appropriate.

Advice and information for an assessment of post-detention education, health and care needs

10.89 As with EHC needs assessments for children and young people in the community, an assessment of post-detention education, health and care needs should be based on a co-ordinated assessment and planning process which puts the detained person, and the child's parent, at the centre. Unless otherwise stated the principles and timescales for assessing detained persons mirror those in the community, as detailed in Chapter 9.

10.90 When securing a detained person's needs assessment the local authority **must** consult the detained person, and where they are a child, the child's parent. The local authority **must** take into account their views, wishes and feelings and **must** ensure that they are fully able to participate in the decision making process.

10.91 Advice and information **must** be sought as follows:

- Educational advice and information from:
    - The head teacher or principal of the school or post-16 or other institution which the detained person attended prior to detention
    - Where this is not available the authority **must** seek advice from a person with experience of teaching children or young people with SEN, or knowledge of the provision which may meet the detained person's needs

    - Where advice from a person with relevant teaching experience or knowledge is not available and the detained person did not attend an educational institution prior to entering detention, the local authority **must** seek educational advice and information from a person who was responsible for educational provision for the detained person prior to detention

    - If the detained person is either vision or hearing impaired, or both, the educational advice and information **must** be given after consultation with a person who is qualified to teach pupils or students with these impairments

- Medical advice and information from a health care professional identified by the home CCG. This should include advice and information gathered from professionals with a role in relation to the detained person's health, including the custodial healthcare provider

- Psychological advice and information from an educational psychologist. The educational psychologist should consult any other psychologists known to be involved with the detained person

- Advice from the person in charge of the relevant youth accommodation, including advice and information from the education provider in that accommodation

- Advice from the YOT responsible for the detained person

- Social care advice and information from or on behalf of the local authority, including, if appropriate, children in need or child protection assessments, or information from a looked after child's care plan. In some cases, a detained person may already have a child in need assessment or a child protection plan from which information should be drawn for the EHC needs assessment

- Advice and information in relation to preparation for adulthood and independent living where the young person would have been in or beyond Year 9 (if not for their detention)

- From any person requested by the appropriate person, where the local authority considers it reasonable to do so (for example, they may suggest consulting a GP or other health professional)

- Any other advice and information which the local authority considers appropriate for a satisfactory assessment (for example, in the case of a looked after child, from the Virtual School Head in the authority that looks after the child)

10.92 The local authority **must** give those providing advice copies of any representations made by the appropriate person, and any evidence submitted by or at the request of the appropriate person. The local authority may also pass on the representations and evidence provided from the person in charge of the relevant youth accommodation, where the person in charge consents to this.

10.93 The whole process, from the point when an assessment is requested (or a detained person is brought to the local authority's attention) until the final EHC plan is issued, **must** take no more than 20 weeks (subject to the exemptions set out paragraph 10.97).

10.94 The following specific requirements also apply:

- Local authorities **must** give their decision in response to any request for an EHC needs assessment within 6 weeks from when the request was received or the point at which a detained person was brought to the their attention
- When local authorities request information as part of the EHC needs assessment process, those supplying the information **must** respond in a timely manner and within 6 weeks from the date of the request
- If a local authority decides, following an EHC needs assessment, not to issue an EHC plan, it **must** inform the appropriate person within 16 weeks from the request for an EHC needs assessment. It **must** also notify those listed in paragraph 10.71

10.95 When notifying the appropriate person of a decision not to issue an EHC plan, the local authority **must** also notify them of their right to appeal that decision and the time limit for doing so. It **must** also provide information concerning mediation and the availability of SEN information and advice. The local authority should ensure that the appropriate person is made aware of the resources available to meet SEN and disability in the community within mainstream provision and through other support as set out in the Local Offer.

10.96 If, following an EHC needs assessment, a local authority decides to issue an EHC plan, the appropriate person **must** be given 15 days, beginning with the day on which the plan was served, to consider and provide views on a draft EHC plan, to ask for a particular school or other institution to be named in it and to request a meeting with the local authority to discuss the plan, if they wish.

10.97 The whole process should be completed within 20 weeks from the date of the request. There may be instances where it may not be reasonable to expect local authorities and other partners to comply with the 20 week time limit. The Special Educational Needs and Disability (Detained Persons) Regulations (2015) set out specific exemptions. These include where:

- the educational institution is closed for at least 4 weeks, (which may delay the submission of information from the school or other institution)
- exceptional personal circumstances affect the detained person or the child's parent. Being detained in youth custody in itself is not an exceptional personal circumstance
- the child's parent is absent from the area for a period of at least 4 weeks

10.98 The appropriate person should be informed if exemptions apply so that they are aware of, and understand, the reason for any delays. All remaining elements of the process should be completed within their prescribed periods wherever possible, regardless of whether exemptions have delayed earlier elements.

10.99 In deciding whether an EHC plan is necessary for the detained person on release from custody, the local authority should take into account whether the special educational provision required to meet their needs can reasonably be provided from within the resources normally available to schools and post-16 institutions or whether an EHC plan may be needed to ensure that support is provided and co-ordinated effectively for them on release from custody. Where, in the light of an assessment of the detained person's EHC needs, it is necessary for special educational provision to be made in accordance with an EHC plan, the local authority **must** prepare a plan.

10.100 Local authorities should take into account that NHS England is the commissioner of health services for detained persons, whereas on release the Clinical Commissioning Group (CCG) where the detained person is ordinarily resident will have responsibility for commissioning the health care element of the EHC plan.

10.101 The views of the home CCG will be crucial to finalising the health content of the EHC plan. The commissioning of the healthcare element of the plan and the duty to ensure it is delivered falls on that CCG after the detained person is released from custody. Although the home CCG does not have statutory commissioning responsibility while the detained person is in the relevant youth accommodation, as a local partner the home CCG **must** co-operate with the local authority that is carrying out an assessment of the detained person's post-detention EHC needs. The views of the home CCG **must** inform the final plan. The local authority and the home CCG should work together with the providers of healthcare in the secure setting to ensure any relevant healthcare information is available to inform the assessment process.

Preparing an EHC plan for a detained person in custody

10.102 In preparing a detained person's EHC plan, local authorities and those contributing to the preparation of the plan should follow the principles and requirements set out in paragraph 9.61.

10.103 As in the community, the format of an EHC plan will be agreed locally. However, as a statutory minimum, EHC plans **must** include the sections set out below, which **must** be separately labelled from each other using the letters below. The content of each is covered in detail in Chapter 9:

Section A: The views, interests and aspirations of the detained person and the child's parent.

Section B: The detained person's special educational needs.

Section C: The detained person's health needs which are related to their SEN.

Section D: The detained person's social care needs which are related to their SEN or to a disability.

Section E: The outcomes sought for the detained person on release. This should include outcomes for adult life. The EHC plan should also identify the arrangements for the setting of shorter term targets by the school, college or other education or training provider.

Section F: The special educational provision required by the detained person on release.

Section G: Any health provision reasonably required on release by the learning difficulties or disabilities which result in the detained person having SEN. Where an Individual Health Care Plan is made for them, that plan should be included.

Section H1: Any social care provision which **must** be made on release for a detained person under 18 resulting from section 2 of the Chronically Sick and Disabled Persons Act 1970.

Section H2: Any other social care provision reasonably required on release by the learning difficulties or disabilities which result in the detained person having SEN. This will include any adult social care provision being provided on release to meet a young person's eligible needs (through a statutory care and support plan) under the Care Act 2014.

Section I: The name and type of the school, post-16 institution or other institution to be attended by the detained person on release and the type of that institution (or, where the name of a school or other institution is not specified in the EHC plan, the type of school or other institution to be attended by the detained person on release).

Section J: Where any provision is to be secured by a Personal Budget post-detention, the details of how the Personal Budget will support particular outcomes, the provision it will be used for including any flexibility in its usage and the arrangements for any direct payments for education, health and social care. The special educational needs and outcomes that are to be met by any direct payment **must** be specified.

Section K: The advice and information gathered during the EHC needs assessment **must** be attached (in appendices). There should be a list of this advice and information.

10.104 In addition, where the detained person would have been in or beyond Year 9, the EHC plan **must** include (in sections F, G, H1 or H2 as appropriate) the provision required by the detained person to assist in preparation for adulthood and independent living, for example, support for finding employment, housing or for participation in society.

10.105 The appropriate person's right to request a particular school, college or other institution in the EHC plan and the process for doing so are the same as set out from paragraph 9.78. The local authority should ensure information is accessible for the detained person.

Provision of information, advice and support

10.106 When securing a detained person's EHC needs assessment the local authority **must** consider whether the child or the appropriate person requires any information, advice and support in order to enable them to take part effectively in the assessment. If it considers that such information, advice or support is necessary the local authority **must** provide it.

10.107 Further guidance on the provision of information, advice and support is covered in Chapter 2.

Finalising the EHC plan

10.108 On completion, the local authority **must** send the finalised EHC plan to the appropriate person, the person in charge of the relevant youth accommodation, the YOT, the governing body, proprietor or principal of any school or other institution named in the EHC plan, the home CCG and NHS England. The YOT should share the plan with the detained person's custodial case manager to inform the work of key personnel who will be involved in delivering the detained person's sentence plan including the health and education providers. Where the EHC needs assessment process is completed after release, the local authority **must** send the finalised EHC plan to the appropriate person, the governing body, proprietor or principal of any school or other institution named in the EHC plan and the CCG, and should send the finalised plan to the YOT.

10.109 Where an EHC plan has been issued while the detained person is still in custody the local authority **must** keep the EHC plan while they remain in custody and arrange the provision in the plan (as set out in paragraphs 10.123 to 10.127). Whilst undertaking these duties they should ensure the least possible disruption to the detained person's education and health support, given that they will already be taking part in a learning programme and receiving any necessary health care that will be based on their assessed needs when they entered into custody.

10.110 When the detained person is released the local authority **must** maintain the EHC plan and review it as soon as possible following the guidance in the section on 'Review on release from youth custody' see (paragraphs 10.134 to 10.138).

Partial assessment on entry to or exit from custody

10.111 Where a detained person is part way through an assessment of special educational needs or the development of an EHC plan on entry to custody, the local authority **must** continue and complete the process following the guidance set out in this section.

10.112 The majority of children and young people in custody will be serving short sentences. In most cases the EHC needs assessment process and plan will not have been completed before the detained person is released. The local authority **must** continue and complete the process in the community following the guidance in Chapter 9 (separate provisions apply if the person is released to a new authority – these are addressed in paragraphs 10.139 to 10.141).

10.113 The timeframes and process for completing an incomplete assessment do not start afresh because a detained person is released or a child or young person is detained. For example, the local authority **must** ensure that any EHC plan is finalised with 20 weeks. It **must** also ensure that a decision on whether or not to secure an EHC needs assessment is made within 6 weeks and that any decision not to secure an EHC plan is made with 16 weeks.

10.114 To achieve this, the Regulations allow a local authority to treat steps taken in respect of an EHC needs assessment in the community as satisfying steps which are required to be taken for a detained persons EHC needs assessment. (Regulation 15(2) and (5) of the Special Educational Needs and Disability (Detained Persons) Regulations 2015.) This is referred to in the Special Educational Needs and

Disability Regulations 2015 'the 2015 Regulations' as 'comparable requirements'. This is intended to provide local authorities with flexibility. For instance, where a local authority has provided notification to the relevant bodies that it intends to carry out an assessment (under Regulation 4(2) of the Special Educational Needs and Disability Regulations 2014 'the 2014 Regulations') there may be no need to do so again under the 2015 Regulations, where the local authority is satisfied that this is reasonable. Where a local authority has consulted a parent or young person at the outset of the process (under Regulation 3 of the 2014 Regulations) there may be no need to do so again following a detention, where the local authority considers this reasonable. A local authority may decide that, given the change in circumstances, it would be better to repeat a step. For example, the authority would like to have input from the youth offending team and the person in charge of the relevant youth accommodation. It is essential that detained persons are assessed as promptly as possible (in detention or upon release) to ensure that any required provision is in place as soon as possible.

Transfer between places of relevant youth accommodation

10.115 The YOT **must** notify the local authority when a detained person has been transferred from one place of relevant youth accommodation to another. If the detained person has an EHC plan the local authority **must** send it to the person in charge of the new relevant youth accommodation within five working days of them becoming aware of the transfer. NHS England should ensure that the new custodial healthcare provider receives the EHC plan.

10.116 If the detained person is part way through an assessment or the development of an EHC plan when they transfer from one place of relevant youth accommodation to another, the local authority and the appropriate CCG **must** continue and complete the process following the guidance set out in this section. The local authority **must** ensure that any EHC plan is finalised within 20 weeks. Anything already completed in relation to an EHC needs assessment by the person in charge of the relevant youth accommodation, including information and advice received, may be treated as having been completed in relation to the new relevant youth accommodation.

Appeals and mediation

10.117 The appropriate person during the period of detention can appeal to the First-tier Tribunal (SEN and Disability) about:

- a decision by a local authority not to carry out an EHC needs assessment
- a decision by a local authority that it is not necessary to issue an EHC plan following an assessment

- the school or other institution or type of school or other institution (such as mainstream school/college) specified in the plan as appropriate for the detained person on their release from custody or that no school or other institution is specified

10.118 Before registering an SEN appeal with the Tribunal the appropriate person **must** consider mediation unless an exemption applies. Further information on mediation and the Tribunal is set out in Chapter 11 on Resolving Disagreements.

10.119 The local authority should work with the YOT and the person in charge of the relevant youth accommodation to ensure that the mediation information session can take place and that the detained person is able to participate in mediation if they choose to go to mediation. When a parent is a party to the mediation, the child (with the agreement of the parent, the mediator and the person in charge of the relevant youth accommodation) may also attend. Young persons placed in relevant youth accommodation may not be able to leave the establishment due to security risks. Most mediation sessions should therefore take place in the relevant youth accommodation and in some cases it may be appropriate for mediation to take place via a video link. However, in such cases, careful consideration should be given as to whether this is accessible for the detained person. The person in charge of the relevant youth accommodation **must** co-operate and support this process by providing local authorities with access to the detained person for the purpose of mediation sessions. The reasonable expenses of the detained person's parent attending mediation **must** be met by the local authority.

10.120 The person in charge of the relevant youth accommodation should also ensure arrangements are in place to enable the young person to attend a Tribunal where an appeal is made. Again, there may be security considerations involved and in some cases a Tribunal hearing could take place via a video link but only where this is accessible the young person.

Keeping an EHC plan and arranging special educational provision

10.121 Where a detained person has an EHC plan at the time of entering custody, or where an EHC plan is finalised in custody, local authorities **must** keep the plan while the detained person is in custody and **must** arrange appropriate special educational provision while they are in custody. They should work closely with the person in charge of the relevant youth accommodation who **must** co-operate with the local authority to enable them to fulfil this duty.

10.122 While the detained person is in custody the local authority **must not** amend the EHC plan, carry out a reassessment or cease to maintain the EHC plan.

10.123 The local authority **must** arrange the special educational provision specified in the EHC plan. In practice the educational provision in relevant youth accommodation, including for additional support that detained persons may need as part of an EHC plan, will be delivered by an education provider under contractual arrangements with the YJB or custodial operator and commissioned and funded centrally. Local authorities should work closely with providers to arrange the provision. The local authority should seek to do this as soon as possible on the detained person entering custody, using the custodial establishment's and YOT's existing planning procedures wherever possible.

10.124 It may not always be practicable to deliver the exact provision set out in the EHC plan, for example, if the EHC plan specifies a named individual in the detained person's home area to provide a service. Where provision is not currently available within the relevant youth accommodation it does not necessarily mean that it is impracticable for it to be arranged. Where it is not practicable to arrange specified provision in the EHC plan, the local authority **must** arrange provision as close as possible to it and should work with the person in charge of the relevant youth accommodation and the education provider to identify how to do so, focusing on the outcomes in the plan. Local authorities should ensure that the appropriate person is fully involved in the process.

10.125 If it appears to the local authority that the special educational provision specified in the plan is no longer appropriate for the person, where for example the detained person's needs have changed since their last EHC plan review or they have previously unidentified needs, the local authority **must** arrange special educational provision that is appropriate for the detained person. Before deciding that the educational provision set out in the EHC plan is no longer appropriate, local authorities should seek appropriate professional advice and work with the custodial case manager, the YOT, the person in charge of the relevant youth accommodation (as well as the education provider) and the appropriate person to review the detained person's needs taking into account the information in the EHC plan, the literacy and numeracy assessment and any other assessment of the detained person's needs. On release, the local authority **must** review the EHC plan and if the special educational provision specified in the plan is no longer appropriate this should also trigger a reassessment of the child or young person's needs.

10.126 Speech and language therapy is usually recorded as education provision in section F of EHC plans (see paragraph 9.74 for further information) and where it is, it **must** be arranged by the local authority. However in practice, when undertaking this duty in relevant youth accommodation, the local authority should work with NHS England, and any providers of speech and language therapy who are contracted and funded centrally by NHS England, to deliver it within the framework of services already provided to the establishment.

10.127 Custodial sentences for detained persons are often short. It is therefore important for decisions to be made as soon as possible to enable the provision to be put in place without delay. Local authorities and the person in charge of the relevant youth accommodation should also ensure that the process for making decisions is clear, robust and transparent. Local authorities should keep records of the decisions they have made and the reasons for those decisions and make those records available to the appropriate person, the YOT and the education or training institution the detained person will be attending upon release.

Arranging health care provision for detained children and young people with EHC plans

10.128 Where a detained person has an EHC plan that specifies healthcare provision, NHS England **must** arrange appropriate health care provision while the detained person is in custody. In practice this will be carried out by a health services provider under its contractual arrangements with NHS England. NHS England should make the arrangements below when commissioning health services in the relevant youth accommodation.

10.129 It may not always be practicable to deliver the exact provision as set out in the EHC plan if, for example, the plan is specific to local health professionals or services. Where it appears impracticable to provide exactly what is in the plan, NHS England's commissioning arrangements **must** ensure that the health care provider arranges provision as close as possible to that in the plan, if it is still appropriate. In practice, although the judgment about what is practical falls to NHS England, its views will be influenced by the advice from the provider.

10.130 If it appears that the health care support specified in the plan is no longer appropriate, NHS England's commissioning arrangements **must** ensure that the health care provider arranges appropriate alternative healthcare support for the detained person. This may be the case if, for example, the health needs have changed since the detained person's last EHC plan review. Again, the assessment of what is no longer appropriate will be informed by the provider's views, although the judgment ultimately falls to NHS England. If it appears that the health care support specified in the plan is no longer appropriate this should trigger a reassessment of the detained person's EHC needs upon release.

10.131 The Comprehensive Health Assessment Tool should remain key when identifying what health provision in the plan can and should continue to be provided for detained persons with an EHC plan in custody. It may also pick up additional health needs. The process for making decisions about health provision should be clear, robust and transparent taking into account the information in the EHC plan, the CHAT assessment and any other assessment of the detained person's needs.

Monitoring provision in custody

10.132 The local authority **must** promote the fulfilment of the detained person's learning potential whilst they are in custody and on their release. Local authorities should use the EHC plan to actively monitor progress towards these and other long term outcomes.

10.133 Where a detained person is in custody within a year of the last review of their EHC plan, the local authority should conduct a monitoring meeting and continue to do so, as a minimum, every 12 months. The monitoring meeting should consider the special educational and health provision arranged for the detained person in custody and the appropriateness of the provision in the EHC plan in light of the detained person's progress or changed circumstances. If the provision in the EHC plan appears inappropriate the local authority should follow the guidance set out in paragraph 10.125. The local authority can request that the person in charge of the relevant youth accommodation or YOT convenes the monitoring meeting. Further guidance on best practice is given in Chapter 9, Education, health and care needs assessments and plans.

Review on release from youth custody

10.134 To support a detained person's transition from custody, the local authority and YOT should seek to review the detained person's educational progress and their continuing special educational and health needs in preparation for their release, using the YOT's existing release planning procedures wherever possible.

10.135 The YOT **must** notify the local authority that a detained person is due to be released from the relevant youth accommodation in order to inform the resettlement process and should ensure all external agencies are aware of their responsibilities under the proposed release plan, and condition of licence or Notice of Supervision. The local authority should inform any relevant community services that the detained person is due to be released.

10.136 If the detained person had an EHC plan before entering custody or was issued with an EHC plan while they were in custody, the responsible local authority **must** keep the plan while the detained person is in custody and **must** review it as soon as possible on release. The review **must** focus on the detained person's progress towards achieving the outcomes specified in the EHC plan and local authorities **must** follow the process set out in Chapter 9, Education, Health and Care needs assessments and plans. Local authorities should work with the YOT to take account of the condition of licence or Notice of Supervision when reviewing the EHC plan. If the EHC plan was issued while the detained person was in custody the review should specifically consider sections I and J of the EHC plan.

10.137 Professionals across education, health and social care are expected to co-operate with local authorities during reviews and the relevant healthcare commissioner **must** agree the healthcare provision to be included in a revised plan.

10.138 Local authorities, CCGs and NHS England **must** co-operate to ensure the health needs of detained persons whilst in custody and on release are considered in developing the local Joint Strategic Needs Assessment and the Joint Health and Wellbeing Strategy.

Moving to a new local authority on release

10.139 If the detained person is due to be released to a new local authority the YOT **must** notify the local authority where the detained person is ordinarily resident (the old local authority) and the new local authority in whose area the YOT expects the detained person to live on release from the relevant youth accommodation. The old authority **must** send the EHC plan to the new authority within 5 working days of being informed of the move. The new authority will become responsible for maintaining the plan and for securing the special educational provision specified in it.

10.140 Where the detained person's move results in a new CCG becoming responsible for the detained person, the new local authority **must** send the EHC plan to the new CCG within 5 working days of becoming responsible for maintaining the plan. Where it is not practicable for the new CCG to secure the health provision specified in the EHC plan, the new CCG **must**, within 15 working days of receiving a copy of the EHC plan, request the new local authority to make an EHC needs assessment or review the EHC plan. The new local authority **must** comply with any request.

10.141 If the detained person is released to a new local authority before the EHC needs assessment process has been completed the new local authority should consider whether it needs to carry out an EHC needs assessment. The new authority should take account of the fact that the old authority decided to carry out an EHC needs assessment (and should seek information concerning the assessment from the old local authority) when making its decision. The new local authority is not bound by the requirements specified in paragraph 10.113. The new local authority should draw on the expertise and knowledge of the YOT to continue the assessment process. (See Chapter 9 for more information about children and young people moving between local authorities).

Looked after children remanded or sentenced to custody

10.142 For the purposes of this section a looked after child refers to a child or young person who is under 18.

10.143 Under the Legal Aid, Sentencing and Punishment of Offenders Act 2012, children remanded to relevant youth accommodation become looked after children for the period for which they are remanded. This includes those who had previously been accommodated under the Children Act 1989. However, if a looked after child, who has previously been accommodated by a local authority under section 20 of the Children Act, is remanded to relevant youth accommodation he or she will no longer be looked after under section 20 as they are no longer voluntarily accommodated by the local authority. (A child who is looked after by a local authority as defined by Section 22 of the Children Act 1989 means a child who is voluntarily accommodated by a local authority or who is subject to a care order or interim care order.) Children who offend and receive a custodial sentence remain looked after if they were under a care order immediately prior to conviction.

10.144 If a looked after child is living in an out-of-authority placement prior to going into custody, the request for an assessment **must** be carried out by the local authority where the child lived before entering custody (i.e. where they are ordinarily resident), which may not be the same as the local authority that looks after the child. The CCG where the child is ordinarily resident has responsibility for the health element of the EHC needs assessment and the development of the health content of the plan. If a disagreement arises, the local authority that looks after the child, will act as the 'corporate parent' in any disagreement resolution, as described in Chapter 11.

10.145 If a looked after child was placed out of authority before going into custody and enters custody with an EHC plan, or one is finalised while they are in custody, the local authority where the child lived before entering custody (i.e. where they are ordinarily resident), **must** arrange appropriate special educational provision for the detained person while he or she is detained. Further information on support for looked after children is set out at the beginning of this chapter.

Transition from youth justice to a custodial establishment for adults

10.146 When a detained person is transferred to an adult custodial establishment the person in charge of the relevant youth accommodation should ensure that all relevant SEN information, including the EHC plan, is passed to the receiving establishment prior to transfer taking place, so that any additional support needs can be taken into account by the receiving establishment. The SEN duties in the Children and Families Act 2014 no longer apply once a young person is transferred to the adult secure estate.

Education on release for those in a custodial establishment for adults

10.147 If a detained person in an adult custodial establishment had an EHC plan immediately before custody, or if they were issued with a plan while in relevant youth accommodation, and if they are still under the age of 25 when they are released from custody, the local authority **must** maintain and review the EHC plan if the young person plans to stay in education. When reviewing the plan local authorities **must** follow the processes set out in Chapter 9, in particular the section on 19- to 25-year-olds.

10.148 If the young person plans to continue their education on release, the Offenders' Learning and Skills Service provider and the National Careers Service provider should liaise to ensure the responsible local authority can review the EHC plan as soon as possible.

Cross-border detention

10.149 Local authorities in England should support detained persons with EHC plans whose home authority is in England but who are detained in Wales in the same way that they support detained persons whose home authority is in England and who are placed in England. Local authorities in England should work with the person in charge of relevant youth accommodation and the Local Health Board to meet the needs of detained persons with EHC plans whose home authority is in England when they are detained in Wales.

10.150 Until the SEN legal framework is changed in Wales, host local authorities in England will be obliged to fulfill their best endeavors duty for detained persons with statements under Section 562C of the Education Act 1996 whose home authority is in Wales but who are detained in Young Offender Institutions in England.

11 Resolving disagreements

What this chapter covers

This chapter is primarily about resolving disagreements between parents or young people and early years providers, schools, colleges, local authorities or health commissioners. It:

- supports early resolution of disagreements at the local level
- explains the independent disagreement resolution arrangements which local authorities **must** make available for disagreements across special educational provision, and health and care provision in relation to Education, Health and Care (EHC) plans
- also explains the independent mediation arrangements which parents and young people can use before deciding whether to appeal to the First-tier Tribunal (Special Educational Needs (SEN) and Disability) ('the Tribunal') and for health and social care complaints in relation to EHC plans
- goes on to describe the conditions for appealing to the Tribunal or making disability discrimination claims. It finishes by describing other complaints procedures and health and social services complaints procedures

Relevant legislation

Primary

The Children and Families Act 2014 Sections 51 – 57 and 60

The Children Act 1989, section 26

The Education Act 1996, Section 496 and 497

The Tribunals, Courts and Enforcement Act 2007

The Equality Act 2010

The Legal Aid, Sentencing and Punishment of Offenders Act 2012

Regulations

The Special Educational Needs Regulations 2014

The Children Act 1989 Representations Procedure Regulations 2006

The Tribunal Procedure (First-tier Tribunal) (Health, Education and Social Care Chamber) Rules 2008

The Local Authority Social Services and National Health Service Complaints Regulations 2009

The Education (Independent School Standards) Regulations 2010

Principles for resolving disagreements

11.1 The guidance in this chapter on resolving disagreements is based on the following principles:

- Decisions about provision for children and young people with SEN or disabilities should be made jointly by providers, parents, and children and young people themselves, taking a person-centred approach, with the views of children, young people and parents taken into account when those decisions are made
- Relations between education, health and social care services and parents and young people should be marked by open communication so that parents and young people know where they are in the decision-making process, their knowledge and experience can be used to support good decision-making and they know the reasons why decisions have been made
- Parents and young people should be given information and, where necessary, support so that they can take part in decision-making and complaints processes. Support can be provided by statutory or voluntary organisations
- Local authorities **must** make known to parents and young people the possibility of resolving disagreements across education, health and social care through disagreement resolution and mediation procedures and education, health and social care providers (such as those listed in paragraph iv. in the Introduction) should have complaints procedures which, along with details about appealing to the Tribunal, should be made known to parents and young people through the local authority's Information, Advice and Support Service (see Chapter 2, Impartial information, advice and support)

11.2 The following table gives a summary of the people and bodies which can consider complaints about decisions and provision in relation to children and young people with education, health and care needs. Text in the rest of this chapter gives more detail about who can deal with complaints. Parents and young people should use the complaints procedures of local providers (schools, colleges etc) before raising their complaints with others.

Children and young people with education, health and care needs – avenues for complaint and redress

	Early years/ school/ college provision	Provision for individual CYP incl those with SEN but no plan	Decision not to assess	Undergoing EHC assessment	Decision not to issue EHC plan	EHC plan	Disability discrimination	Health complaints	Social care complaints
Early years provider	✓	✓					✓		
School	✓	✓					✓		
College	✓	✓					✓		
DfE/School Complaints Unit	✓ (LA maintained schools)	✓ (LA maintained schools)							
EFA	✓ (Academies, sixth form colleges)	✓ (Academies, sixth form colleges)							
SFA	✓ (General FE colleges)	✓ (General FE colleges)							
Secretary of State	✓ (Independent Schools)	✓	✓	✓	✓	✓	✓ (in LA maintained schools)		
Ofsted	✓ (Early years & LA maintained schools and academies as a whole)								
Local authority	✓ (LA maintained schools)		✓	✓	✓	✓ (about non-provision of education & social care)			✓

	Early years/ school/ college provision	Provision for individual CYP incl those with SEN but no plan	Decision not to assess	Undergoing EHC assessment	Decision not to issue EHC plan	EHC plan	Disability discrimination	Health complaints	Social care complaints
Local Government Ombudsman			✓ (maladministration, delay etc)	✓ (maladministration)	✓ (maladministration)	✓ (about non provision of education & social care)			✓
Disagreement resolution services	✓ (how providers carry out duties)	✓	✓	✓	✓	✓ (about sections E, H and C in the plan)			
Mediation			✓		✓	✓ (about sections E, H and C in the plan)			
First-tier Tribunal (SEND)			✓		✓	✓ (about education in the plan)	✓ (in schools)		
County Court							✓ (in early years, post-16, LAs)		
NHS complaints						✓ (about health provision in plan)		✓	
Parliamentary and Health Service Ombudsman						✓ (with the LGO)		✓	

Early resolution of disagreements

11.3 Decisions about provision for children and young people with SEN should be made as soon as possible. In most cases this will be achieved by early years providers, schools, colleges, local authorities and clinical commissioning groups (CCGs) working closely together and agreeing what should be provided with parents and young people.

11.4 However, where agreement cannot be reached, early resolution of disagreements benefits parents and young people and can avoid unnecessary stress and expense. The local Information, Advice and Support Service, described in Chapter 2, can provide access to support for parents and young people in arranging and attending meetings.

Disagreement resolution arrangements and mediation

11.5 While 'disagreement resolution' and 'mediation' are often used interchangeably, under the Children and Families Act 2014 they refer to different processes. Disagreement resolution arrangements apply more widely and are distinct from the mediation arrangements set out in paragraphs 11.13 to 11.38 below which apply specifically to parents and young people who are considering appealing to the Tribunal about EHC needs assessments and the special educational element of an EHC plan or who want mediation on the health and social care elements of an EHC plan. However, local authorities may contract disagreement resolution services and mediation from the same providers. Whereas parents and young people **must** contact a mediation adviser before registering an appeal about EHC needs assessments or the SEN element of an EHC plan they do not have to engage with the disagreement resolution services at any time, including before registering an appeal.

Disagreement resolution services

11.6 Local authorities **must** make disagreement resolution services available to parents and young people. Use of the disagreement resolution services is voluntary and has to be with the agreement of all parties. The service, while commissioned by it, **must** be independent of the local authority – no-one who is directly employed by a local authority can provide disagreement resolution services. Parents and young people can also access informal support in resolving disagreements through the local impartial Information, Advice and Support Service and, between 2014 and 2016, with the help of independent supporters.

11.7 Disagreement resolution arrangements cover all children and young people with SEN, not just those who are being assessed for or have an EHC plan, and a range of disagreements, as set out in paragraph 11.8. They are available to parents and young people to resolve disagreements about any aspect of SEN provision, and health and social care disagreements during the processes related to EHC needs assessments and EHC plans set out in Chapter 9. They can provide a quick and non-adversarial way of resolving disagreements. Used early in the process of EHC needs assessment and EHC plan development they can prevent the need for mediation, once decisions have been taken in that process, and appeals to the Tribunal.

11.8 The disagreement resolution service is to help resolve four types of disagreement or to prevent them from escalating further:

- The first is between parents or young people and local authorities, the governing bodies of maintained schools and maintained nursery schools, early years providers, further education institutions or the proprietors of academies (including free schools), about how these authorities, bodies or proprietors are carrying out their education, health and care duties for children and young people with SEN, whether they have EHC plans or not. These include duties on the local authority to keep their education and care provision under review, the duties to assess needs and draw up EHC plans and the duty on governing bodies and proprietors to use their best endeavours to meet children and young people's SEN

- The second is disagreements between parents or young people and early years providers, schools or post-16 institutions about the special educational provision made for a child or young person, whether they have EHC plans or not

- The third is disagreements between parents or young people and CCGs or local authorities about health or social care provision during EHC needs assessments, while EHC plans are being drawn up, reviewed or when children or young people are being reassessed. Disagreement resolution services can also be used to resolve disagreements over special educational provision throughout assessments, the drawing up of EHC plans, while waiting for Tribunal appeals and at review or during re-assessments

- the fourth is disagreements between local authorities and health commissioning bodies during EHC needs assessments or re-assessments, the drawing up of EHC plans or reviews of those plans for children and young people with SEN. In relation to EHC plans, this includes the description of the child or young person's education, health and care needs and any education, health and care provision set out in the plan. These disagreements do not involve parents and young people.

11.9 Local authorities **must** make the availability of disagreement resolution services known to parents, young people, headteachers, governing bodies, proprietors and principals of schools and post-16 institutions in their areas and should make them known to others they think appropriate. Details of the disagreement resolution arrangements **must** be set out in the Local Offer.

11.10 A decision by parents and young people not to use disagreement resolution services has no effect on their right to appeal to the Tribunal and no inference will be drawn by the Tribunal if the parties to a disagreement have not used the disagreement resolution services. Disagreement resolution meetings are confidential and without prejudice to the Tribunal process and the Tribunal will disregard any offers or comments made during them. Partial agreement achieved by use of disagreement resolution services can help to focus on the remaining areas of disagreement in any subsequent appeals to the Tribunal.

Contracting disagreement resolution services

11.11 In contracting an effective disagreement resolution service, local authorities should:

- take responsibility for the overall standard of the service
- have clear funding and budgeting plans for the service – parents and young people should not be charged for the use of the service and schools, colleges and early years providers should be clear about how the service can be accessed and how it will be funded
- ensure that the service is impartial
- ensure that the service has a development plan which sets out clear targets and is regularly reviewed
- ensure that the independent persons appointed as facilitators:
    - have the appropriate skills, knowledge and expertise in disagreement resolution
    - have an understanding of SEN processes, procedures and legislation
    - have no role in the decisions taken about a particular case, nor any vested interest in the terms of the settlement
    - maintain confidentiality

    - carry out the process quickly and to the timetable decided by the parties

- establish protocols and mechanisms for referring parents and young people to disagreement resolution and, where necessary, provide advocacy support to help them take part

- establish a service level agreement for delivering the service which sets out the appropriate standards expected of, and the responsibilities delegated to, the provider. There should be appropriate arrangements for overseeing, regularly monitoring and reviewing the performance of the service, taking account of local and national best practice, and

- seek feedback from the service to inform and influence local authority and provider decisions on SEN policies, procedures and practices

11.12 Parents and young people can also use the complaints procedures set out in paragraphs 11.67 to 11.111 in addition to these disagreement resolution arrangements. There is no requirement to have used the disagreement resolution services before using those other complaints procedures, and disagreement resolution services can be used before, at the same time or after those procedures.

Mediation

11.13 As paragraph 11.5 points out, the Children and Families Act 2014 makes a distinction between disagreement resolution arrangements and mediation. If parents or young people want it to, mediation can take place following decisions by a local authority not to carry out an EHC needs assessment, not to draw up an EHC plan, after they receive a final EHC plan or amended plan, following a decision not to amend an EHC plan or a decision to cease to maintain an EHC plan. These mediation arrangements complement the disagreement resolution arrangements set out in paragraphs 11.5 to 11.10. The disagreement resolution arrangements are designed to resolve disagreements about the performance of duties, SEN provision, disagreements over health and social care provision and disagreements between health commissioners and local authorities and are voluntary for both parties (see paragraph 11.8). The mediation arrangements are specifically linked to decisions about EHC needs assessments and plans. Disagreement resolution services can be used at any time, if both parties agree, including while an EHC needs assessment is being conducted, while the plan is being drawn up, after the plan is finalised or while an appeal is going through the Tribunal process.

Contracting services for mediation and mediation information

11.14 Local authorities **must** make arrangements for parents and young people to receive information about mediation so that they can take part in mediation if they so choose before a possible appeal to the Tribunal.

11.15 Local authorities and relevant health commissioners are free to choose how they make arrangements to provide mediation information and mediation, whether that is by contracting a mediation provider or providers or otherwise. Any mediation provision – by a mediation adviser (providing information) or mediator (conducting mediation) – **must** be independent of local authorities in England and/or relevant health commissioners. No one who is directly employed by a local authority in England can be a mediation adviser and no one who is directly employed by a local authority in England or a relevant health commissioner can act as a mediator. People who are contracted to act as mediators should have received accredited mediation training. The guidance on arranging effective disagreement resolution services (paragraph 11.11) provides a good guide for the arrangements which should be made for mediation services.

11.16 Local authorities must set out the arrangements they have made for securing mediation information services and mediation itself in the Local Offer.

Routes to mediation

11.17 The Children and Families Act 2014 sets out two pathways for going to mediation depending on whether the parent or young person wants to go to mediation about the matters which can be appealed to the Tribunal (see paragraph 11.45) or whether they want to go to mediation about the health and social care elements of EHC plans.

Mediation on matters which can be appealed to the Tribunal

11.18 Parents and young people who wish to make an appeal to the Tribunal (see paragraphs 11.39 to 11.52) may do so only after they have contacted an independent mediation adviser and discussed whether mediation might be a suitable way of resolving the disagreement.

11.19 When the local authority sends the parent or young person notice of a decision which can be appealed to the Tribunal it **must** tell the parent or young person of their right to go to mediation and that they **must** contact a mediation adviser before registering an appeal with the Tribunal. The notice **must** give the contact details of a mediation adviser, contain the timescales for requesting mediation and the contact details of any person acting on behalf of the local authority who the parent or young person should contact if they wish to pursue mediation. The notice should also make clear that parents' and young people's right to appeal is not affected by entering into mediation.

11.20 If the parent or young person is considering registering an appeal and has contacted the mediation adviser, the adviser will provide information on mediation and answer any questions which the parent or young person may have. The information will normally be provided on the telephone, although information can be provided in written form, through face-to-face meetings or through other means if the parent or young person prefers.

Mediation advice before mediation

11.21 The mediation information which is given to parents and young people:

- should be factual and unbiased, and
- should not seek to pressure them into going to mediation. Where there is more than one available, the mediation adviser should not try to persuade the parents or young people to use any particular mediator

11.22 The mediation adviser should be ready to answer any questions from the parent or young person and explain:

- that mediation is an informal, non-legalistic, accessible and simple disagreement settlement process run by a trained third party and designed to bring two parties together to clarify the issues, and reach a resolution
- that the parent or young person's use of mediation is voluntary
- the timescales which must be met and the certificate, and
- that the local authority will pay reasonable travel expenses and other expenses to the parent or young person taking part in mediation

11.23 Once the information has been provided it is for the parent or young person to decide whether they want to go to mediation before any appeal they might make to the Tribunal. Parents and young people have the right to appeal to the Tribunal but are not able to register an appeal without a certificate and the local authority must tell them this in the notice referred to in paragraph 11.19. Where the parent or young person decides not to go to mediation during or following contact with the mediation adviser the adviser will issue a certificate, within three working days of the parent or young person telling them that they do not want to go to mediation, confirming that information has been provided. The certificate will enable the parent or young person to lodge their appeal, either within two months of the original decision being sent by the local authority or within one month of receiving the certificate whichever is the later.

Exceptions to the requirement to contact a mediation adviser

11.24 Parents and young people do not have to contact the mediation adviser prior to registering their appeal with the Tribunal if their appeal is solely about the name of the school, college or other institution named on the plan, the type of school, college or other institution specified in the plan or the fact that no school or other institution is named. Parents and young people will already have had the opportunity to request a school, college or other institution and to discuss this in detail with the local authority. The disagreement resolution arrangements, as set out in paragraphs 11.5 to 11.10, would be available if parents or young people and local authorities wanted to attempt to resolve the dispute about the placement by making use of these arrangements.

11.25 The mediation advice arrangements do not apply to disability discrimination claims.

Going to mediation about matters which can be appealed to the Tribunal

11.26 If the parent or young person decides to proceed with mediation then the local authority **must** ensure that a mediation session takes place within 30 days of the mediation adviser informing the local authority that the parent or young person wants to go to mediation, although it may delegate the arrangement of the session to the mediator. Parents or young people do not have to pay for the mediation session(s). The local authority **must** attend the mediation.

11.27 If the parent or young person wants to go to mediation then the local authority **must** also take part. If the local authority is unable to arrange mediation in a case which involves a disagreement on a matter which can be appealed to the Tribunal within 30 days it **must** tell the mediator. The mediation adviser **must** then issue a certificate within three days. On receipt of the certificate the parent or young person could decide whether to appeal immediately or to wait for mediation to take place. If the parent or young person initially indicates that they want to go to mediation about a matter which can be appealed to the Tribunal but changes their mind, they can contact the mediation adviser who can then issue a certificate with which an appeal can be registered.

11.28 A mediation session or sessions which arise out of these arrangements **must** be conducted by independent mediators. Once mediation is completed about a matter which can be appealed to the Tribunal the mediation adviser **must** issue a certificate to the parent or young person within three working days confirming that it has concluded. Mediation will not always lead to complete agreement between the parties and if the parent or young person still wants to appeal to the Tribunal following mediation they **must** send the certificate to the Tribunal when they register their appeal.

11.29 Parents and young people have one month from receiving the certificate to register an appeal with the Tribunal or two months from the original decision by the local authority whichever is the later. The certificate will not set out any details about what happened in the mediation – it will simply state the mediation was completed at a given date. When cases are registered with the Tribunal following mediation the Tribunal will deal with the appeal on the facts of the case. The Tribunal may cover similar ground to that explored in the mediation but will reach its own independent findings and conclusions. Mediation meetings are confidential and without prejudice to the Tribunal process and the Tribunal will disregard any offers or comments made during them. Partial agreement achieved through mediation can help to focus any subsequent appeals to the Tribunal on the remaining areas of disagreement.

11.30 The Special Educational Needs and Disability Regulations 2014 set out time limits for local authorities to implement agreements made at mediation. If the local authority does not implement the agreements within the set time limits, or ones which have been agreed with the parents or young people instead, the parents or young person can appeal to the Tribunal if it is a matter which can be appealed (see paragraphs 11.45 and 11.46).

Mediation on the health and social care elements of an EHC plan

11.31 Parents and young people can also go to mediation about the health and social care elements of an EHC plan. However, unlike matters which can be appealed to the Tribunal, parents and young people do not have to receive mediation advice before going to mediation. (Health and social care provision which educates or trains a child or young person is treated as special educational provision, rather than health and social care provision, and can be appealed to the Tribunal and the parent or young person would have to contact a mediation adviser before appealing about that provision.)

11.32 The notice which is sent to the parent or young person by the local authority with the final EHC plan or the final amended plan **must** tell the parent or young person that they can go to mediation about the health and care aspects of the plan and give contact details of someone acting on behalf of the local authority who the parent or young person should contact if they want to go to mediation. When contacting the local authority the parent or young person **must** tell the local authority about the matters they wish to go to mediation about. In particular, they **must** inform the local authority if they want to go to mediation about the fact that no health care provision or no health care provision of a particular kind, is specified in the plan and they **must** also inform the local authority of the health care provision which he or she wishes to be specified in the plan.

11.33 If the parent or young person wants to go to mediation about the health care matters set out in paragraph 11.32 then the local authority **must** inform each relevant commissioning body within three working days about those matters.

11.34 If the parent or young person has told the local authority that they disagree with either the education and social care element of the plan or the health and one or both of the education and social care elements then the local authority **must** arrange the mediation, after the parent or young person has contacted the mediation adviser in a case involving the education element of the plan. If the parent or young person only wants to appeal about the health care aspect of the plan then the responsible health commissioning body or bodies **must** arrange for mediation between them and the parent or young person, ensure that the mediation is conducted by an independent person who is not employed by a clinical commissioning group or the National Health Service Commissioning Board, and take part in the mediation. The health commissioning body or bodies **must** also take part in the mediation arranged by the local authority if the mediation is about the health care element of the plan and either or both of the education or social care parts of the plan. They **must** pay the reasonable expenses of the parent or young person where they arrange the mediation.

11.35 If the responsible health commissioning body or bodies are responsible for arranging a mediation which is solely about the health care elements of the plan then they **must** do so within 30 days of being informed by the local authority.

11.36 Mediation offers a relatively quick way of resolving disagreements about the health and social care elements of an EHC plan. It may not resolve those disagreements or may not resolve all of them. If there is no resolution of the parent's or young person's disagreement with the health and/or social care elements of the plan then they cannot appeal to the Tribunal. Parents and young people could at this point request that the responsible commissioning body in the case of the health care element of the plan or the local authority in the case of the social care element goes to disagreement resolution, although the health commissioning body and the local authority would be under no duty to do so and given that the disagreements have not been resolved at mediation the health commissioning body and the local authority are unlikely to agree. The mediation arrangements for the health and social care elements of an EHC plan lie alongside the health and social care arrangements set out in paragraphs 11.101 to 11.111. Going to mediation about the health and social care elements of an EHC plan does not prevent a parent or young person also complaining via the routes set out in paragraphs 11.101 to 11.111 and vice versa nor does going to mediation prevent a parent or young person subsequently complaining via those routes.

11.37 Despite there being two routes to mediation the right to go to mediation about the education, health and social care elements of an EHC plan provides an opportunity for disagreements about a plan to be dealt with at one venue and dealt with holistically. Where parents or young people have disagreements about more than one element of the plan, including the educational element, the local authority should not arrange the mediation until the parent or young person has contacted the mediation adviser and decided whether they want to go to mediation about the educational element of the plan, so that one mediation can be arranged covering all areas of disagreement.

Effective mediation

11.38 For mediation to work well:

- the mediation session should be arranged, in discussion with the parents or young people, at a place and a time which is convenient for the parties to the disagreement. The body (or bodies) arranging the mediation **must** inform the parent or young person of the date and place of the mediation at least 5 working days before the mediation unless the parent or young person consents to this period of time being reduced
- the mediator should play a key role in clarifying the nature of the disagreement and ensuring that both sides are ready for the mediation session. The mediator should agree with the parties on who needs to be there
- mediators **must** have sufficient knowledge of the legislation relating to SEN, health and social care to be able to conduct the mediation
- the local authority and health commissioner representative(s) should be sufficiently senior and have the authority to be able to make decisions during the mediation session
- the parents or young person may be accompanied by a friend, adviser or advocate and, in the case of parents, the child, where the parent requests this and the local authority has no reasonable objection. In cases where parents are the party to the mediation and it is not appropriate for the child to attend in person the mediator should take reasonable steps (within terms of time, difficulty, expense etc) to obtain the views of the child. Young people with learning difficulties, in particular, may need advocacy support when taking part in mediation

- both parties should be open about all the aspects of the disagreement and not hold anything back for a possible appeal to the Tribunal on the SEN aspects of EHC plans
- where a solicitor has acted as the mediator, under the Solicitors' Code of Conduct (rule 3 Conflict of interests), he or she should not also represent either party at the Tribunal
- generally, legal representation should not be necessary at the mediation, but this will be a matter for the parties and the mediator to agree. If either party does have legal representation they will have to pay for it themselves

Children and young people in youth custody

Please see Chapter 10, paragraphs 10.76 to 10.78.

Registering an appeal with the Tribunal

11.39 Parents and young people have two months to register an SEN appeal with the Tribunal, from the date when the local authority sent the notice containing a decision which can be appealed or one month from the date of a certificate which has been issued following mediation or the parent or young person being given mediation information, whichever is the later. In some cases parents and young people will not register the appeal within the two-month limit. Where it is fair and just to do so the Tribunal has the power to use its discretion to accept appeals outside the two-month time limit.

11.40 The Tribunal will not take account of the fact that mediation has taken place, or has not been taken up, nor will it take into account the outcome of any mediation. Parents and young people will not be disadvantaged at the Tribunal because they have chosen not to go to mediation.

Parents' and young people's right to appeal to the Tribunal about EHC needs assessments and EHC plans

The First-tier Tribunal (SEN and Disability)

11.41 The Tribunal forms part of the First-tier Tribunal (Health, Education and Social Care Chamber). Tribunals are overseen by Her Majesty's Courts and Tribunals Service.

The role and function of the Tribunal

11.42 The Tribunal hears appeals against decisions made by the local authorities in England in relation to children's and young people's EHC needs assessments and EHC plans. It also hears disability discrimination claims against schools and against local authorities when the local authority is the responsible body for a school.

11.43 The Tribunal seeks to ensure that the process of appealing is as user friendly as possible, and to avoid hearings that are overly legalistic or technical. It is the Tribunal's aim to ensure that a parent or young person should not need to engage legal representation when appealing a decision. Parents and young people may find it helpful to have support from a voluntary organisation or friend at a hearing.

Who can appeal to the Tribunal about EHC needs assessments and plans

11.44 Parents (in relation to children from 0 to the end of compulsory schooling) and young people (over compulsory school age until they reach age 25) can appeal to the Tribunal about EHC needs assessments and EHC plans, following contact with a mediation adviser in most cases (see paragraph 11.18). Young people can register an appeal in their name but can also have their parents' help and support if needed. Chapter 8, paragraphs 8.15 to 8.18 , gives further guidance on the rights of young people under the Children and Families Act 2014 and the involvement and support of parents.

What parents and young people can appeal about

11.45 Parents and young people can appeal to the Tribunal about:

- a decision by a local authority not to carry out an EHC needs assessment or re-assessment
- a decision by a local authority that it is not necessary to issue an EHC plan following an assessment
- the description of a child or young person's SEN specified in an EHC plan, the special educational provision specified, the school or other institution or type of school or other institution (such as a mainstream school/college) specified in the plan or that no school or other institution is specified
- an amendment to these elements of the EHC plan

- a decision by a local authority not to amend an EHC plan following a review or re-assessment
- a decision by a local authority to cease to maintain an EHC plan

The Tribunal does not hear appeals about Personal Budgets, but will hear appeals about the special educational provision to which a Personal Budget may apply (see paragraph 9.108).

11.46 Parents and young people who are unhappy with decisions about the health and social care elements of an EHC plan can go to mediation (see paragraphs 11.31 to 11.35). They can also complain through the health and social care complaints procedures, set out in paragraphs 11.101 to 11.104 and 11.105 to 11.111.

Conditions related to appeals

11.47 The following conditions apply to appeals:

- the parent or young person can appeal to the Tribunal when the EHC plan is initially finalised, following an amendment or a replacement of the plan
- appeals **must** be registered with the Tribunal within two months of the local authority sending a notice to the parent or young person of the decision about one of the matters that can be appealed to the Tribunal or within one month of a certificate being issued following mediation or the parent or young person being given mediation information
- the right to appeal a refusal of an EHC needs assessment will be triggered only where the local authority has not carried out an assessment in the previous six months
- when the parent or young person is appealing about a decision to cease to maintain the EHC plan the local authority has to maintain the plan until the Tribunal's decision is made

Decisions the Tribunal can make

11.48 The Tribunal has prescribed powers under the Children and Families Act 2014 to make certain decisions in relation to appeals. The Tribunal can dismiss the appeal, order the local authority to carry out an assessment, or to make and maintain an EHC plan, or to maintain a plan with amendments. The Tribunal can also order the local authority to reconsider or correct a weakness in the plan, for example, where necessary information is missing. Local authorities have time limits within which to comply with decisions of the Tribunal (see the Special Educational Needs Regulations 2014).

11.49 In making decisions about whether the special educational provision specified in the EHC plan is appropriate, the Tribunal should take into account the education and training outcomes specified in Section E of the EHC plan and whether the special educational provision will enable the child or young person to make progress towards their education and training outcomes. The Tribunal can consider whether the education and training outcomes specified are sufficiently ambitious for the child or young person. When the Tribunal orders the local authority to reconsider the special educational provision in an EHC plan, the local authority should also review whether the outcomes remain appropriate.

How parents and young people can appeal

11.50 When appealing to the Tribunal parents and young people **must** supply a copy of the decision that they are appealing against and the date when the local authority's decision was made, or the date of the mediation certificate. The parent or young person who is appealing (the appellant) will be required to give the reasons why they are appealing. The reasons do not have to be lengthy or written in legal language but should explain why the appellant disagrees with the decision. Parents and young people have to send all relevant documents, such as copies of assessments, to the Tribunal.

11.51 Once the appeal is registered the local authority will be sent a copy of the papers filed and will be given a date by which they **must** respond and asked to provide details of witnesses – this will apply to all parties. The parties will also be told of the approximate hearing date. Hearings are heard throughout the country at Her Majesty's Courts and Tribunals Service buildings. The Tribunal will try to hold hearings as close to where the appellant lives as possible. Appeals are heard by a judge and a panel of Tribunal members who have been appointed because of their knowledge and experience of children and young people with SEN or disabilities. The local authority will provide a bundle of papers for each of the panel members and the parent, including any document requested by the parent. Advice on making SEN appeals to the Tribunal is available from the Ministry of Justice website – a link is given in the References section under General.

11.52 A video is available from the Ministry of Justice website which gives appellants some guidance on what happens at a hearing – a link to it is given in the References section under Chapter 11. A DVD of this video can be requested from the Tribunal by writing to:

First-tier Tribunal (Special Educational Needs and Disability)
Darlington Magistrates Court
Parkgate
Darlington
DL1 1RU

Disability discrimination claims

11.53 The parents of disabled children and disabled young people in school have the right to make disability discrimination claims to the Tribunal if they believe that their children or the young people themselves have been discriminated against by schools or local authorities when they are the responsible body for a school. Claims **must** be made within six months of the alleged instance of discrimination. The parents of disabled children, on behalf of their children, and disabled young people in school can make a claim against any school about alleged discrimination in the matters of exclusions, the provision of education and associated services and the making of reasonable adjustments, including the provision of auxiliary aids and services. They can also make claims to the Tribunal about admissions to independent and non-maintained special schools. Claims about admissions to state-funded schools are made to local admissions panels.

11.54 Disability discrimination claims by young people against post-16 institutions, and by parents about early years provision and about their treatment as a parent in being provided with an education service for their child, are made to the county courts. Claims by parents and young people against local authorities about the policies the authorities have adopted also go to the county courts.

11.55 Guidance on how to make a disability discrimination claim to the Tribunal is available from the Ministry of Justice website, via the link to information about the Tribunal given in the References section under General.

Exclusion

11.56 The Government issues statutory guidance on school exclusion, which can be found on the GOV.UK website – a link is given in the References section under Chapter 11.

11.57 The guidance sets out details of the permanent exclusion review panel process, including parents' right to ask for an SEN expert to attend. In addition, claims for disability discrimination in relation to permanent and fixed-period exclusions may be made to the Tribunal.

11.58 Local authorities have a duty to arrange suitable, full-time education for pupils of compulsory school age who would not otherwise receive such education, including from the sixth day of a permanent exclusion. Schools have a duty to arrange suitable, full-time education from the sixth day of a fixed period exclusion (see Chapter 10, paragraphs 10.47 to 10.52 on alternative provision). Suitable education means efficient education suitable to a child's age, ability and aptitude and to any SEN the child may have.

Please note that the following figure shows the maximum time it would take to register an appeal at the Tribunal both with and without mediation and have the appeal heard. Most registrations of an appeal, even where the case goes to mediation will take a far shorter time than this. The top half the diagram is for appeals after receipt of a finalised EHC plan.

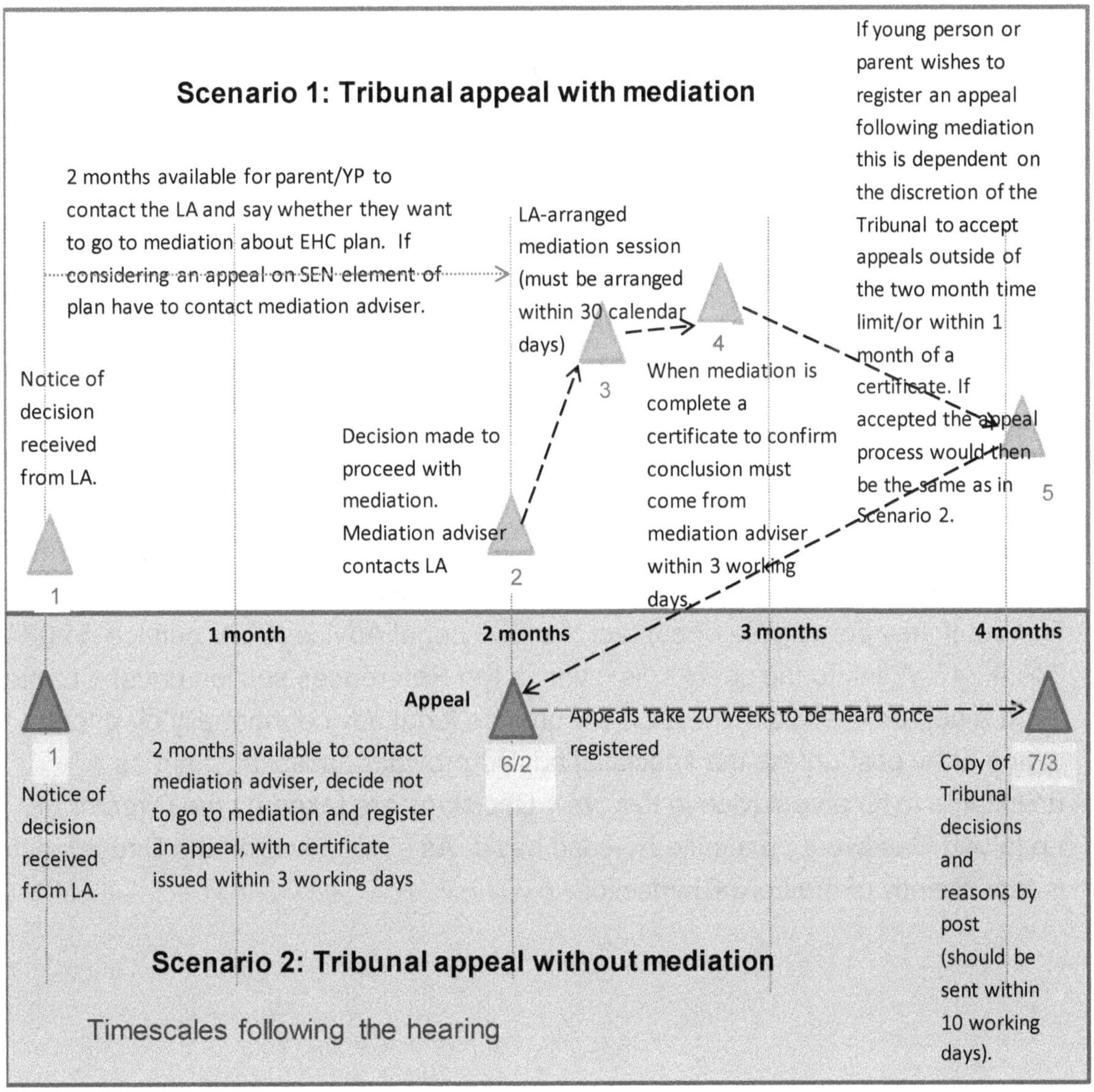

11.59 The young person or parent making the appeal and the local authority should both receive a copy of the Tribunal's decision and reasons by post within 10 working days of the hearing. Along with the decision notice the Tribunal will send a leaflet which will explain the application process for permission to appeal the Tribunal decision to the Upper Tribunal, if the appellant considers that the decision made was wrong in law. Local authorities can also appeal to the Upper Tribunal on the same grounds.

11.60 Step-by-step guidance on the process of appealing to the Tribunal and what it involves can be found at the Ministry of Justice website – a link is given in the References section under General.

Legal aid

11.61 If a parent or young person has decided to appeal, legal aid may be available to assist with that appeal. Legal aid can fund legal advice and assistance in preparing an appeal to the Tribunal, but not representation at the Tribunal.

11.62 Before someone can be granted legal aid they **must** pass a financial means assessment. The case **must** also satisfy a merits test of whether it has a reasonable chance of succeeding.

11.63 If the parent or young person's appeal to the Tribunal is unsuccessful, and they wish to mount a further appeal to the Upper Tribunal (or beyond to the Court of Appeal or Supreme Court), then legal aid can provide advice, assistance and representation, subject to the means and merits tests being met.

11.64 Legal aid for disability discrimination cases may also be available on the same basis set out above.

11.65 A parent or young person seeking access to legal aid for an SEN case or disability discrimination case should go to the legal aid checker on the GOV.UK website to find out if they are eligible or contact the Civil Legal Advice (CLA) service on 0845 345 4 345. A link to the checker is given in the References section under Chapter 11. If a person is eligible, the CLA will provide legal advice, normally by phone, online or by post unless the specialist advice provider assesses them as unsuitable to receive advice in this way. Decisions are taken by the Director of Legal Aid Casework on a case-by-case basis. As a civil servant, the Director acts independently of the Lord Chancellor.

11.66 The following groups do not have to apply via CLA – they can seek advice directly from a face- to-face provider:

- young people under 18, and
- those assessed by the CLA in the previous 12 months as requiring face-to-face advice, who have a further linked problem, and are seeking further help from the same face-to-face provider

Complaints procedures

Early education providers' and schools' complaints procedures

11.67 The Early Years Foundation Stage (EYFS) Statutory Framework requires all registered childcare providers to have a complaints procedure.

11.68 For childcare provision registered with Ofsted concerns should be raised directly with the manager or provider in the first instance. For complaints in writing the nursery provider **must** respond within 28 days. Where the childcare provision is run by a school, the school's complaints procedure should be used.

11.69 All state-funded schools are required to have a procedure to deal with complaints and to publish details of their procedure. The governing bodies of maintained schools should make efforts to ensure that anyone who wishes to make a complaint, including a complaint in relation to children and young people with SEN, whether they have EHC plans or not, is treated fairly, given the chance to state their case, provided with a written response (including the rationale for any decisions) and informed of their appeal rights. If the complainant remains concerned after following the local complaints procedure, he or she could ask the Department for Education's School Complaints Unit to take up the matter.

11.70 Further details on making complaints to the Department about schools are available from the GOV.UK website – a link is given in the References section under Chapter 11.

11.71 The proprietors of academies, free schools and independent schools **must**, under the Education (Independent School Standards) Regulations 2010,ensure that a complaints procedure is drawn up which is in writing and is made available to parents. The procedure **must** allow for a complaint to be considered informally in the first instance and then, if the parent remains dissatisfied, there should be a formal procedure for the complaint to be made in writing. If the parent is still dissatisfied the complaint can then be heard in front of a panel of at least three people one of whom **must** be independent of the management and running of the school. Should the parent still not be satisfied they can complain, in the case of academies and free schools, to the Education Funding Agency (EFA) acting on behalf of the Secretary of State, or, in the case of independent schools, to the Secretary of State directly. Both the EFA and the Secretary of State will look at whether the school handled the complaint properly, rather than the substance of the complaint. Further details on making a complaint to the EFA about academies and free schools are also available at the website address given in the previous paragraph.

11.72 Early years and schools complaints procedures are available for use in relation to children and young people who have SEN but without EHC plans.

Complaints to the Secretary of State

11.73 If disagreements have not been resolved at the local level, under sections 496 and 497 of the Education Act 1996 complaints can be made to the Secretary of State for Education that either the governing body of a maintained school or a local authority has acted unreasonably or has failed to carry out one of its duties under the Education Acts, including their SEN duties. The Secretary of State can also consider complaints about disability discrimination in relation to a pupil at a school by virtue of Section 87 of the Equality Act 2010. Sections 496 and 497 of the Education Act 1996 apply only to maintained schools, not other state-funded schools or independent schools.

11.74 Unreasonableness has been defined by the Courts as acting in a way in which no reasonable governing body or local authority would have acted in the circumstances.

11.75 The Secretary of State can issue directions about the exercise of a power or the performance of a duty by the governing body of a maintained school or a local authority. Any directions the Secretary of State issues **must** be 'expedient' – that is, the direction can make a material difference in remedying the matter. The Secretary of State would not intervene in a case where there is another avenue of redress, such as the Tribunal.

Complaints to Ofsted

11.76 Ofsted can consider complaints from parents and others about early years providers and schools, but only where the complaint is about the early years provision or the school as a whole rather than in relation to individual children, and where the parent or other complainant has tried to resolve the complaint through the early years provider's or school's own complaints procedure.

11.77 Further information about complaints to Ofsted about early years or childcare provision can be found at Ofsted's website – a link is given in the References section under Chapter 11.

11.78 Further details about school complaints can be found at Ofsted's website – a link is given in the References section under Chapter 11.

11.79 Examples of circumstances where complaints might relate to the school as a whole include:

- the school not providing a good enough education
- the pupils not achieving as much as they should, or their different needs not being met
- the school not being well led and managed, or wasting money
- the pupils' personal development and wellbeing being neglected

11.80 Ofsted can respond to a complaint that relates to the whole school by bringing forward an inspection, or it could decide to look at the matters raised when next inspecting the school.

11.81 Complainants can contact Ofsted on 08456 404045 or by email enquiries@ofsted.gov.uk

11.82 Complainants can make a formal complaint by writing to:

Enquiries
National Business Unit
Ofsted
Piccadilly Gate
Store Street
Manchester M1 2WD

Post-16 institution complaints

11.83 Complaints at general further education colleges can be made informally to the teacher or the Principal, or through the college's formal complaints procedure. If the complainant is dissatisfied after going through the college's own procedure they can take this up with the Skills Funding Agency. A copy of the Skills Funding Agency's procedure for handling complaints made against colleges is available on their website – a link is given in the References section under Chapter 11.

11.84 Complaints at sixth form colleges and some other Education Funding Agency (EFA)-funded providers can be made informally to the teacher or the Principal, or through the college's formal complaints process. If the complainant is dissatisfied after going through the provider's own procedure they can take this up with the EFA. A copy of the EFA's procedure for handling complaints is available on the GOV.UK website – a link is given in the References section under Chapter 11.

Local Authority complaints procedures

11.85 Some, but not all, local authorities offer a service that investigates the way in which a complaint was handled by a local authority maintained school. This may form part of a school's complaints procedure.

11.86 All local authorities have responsibility to consider complaints about decisions made in relation to the following:

- admission to schools (except in Voluntary Aided Schools)
- EHC needs assessments
- exclusion of pupils from schools
- child protection/allegations of child abuse
- complaints about the action of the Governing Body, and
- school transport

11.87 The Local Offer will make clear whether a particular local authority offers this service.

11.88 The Local Government Ombudsman provides 'top tips' for making a complaint to a local authority on its website – a link is provided in the References section under Chapter 11.

Local Government Ombudsman

11.89 The Local Government Ombudsman (LGO) can investigate complaints against local authorities where the complaint has not been resolved by the local authority's complaints procedure. The LGO investigates the process by which local authority decisions were made and whether there has been maladministration, rather than examining the merits of a decision which has been properly taken. The LGO will decide whether there has been an injustice to the complainant and/or there is evidence of maladministration. Maladministration can include delay, failure to take action and failure to follow procedures. The LGO does not investigate the merits of decisions which have been properly taken, but which the complainant thinks are wrong, but does look at the decision-making process and the delivery of provision set out in EHC plans.

11.90 The LGO does not investigate matters which can be appealed to the Tribunal, such as a decision not to carry out an assessment (see paragraph 11.45). The LGO can investigate complaints that the special educational provision set out in EHC plans is not being delivered and, in doing so, can investigate what part the school may have played in the provision not being delivered. (The LGO cannot, otherwise, investigate complaints about schools' SEN provision and has no powers to make recommendations to a school.) In association with the Parliamentary and Health Service Ombudsman (PHSO), the LGO can also investigate complaints about the delivery of health provision set out in plans. As set out in the previous paragraph, the LGO, in association with the PHSO with regard to health, does not investigate the merits of a decision which has been properly taken, but does look at the decision-making process and the delivery of provision set out in EHC plans.

11.91 Complaints can be made to the Local Government Ombudsman via its website – a link is given in the References section under Chapter 11. Help in making complaints is available on this number: **0300 061 0614**.

11.92 Alternatively, complaints can be made in writing to the following address:

PO Box 4771
Coventry
CV4 0EH

11.93 If the LGO finds evidence of fault in the way a decision has been made, it will generally ask the local authority to reconsider the decision and consider if other remedies are available. Where there is evidence of systemic failings, LGO recommendations could include review of systems, policy and procedures. In addition, if during the course of an investigation the LGO identifies other children who are similarly affected they can widen the scope of their investigation to include them.

11.94 The LGO cannot make local authorities carry out its recommendations following investigation of a complaint but in practice authorities almost always do so.

The Parliamentary and Health Service Ombudsman

11.95 The role of the Parliamentary and Health Service Ombudsman (PHSO) is to investigate complaints that individuals have been treated unfairly or have received a poor service from government departments and other public organisations in the UK, and the NHS in England.

11.96 The PHSO can investigate complaints about the commissioning and provision of healthcare. As mentioned in paragraph 11.90, the PHSO can conduct joint investigations with the LGO where a complaint includes concerns about the delivery of the health provision in EHC plans. They will normally investigate a complaint only once the NHS organisation has had a chance to resolve the issue first.

11.97 The PHSO can also investigate a number of other organisations which have to have regard to this Code: Ofsted, the Education Funding Agency, the Skills Funding Agency, and the Department for Education (including its School Complaints Unit and the Secretary of State for Education). The PHSO will generally expect the individual to have completed the organisation's own complaints procedure first. Complaints about government departments and public organisations **must** be referred by an MP. If someone has any difficulties getting in touch with an MP, they can contact the PHSO for help.

11.98 The PHSO can investigate complaints that the Tribunal's administrative staff have got something wrong or acted in an unreasonable manner, although they cannot look into the actions of Tribunal members or the decisions made by the Tribunal. PHSO would generally expect the complaint to have been made to Her Majesty's Courts and Tribunals Service first. These complaints will also need to be referred by an MP.

11.99 More information on the role of the PHSO is available from their website – a link is given in the References section under Chapter 11.

Judicial review

11.100 Parents and young people can make an application to the Administrative Court for Judicial Review. The Administrative Court can consider decisions of local authorities in the exercise of their duties including decisions on special education for children and young people. For example, a judicial review in relation to EHC plans would be a review of the way in which decisions that are reflected in the plan were made rather than the content of these decisions. An application for judicial review will be considered only once all other options for remedy have been exhausted. Any application for judicial review is time bound. Guidance on making an application for Judicial Review is available from the Ministry of Justice website – a link is given in the References section under Chapter 11.

NHS Complaints

11.101 The NHS complaints arrangements cover the health services which a child or young person receives under an EHC plan. A complaint may be made to a service provider (for example, the NHS Hospital Trust), where there are concerns about the service provided, or to the CCG, where there is a concern about the way in which a service is commissioned or provided, and this might include concerns about the appropriateness of the services in an EHC plan.

11.102 Local Healthwatch has a statutory role to provide patients with advice on how to take forward a complaint, or resolve an issue (local Healthwatch may also notify Healthwatch England of concerns which need to be considered at a national level). Contact details for local Healthwatch are available on the Healthwatch for England website and should also be available with the Local Offer – a link to the Healthwatch for England website is provided in the References section under Chapter 11.

11.103 Each CCG will have available information about its complaints arrangements and will deal with complaints about any of its functions (providers of NHS services will have patient advice and liaison services, and handle complaints about the services they provide). Just as the arrangements for commissioning services for SEN integrate the contributions of education, health and care, so the local authority and CCG should consider integrating their arrangements for providing patient advice, liaison and complaints handling in this area. Support in making a complaint about health services can also be provided by NHS Complaints Advocacy Services (each local authority will have details of services in their own local areas).

11.104 If a complainant is dissatisfied with the way in which the NHS has dealt with their complaint, they can contact the PHSO, though usually the NHS will need to have had a chance to resolve it locally. In line with the Ombudsman's Principles of Good Administration, in considering a complaint in relation to health services in an EHC plan, the Ombudsman will take into account this Code of Practice, and relevant legislation.

Complaints about social services provision

11.105 The Children Act 1989 places a duty on children's social care services to safeguard and protect children. Someone who is unhappy with the way in which they or their family have been treated by these services, including during EHC needs assessments and the drawing up of plans, has the right to make a formal complaint under the 'Local Authority Complaints Procedure'. They can write to either the Director of Children's Services or the Designated Complaints Officer for the local authority concerned. The authority **must** then consider the complaint, appointing at least one person independent of the local authority to take part in dealing with the issues raised and provide the complainant with a written response within 28 days.

11.106 If the complainant is unhappy with the authority's response, they can request a panel hearing by writing to the authority within 28 days of the response. The panel should be chaired by an independent person. If the complainant remains dissatisfied with the handling of their complaint under the local procedures and they think a local authority has treated them unfairly as a result of bad or inefficient management ('maladministration'), and that this has caused them injustice (such as loss, injury or upset), they can refer their complaint to the Local Government

Ombudsman (LGO). See Local Government Ombudsman, paragraphs 11.89 to 11.94.

11.107 Young people aged 18 and over can complain under regulations which prescribe:

- a procedure before investigation, and
- an investigation and response process

11.108 The provider **must** acknowledge the complaint within three days and they **must** offer the complainant the opportunity to discuss the timing and procedure for resolving the complaint. Once that has been agreed, the complaint **must** be investigated and, as soon as possible after completing the investigation, a written report **must** be sent to the complainant explaining how the complaint has been considered, the conclusions of the report and any remedial action which has been taken or is proposed to be taken.

11.109 A complainant who is dissatisfied with the outcome of this process can also take their case to the Local Government Ombudsman.

11.110 Parents and young people who wish to complain about the way in which their concerns about the social care elements of EHC plans have been dealt with can use these complaint procedures whether they go to mediation about the social care elements of the plan or not.

11.111 From 2016 there will also be a new system for appealing local authority decisions made under part 1 of the Care Act. This will be detailed in future updates to Statutory Guidance on the Care Act 2014.

Annex 1: Mental Capacity

Young people over compulsory school age have the right to participate in decisions about the provision that is made for them and be consulted about provision in their areas, although there is nothing to stop them asking their parents, or others to help them make the decision. However, some young people, and possibly some parents, will not have the mental capacity to make certain decisions. Provision is made in the Children and Families Act to deal with this. Under the Act, lacking mental capacity has the same meaning as in the Mental Capacity Act (MCA) 2005. A separate Code of Practice provides guidance on how the MCA works on a day-to-day basis. Professionals and anyone who is paid for the work they do with someone who lacks capacity has a duty to 'have regard' to that Code. The Code is available from the Ministry of Justice website – a link is given in the References section under Annex 1.

In cases where a person lacks mental capacity to make a particular decision, that decision will be taken by a representative on their behalf. The representative will be a deputy appointed by the Court of Protection, or a person who has a lasting or enduring power of attorney for the person. In the case of a young person who does not have such a representative, the decision will be taken by the young person's parent. It is also likely that where a young person does have a representative, that representative will be the young person's parent. Therefore in most cases, where a young person lacks capacity, decisions will be taken on their behalf by their parent. However, it is important that people are helped to make decisions themselves wherever possible.

The MCA sets out five key principles which **must** underlie everything someone does in relation to someone who may lack capacity to make some decisions. The five key principles are:

- It should be assumed that everyone can make their own decisions unless it is proved otherwise
- A person should have all the help and support possible to make and communicate their own decision before anyone concludes that they lack capacity to make their own decision
- A person should not be treated as lacking capacity just because they make an unwise decision
- Actions or decisions carried out on behalf of someone who lacks capacity **must** be in their best interests
- Actions or decisions carried out on behalf of someone who lacks capacity should limit their rights and freedom of action as little as possible

If there is doubt about a person's mental capacity, consideration needs to be given as to whether the person lacks capacity to make that particular decision, as they may have capacity to make some decisions but not others. This does not necessarily mean that a person's mental capacity has to be reassessed each time a decision needs to be taken. If there is a reasonable belief that the person lacks the capacity to make a decision based on prior knowledge of that person then the decision can be made by a parent or representative, as appropriate. **Subject to the principles above,** there are four key questions to consider in determining whether someone is able to make a decision:

- Can the person understand information relevant to the decision, including understanding the likely consequences of making, or not making the decision?
- Can they retain this information for long enough to make the decision?
- Can they use and weigh the information to arrive at a choice?
- Can they communicate their decision in any way?

If the answer to any of these questions **is 'no' (bearing in mind that if an individual needs a lot of support to make and communicate a decision it does not mean they are incapable of making a decision)** then the person lacks capacity to make that decision at that time.

The Special Educational Needs and Disability Regulations 2014 specify the particular occasions when a representative or parent has to act on behalf of a young person who lacks capacity or a representative if the child or young person's parent lacks capacity.

There are some occasions when a local authority **must** take account of the views of the young person as well as any representative. These are when the local authority is:

- having regard to the views and wishes of a child, the child's parent or a young person when carrying out its functions under Part III of the Act (Section 19)
- consulting children, their parents and young people when carrying out its duty to keep education and care provision for disabled children and young people and those with SEN under review (Section 27)
- publishing the comments of children, their parents and young people about its Local Offer and involving these people in preparing and reviewing the Local Offer (Section 30), and

- arranging for information and advice to be provided to children, their parents and young people and taking steps to make information and advice services known to those people (Section 32)

The Regulations also specify the following occasions when the local authority considers the views of the representative instead of the parent or young person. These are where the child's parent or young person is:

- expressing their wishes, being notified, consulted and copied documents, agreeing or taking decisions in relation to needs assessments, re-assessments and EHC plans (Sections 33, 36, 38, 39, 40, 42 and 44)
- being admitted to special provision where they do not have an EHC plan (Section 34)
- requesting a Personal Budget (Section 49)
- appealing to the Tribunal (Section 51)
- participating in mediation and resolving disagreements (Sections 52, 53, 54, 55, 56 and 57)
- being consulted about making special educational provision otherwise than in a school or post-16 institution (Section 61)
- being informed that special educational provision is being made for them or their child (Section 68)
- similar provisions in relation to detained persons

Further advice about the MCA is available from the Ministry of Justice website – a link is given in the References section under Annex 1.

Annex 2: Improving practice and staff training in education settings

Early years providers, schools and colleges are responsible for deciding what external support to seek and for setting their own priorities for the continuous professional development of their staff. The support described in this guidance can be delivered most effectively in education settings which adopt structured approaches to engaging parents and children, tracking and measuring progress of pupils with SEN, and where there is a good level of knowledge across all staff of different types of SEN and suitable teaching approaches and interventions. Where a setting has a SENCO, they should play an important role in advising on and contributing to the broader support provided by schools and the professional development of other teachers and staff.

A range of organisations offer support and training to schools on overall identification and teaching approaches for pupils with SEN as well as on specific conditions.

Many aspects of the approach set out in Chapter 6 draw on learning from the piloting and subsequent work of Achievement for All (www.afa3as.org.uk). This demonstrates that when a whole-school approach to supporting pupils with SEN is taken, along with effective engagement with parents, there can be a clear impact on attainment.

Schools, colleges and early years providers who need to improve the knowledge and skills of staff in relation to specific conditions can access information, advice and training materials that have been developed through the Department for Education's voluntary and community sector grants programme. NASEN provides a SEN Gateway that enables access to a broad range of materials and support services across the range of SEN (www.sendgateway.org.uk).

The Excellence gateway provides access to resources to support professional development in the FE and Skills sector (www.excellencegateway.org.uk).

Early Support provides a range of information materials to families and professionals www.ncb.org.uk/earlysupport.

The following organisations provide advice, information and training on specific impairments:

- The Autism Education Trust for children and young people on the Autism Spectrum (www.autismeducationtrust.org.uk)
- The Communications Trust for speech, language and communication difficulties (www.thecommunicationtrust.org.uk)

- The Dyslexia SpLD Trust on dyslexia and literacy difficulties (www.thedyslexia-spldtrust.org.uk)
- The National Sensory Impairment Partnership for vision impairment, hearing impairment and multi-sensory impairment (www.natsip.org.uk)

Each of these organisations is working with funding from the Department for Education to support the reforms to the SEN system.

MindEd (www.minded.org.uk) is an e-learning portal aimed at supporting all adults working with children and young people. It provides simple, clear guidance on children and young people's mental health, wellbeing and development.

Glossary of terms

Academy: A state-funded school in England that is directly funded by the Department for Education, through the Education Funding Agency. Academies are self-governing and independent of local authority control.

Access to Work: An Access to Work grant from the Department for Work and Pensions helps to pay for practical support for young people and adults who have a disability, health or mental health condition so they can start work, stay in work or start their own business. It can pay for things like special equipment, fares to work if public transport is not practical, a support worker or coach in the workplace or a communicator at a job interview.

Annual review: the review of an EHC plan which the local authority must make as a minimum every 12 months.

Armed Forces Covenant: The armed forces covenant sets out the relationship between the nation, the government and the armed forces. It recognises that the whole nation has a moral obligation to members of the armed forces and their families and it establishes how they should expect to be treated. The Covenant states that the children of service personnel should have the same standard of, and access to, education (including early years services) as any other UK citizen in the area in which they live.

Care Plan: A record of the health and/or social care services that are being provided to a child or young person to help them manage a disability or health condition. The Plan will be agreed with the child's parent or the young person and may be contained within a patient's medical record or maintained as a separate document. Care Plans are also maintained by local authorities for looked after children – in this instance the Care Plan will contain a Personal Education Plan in addition to the health and social care elements.

Child and Adolescent Mental Health Services (CAMHS): These services assess and treat children and young people with emotional, behavioural or mental health difficulties. They range from basic pastoral care, such as identifying mental health problems, to specialist 'Tier 4' CAMHS, which provide in-patient care for those who are severely mentally ill.

Children and young people's secure estate: This comprises three types of establishment – secure children's homes, secure training centres and young offender institutions.

Comprehensive Health Assessment Tool (CHAT): An assessment tool for young people in the youth justice system. It ensures that young people in the secure estate and in the community receive a comprehensive assessment of their physical and mental health, substance misuse and neuro-disability needs on entry to the system.

Compulsory school age: A child is of compulsory school age from the beginning of the term following their 5th birthday until the last Friday of June in the year in which they become 16, provided that their 16th birthday falls before the start of the next school year.

Disabled Students Allowance (DSA): An allowance for undergraduate or post-graduate students who have a disability or long-term health condition, mental health condition or specific learning difficulty such as dyslexia or dyspraxia which affects their ability to study. It can be used to pay for things such as special equipment, a note-taker or transport costs.

Disagreement resolution: This is a statutory service commissioned by local authorities to provide a quick and non-adversarial way of resolving disagreements between parents or young people and bodies responsible for providing education, whether the child or young person has an EHC plan or not, or health and social care in relation to EHC assessments and plans. Disagreement resolution services can also be used in cases of disagreement between local authorities and health commissioning bodies during EHC needs assessments, the drawing up of EHC plans or the reviewing of those plans.

Early Help Assessment: A social care assessment of a child and his or her family, designed to identify needs at an early stage and enable suitable interventions to be put in place to support the family.

Early Support Programme: The Early Support Programme co-ordinates health, education and social care support for the parents and carers of disabled children and young people from birth to adulthood. A key worker is assigned to families that join the Programme.

Early Years Foundation Stage (EYFS): The foundation stage begins when children reach the age of three. Many children attend an early education setting soon after their third birthday. The foundation stage continues until the end of the reception year and is consistent with the National Curriculum. It prepares children for learning in Year 1, when programmes of study for Key Stage 1 are taught.

Early years provider: A provider of early education places for children under five years of age. This can include state-funded and private nurseries as well as child minders.

Education Funding Agency (EFA): An arm of the Department for Education that manages the funding for learners between the ages of 3 and 19 years and for those with SEN or disabilities between the ages of 3 and 25. The EFA allocates funding to 152 local authorities for maintained schools and voluntary aided schools. It is also responsible for funding and monitoring academies, University

Technical Colleges, studio schools and free schools, as well as building maintenance programmes for schools and sixth-form colleges.

Education, Health and Care plan (EHC plan): An EHC plan details the education, health and social care support that is to be provided to a child or young person who has SEN or a disability. It is drawn up by the local authority after an EHC needs assessment of the child or young person has determined that an EHC plan is necessary, and after consultation with relevant partner agencies.

Elected members: The elected members of a county council or unitary local authority (as opposed to the salaried officials of the council or local authority). Some elected members have a lead responsibility for specific areas of policy, for example the Lead Member for Children's Services.

First-tier Tribunal (Special Educational Needs and Disability): An independent body which has jurisdiction under section 333 of the Education Act 1996 for determining appeals by parents against local authority decisions on EHC needs assessments and EHC plans. The Tribunal's decision is binding on both parties to the appeal. The Tribunal also hears claims of disability discrimination under the Equality Act 2010.

Free school: A free school is a type of academy, which is free to attend, but is not controlled by the local authority. Free schools receive state funding via the Education Funding Agency. Parents, teachers, businesses or charities can submit an application to the Department for Education to set up a free school.

Further education (FE) college: A college offering continuing education to young people over the compulsory school age of 16. The FE sector in England includes general further education colleges, sixth form colleges, specialist colleges and adult education institutes.

Graduated approach: A model of action and intervention in early education settings, schools and colleges to help children and young people who have special educational needs. The approach recognises that there is a continuum of special educational needs and that, where necessary, increasing specialist expertise should be brought to bear on the difficulties that a child or young person may be experiencing.

Health and Wellbeing Board: A Health and Wellbeing Board acts as a forum where local commissioners across the NHS, social care and public health work together to improve the health and wellbeing of their local population and reduce health inequalities. The boards are intended to increase democratic input into strategic decisions about health and wellbeing services, strengthen working relationships between health and social care and encourage integrated commissioning of health and social care services.

Healthwatch England: Healthwatch England is an independent consumer champion, gathering and representing the views of the public about health and social care services in England. It operates both at a national and local level and ensures the views of the public and people who use services are taken into account. Healthwatch England works as part of the Care Quality Commission.

Healthy Child Programme: The Healthy Child Programme covers pregnancy and the first five years of a child's life, focusing on a universal preventative service that provides families with a programme of screening, immunisation, health and development reviews, supplemented by advice around health, wellbeing and parenting.

Independent Reviewing Officer (IRO): The appointment of an IRO is a statutory requirement for local authorities under the Adoption and Children Act 2002. IROs make an important contribution to the goal of significantly improving outcomes for looked after children. Their primary focus is to quality assure the care planning process for each child, and to ensure that his or her current wishes and feelings are given full consideration.

Independent school: A school that is not maintained by a local authority and is registered under section 464 of the Education Act 1996. Section 347 of the Act sets out the conditions under which an independent school may be approved by the Secretary of State as being suitable for the admission of children with EHC plans.

Independent supporter: A person recruited locally by a voluntary or community sector organisation to help families going through an EHC needs assessment and the process of developing an EHC plan. This person is independent of the local authority and will receive training, including legal training, to enable him or her to provide this support.

Information, Advice and Support Services: Information, Advice and Support Services provide advice and information to children with SEN or disabilities, their parents, and young people with SEN or disabilities. They provide neutral and factual support on the special educational needs system to help the children, their parents and young people to play an active and informed role in their education and care. Although funded by local authorities, Information, Advice and Support Services are run either at arm's length from the local authority or by a voluntary organisation to ensure children, their parents and young people have confidence in them.

Joint Strategic Needs Assessment (JSNA): Joint strategic needs assessments (JSNAs) analyse the health needs of populations to inform and guide commissioning of health, wellbeing and social care services within local authority areas. The JSNA's central role is to act as the overarching primary evidence base for health and wellbeing boards to decide on key local health priorities.

Local Offer: Local authorities in England are required to set out in their Local Offer information about provision they expect to be available across education, health and social care for children and young people in their area who have SEN or are disabled, including those who do not have Education, Health and Care (EHC) plans. Local authorities must consult locally on what provision the Local Offer should contain.

Maintained school: For the purposes of this Code, schools in England that are maintained by a local authority – any community, foundation or voluntary school, community special or foundation special school.

Mediation: This is a statutory service commissioned by local authorities which is designed to help settle disagreements between parents or young people and local authorities over EHC needs assessments and plans and which parents and young people can use before deciding whether to appeal to the First-Tier Tribunal about decisions on assessment or the special educational element of a plan. Mediation can cover any one or all three elements of an EHC plan and must be offered to the parent or young person when the final plan is issued, but they are not able to appeal to the Tribunal about the health and social care aspects of the plan.

National curriculum: This sets out a clear, full and statutory entitlement to learning for all pupils, determining what should be taught and setting attainment targets for learning. It also determines how performance will be assessed and reported.

National Offender Management Service (NOMS): NOMS is an executive agency of the Ministry of Justice. It is responsible for the running of prison and probation services, rehabilitation services for prisoners leaving prison, ensuring support is available to stop people re-offending, contract managing private sector prisons and services such as the Prisoner Escort Service and electronic tagging, and contract managing 35 Probation Trusts.

NHS Continuing Care: NHS Continuing Care is support provided for children and young people under 18 who need a tailored package of care because of their disability, an accident or illness.

NHS Continuing Healthcare: NHS Continuing Healthcare is the name given to a package of care that is arranged and funded solely by the NHS for individuals aged 18 and over who are not in hospital but have complex ongoing healthcare needs. It can be provided in any setting, for example in the home or in a residential care home.

NHS England: NHS England is an independent body, at arm's length to the government and held to account through the NHS Mandate. Its main role is to improve health outcomes for people in England by providing national leadership for improving outcomes and driving up the quality of care; overseeing the operation of clinical commissioning groups; allocating resources to clinical commissioning groups, and commissioning primary care and specialist services.

NHS foundation trust: NHS foundation trusts are not-for-profit corporations that provide NHS hospital, mental health and ambulance services. NHS foundation trusts are not directed by the Government, but are accountable to their local communities through their members and governors, to their commissioners through contracts and to Parliament through their annual report and accounts. Foundation trusts are registered with and inspected by the Care Quality Commission.

NHS Mandate: The NHS Mandate is issued by the government to NHS England. It sets out the government's ambition for the National Health Service and provides direction to NHS England. The mandate will be reviewed annually.

NHS trust: NHS trusts are public sector bodies that provide community health, hospital, mental health and ambulance services on behalf of the NHS in England and Wales. Each trust is headed by a board consisting of executive and non-executive directors, and is chaired by a non-executive director.

Non-maintained special school: Schools in England approved by the Secretary of State under section 342 of the Education Acct 1996 as special schools which are not maintained by the state but charge fees on a non-profit-making basis. Most non-maintained special schools are run by major charities or charitable trusts.

Ofsted: Office for Standards in Education, a non-Ministerial government department established under the Education (Schools) Act 1992 to take responsibility for the inspection of all schools in England. Her Majesty's Inspectors (HMI) form its professional arm.

Parent: Under section 576 of the Education Act 1996, the term 'parent' includes any person who is not a parent of the child, but has parental responsibility (see below) or who cares for him or her.

Parent Carer Forum: A Parent Carer Forum is a group of parents and carers of disabled children who work with local authorities, education, health and other providers to make sure the services they plan and deliver meet the needs of disabled children and families.

Parental responsibility: Parental responsibility is defined under Section 3 (1) of the Children Act 1989 as meaning all the duties, rights, powers, responsibilities and authority which parents have with respect to their children and their children's property. Under Section 2 of the Children Act 1989, parental responsibility falls upon:

- all mothers and fathers who were married to each other at the time of the child's birth (including those who have since separated or divorced)

- mothers who were not married to the father at the time of the child's birth, and
- fathers who were not married to the mother at the time of the child's birth, but who have obtained parental responsibility either by agreement with the child's mother or through a court order

Under Section 12 of the Children Act 1989, where a court makes a residence order in favour of any person who is not the parent or guardian of the child, that person has parental responsibility for the child while the residence order remains in force.

Under section 33 (3) of the Children Act 1989, while a care order is in force with respect to a child, the social services department designated by the order will have parental responsibility for that child, and will have the power (subject to certain provisions) to determine the extent to which a parent or guardian of the child may meet his or her parental responsibility for the child. The social services department cannot have parental responsibility for a child unless that child is the subject of a care order, except for very limited purposes where an emergency protection order is in force under Section 44 of the Children Act 1989.

Personal Budget: A Personal Budget is an amount of money identified by the local authority to deliver provision set out in an EHC plan where the parent or young person is involved in securing that provision. The funds can be held directly by the parent or young person, or may be held and managed on their behalf by the local authority, school, college or other organisation or individual and used to commission the support specified in the EHC plan.

Personal Education Plan: An element of a Care Plan maintained by a local authority in respect of a looked after child, which sets out the education needs of the child. If a looked after child has an EHC plan, the regular reviews of the EHC plan should, where possible, coincide with reviews of the Personal Education Plan.

Portage: Planned, home-based educational support for pre-school children with special educational needs. Local authorities usually provide Portage services. The Portage service is named after the town of Portage, Wisconsin, USA. There is an active and extensive network of Portage services in the UK, developed by the National Portage Association, which provides a Code of Practice and accredited training.

Pupil Referral Unit (PRU): Any school established and maintained by a local authority under section 19 (2) of the Education Act 1996 which is specially organised to provide education for pupils who would otherwise not receive suitable education because of illness, exclusion or any other reason.

Service Children's Education (SCE): SCE oversees the education of UK Service children abroad. It is funded by the Ministry of Defence and operates its own schools as well as providing advice to parents on UK and overseas schools.

Special Educational Needs (SEN): A child or young person has SEN if they have a learning difficulty or disability which calls for special educational provision to be made for him or her. A child of compulsory school age or a young person has a learning difficulty or disability if he or she has a significantly greater difficulty in learning than the majority of others of the same age, or has a disability which prevents or hinders him or her from making use of educational facilities of a kind generally provided for others of the same age in mainstream schools or mainstream post-16 institutions.

Special Educational Needs Co-ordinator (SENCO): A qualified teacher in a school or maintained nursery school who has responsibility for co-ordinating SEN provision. In a small school, the headteacher or deputy may take on this role. In larger schools there may be a team of SENCOs. Other early years settings in group provision arrangements are expected to identify an individual to perform the role of SENCO and childminders are encouraged to do so, possibly sharing the role between them where they are registered with an agency.

Special educational provision: Special educational provision is provision that is different from or additional to that normally available to pupils or students of the same age, which is designed to help children and young people with SEN or disabilities to access the National Curriculum at school or to study at college.

Special school: A school which is specifically organised to make special educational provision for pupils with SEN. Special schools maintained by the local authority comprise community special schools and foundation special schools, and non-maintained (independent) special schools that are approved by the Secretary of State under Section 342 of the Education Act 1996.

Speech and language therapy: Speech and language therapy is a health care profession, the role and aim of which is to enable children, young people and adults with speech, language and communication difficulties (and associated difficulties with eating and swallowing) to reach their maximum communication potential and achieve independence in all aspects of life.

Virtual School Head (VSH): The Virtual School Head (VSH) is an officer of a local authority who leads a virtual school team that tracks the progress of children looked after by the authority as if they attended a single school. The Children and Families Act 2014 requires every local authority to appoint an officer who is an employee of that or another authority to discharge this duty.

Young person: A person over compulsory school age (the end of the academic year in which they turn 16). From this point the right to make decisions about matters covered by the Children and Families Act 2014 applies to the young person directly, rather than to their parents.

Youth Justice Board (YJB): The Youth Justice Board for England and Wales is an executive non-departmental public body. Its board members are appointed by the Secretary of State for Justice. The YJB oversees the youth justice system in England and Wales, works to prevent offending and reoffending by children and young people under the age of 18 and ensures that custody for them is safe, secure and addresses the causes of their offending behaviour.

Youth Offending Team (YOT): Youth offending teams are part of local authorities and are separate from the police and the justice system. They work with local agencies including the police, probation officers, health, children's services, schools and the local community, to run local crime prevention programmes, help young people at the police station if they're arrested, help young people and their families at court, supervise young people serving a community sentence and stay in touch with a young person if they're sentenced to custody.

References

General

These references are used many times across the Code and are therefore not repeated under individual chapters:

Care Act 2014

Children and Families Act 2014

Education Act 1996

Equality Act 2010

First-tier Tribunal (Special Educational Needs and Disability)

Office for Standards in Education (Ofsted)

Pathfinder information packs

Special Educational Needs (Personal Budgets) Regulations 2014

Special Educational Needs and Disability Regulations 2014

Introduction

Children Act 1989 Guidance and Regulations Volume 2 (Care Planning, Placement and Case Review)

Children Act 1989 Guidance and Regulations Volume 3 (Planning Transition to Adulthood for Care Leavers)

Equality Act 2010: Advice for Schools

Mental Capacity Act Code of Practice: Protecting the Vulnerable 2007

Reasonable adjustments for disabled pupils 2012:

Supporting pupils at school with medical conditions

Transition to the new 0-25 special educational needs and disability system (DfE guidance)

Working Together to Safeguard Children 2013

Chapter 1: Principles

Contact a Family

National Network of Parent Carer Forums

School Admissions Code of Practice

United Nations Convention on the Rights of Persons with Disabilities

United Nations Convention on the Rights of the Child

Chapter 2: Impartial information, advice and support

Children's Education Advisory Service (CEAS)

Early Support Programme

Family Information Services

Information, Advice and Support Services Network – guidance on impartial information, advice and support

Patient Advice and Liaison Service (PALS)

Chapter 3: Working together across education, health and care for joint outcomes

Campbell Collaboration

Child and Maternal Health Intelligence Network (ChiMat)

Children Act 1989

Children Act 2004

Chronically Sick and Disabled Persons Act 1970

Cochrane Collaboration

Commissioning support resources (BOND/Young Minds):

Health and Social Care Act 2012

Improving Children and Young People's Health Outcomes: a system-wide response (Children and Young People's Outcome Forum)

In Control examples of approaches to Personal Budgets

JSNA guidance

Making it personal (Kids website)

National Development Team for Inclusion (NDTI)

National Health Service Act 2006

Procurement, Patient Choice and Competition Regulations: guidance and hypothetical case scenarios (Monitor)

Public health in local government – factsheet for local authorities

Transforming Participation in Health and Care (NHS England)

Who Pays? Determining responsibility for payments to providers (August 2013)

Winterbourne Concordat

Chapter 4: The Local Offer

Access to Work fund (DWP)

Breaks for Carers of Disabled Children Regulations 2011

School Organisation (Maintained Schools) guidance (DfE)

Chapter 5: Early years providers

Statutory Framework for the Early Years Foundation Stage

Early years outcomes guide

Healthy Child Programme

National Children's Bureau

Chapter 6: Schools

Achievement for All

Autism Education Trust

Bullying guidance

Communication Trust

Data Protection Act 1998

Dyslexia SpLD Trust

I CAN – the children's communications charity

Mental Health and Behaviour Guidance (DfE)

MindEd

National Award for SENCO Co-ordination: learning outcomes

National Sensory Impairment Partnership

Provision mapping resources

Social Care for Deafblind Children and Adults guidance 2009 (DoH)

Supporting pupils at school with medical conditions

Chapter 7: Further Education

16 to 19 funding guidance (DfE)

Disabled Students Allowance (DSA)

Education Funding Agency (EFA)

Higher Education Funding Council for England (HEFCE)

Skills Funding Agency (SFA)

Chapter 8: Preparing for adulthood from the earliest years

16 to 19 study programmes: advice for further education colleges

Access to Work (DWP)

Autism Strategy 2014

Care Act 2014 – Personal Budget Guidance (draft)

Care Act 2014 – Transition Guidance (draft)

Mental Capacity Act 2005

Mental Health Action Plan – Closing the Gap 2014

Ordinary Residence Guidance 2013 (DoH)

Participation of young people in education, employment and training (DfE guidance)

Preparing for Adulthood

Supported internships – DfE advice (2014)

Chapter 9: Education, health and care needs assessments and plans

Chronically Sick and Disabled Persons Act 1970

Community Care, services for Carers and Children's Services (Direct Payments) Regulations 2009

Disabled Persons (Services, Consultation and Representation) Act 1986

Education and Inspections Act 2006

Information sharing for practitioners and managers (DfE)

Local Government Act 1974

National Health Service (Direct Payments) Regulations 2013

Picture Exchange Communication System

Support and aspiration – introducing Personal Budgets

Chapter 10: Children and young people in specific circumstances

Alternative provision guidance (DfE)

Apprenticeships, Skills and Learning Act 2009

Children and Young Persons Act 2008

Children's Education Advisory Service (CEAS)

Comprehensive Health Assessment Tool (CHAT)

Crime and Disorder Act 1998

Designated Teacher (Looked After Pupils etc) Regulations 2009

Education (Pupil Information) Regulations 2005

Preparing for Adulthood Factsheet – 'Links Between the Children and Families Act 2014 and the Care Act'

Preparing for Adulthood

Raising the Participation Age – useful information

Standards for the healthcare of children and young people in secure settings (Royal College of Paediatrics and Child Health)

Chapter 11: Resolving disagreements

Care Act – Statutory Guidance (draft)

Children Act 1989 Representations Procedure (England) Regulations 2006:

Complaints about schools (DfE)

Complaints to local authorities (LGO tips)

Complaints to Ofsted about early years or childcare provision

Complaints to Ofsted about schools

Complaints to the EFA

Complaints to the SFA

Education (Independent School Standards) Regulations 2010:

Exclusions guidance (DfE)

Healthwatch for England

Judicial review guidance (MoJ)

Legal aid checker

Legal Aid, Sentencing and Punishment of Offenders Act 2012:

Local Authority Social Services and National Health Service Complaints (England) Regulations 2009

Local Government Ombudsman (LGO)

Ministry of Justice – Tribunal video

Parliamentary and Health Service Ombudsman (PHSO)

Tribunal Procedure (First-tier Tribunal)(Health, Education and Social Care Chamber) Rules 2008

Tribunals, Courts and Enforcement Act 2007

Annex 1: Mental Capacity

Mental Capacity Act 2005 (MoJ)

Adapted and published by GRANGIS under the OGL Licence.
GRANGIS - UK PUBLISHING 2022.
Thank you for taking the time to leave us a review regarding this edition"

★★★★★

For further inquiries, please feel free to contact us at:
www.grangis.com / contact@grangis.com

www.ingramcontent.com/pod-product-compliance
Lightning Source LLC
LaVergne TN
LVHW060211210926
848481LV00008B/2690